The Arab Uprisings and Malaysia's Islamist Movements

This book examines the attitude of Malaysia's Islamist movements – The Pan-Malaysian Islamic Party (PAS); The National Trust Party (AMANAH); The Muslim Youth Movement of Malaysia (ABIM) and the Malaysian Muslim Solidarity Front (ISMA) – towards the Arab Uprisings in the Middle East and North Africa.

The book analyses the perceptions of Islamist movement activists, politicians and members in Malaysia towards the 2011 Arab Uprisings, popularly known as the 'Arab Spring'. A questionnaire-based survey as well as in-depth interviews with activists and leaders ranging from individuals in opposing political parties (PAS and AMANAH) to non-government Islamist organisations (ABIM and ISMA) informs the findings of the book. Using quantitative and qualitative methods, the author analyses how the events impacted the activism, political approach and attitudes of the members of Islamic movements towards the issues of regime change, civil disobedience, political revolution, democracy, Islamism and political stability. The book demonstrates that Malaysian Islamists are mainly in support of free and democratic elections as a medium for political change as opposed to overthrowing the previous BN-led regime via civil disobedience, street demonstration or 'revolution'.

A novel approach in examining the connections between Islamic movements in Southeast Asia and the Middle East and Africa, this book will be of interest to academics in the fields of Politics, History, Social Movements, Political Islam, Middle Eastern Studies and Southeast Asian Studies.

Mohd Irwan Syazli Saidin is an Honorary Research Fellow at the Institute of Arab and Islamic Studies, University of Exeter, UK, and a senior lecturer in Middle East Politics in the Faculty of Social Sciences and Humanities, Universiti Kebangsaan Malaysia.

Routledge Contemporary Southeast Asia Series

The aim of this series is to publish original, high-quality work by both new and established scholars on all aspects of Southeast Asia.

Power Interconnection in Southeast Asia
Anthony David Owen, Anton Finenko and Jacqueline Tao

Contemporary Inter-regional Dialogue and Cooperation between the EU and ASEAN on Non-traditional Security Challenges
Naila Maier-Knapp

Securitising Singapore
State Power and Global Threats Management
Syed Mohammed Ad'ha Aljunied

The European Union and Myanmar
Interactions via ASEAN
Edited by Ludovica Marchi Balossi Restelli

The State and Religious Violence in Indonesia
Minority Faiths and Vigilantism
A'an Suryana

Science and Development in Thai and South Asian Buddhism
David L. Gosling

The Arab Uprisings and Malaysia's Islamist Movements
Influence, Impact and Lessons
Mohd Irwan Syazli Saidin

For more information about this series, please visit: www.routledge.com/Routledge-Contemporary-Southeast-Asia-Series/book-series/RCSEA

The Arab Uprisings and Malaysia's Islamist Movements
Influence, Impact and Lessons

Mohd Irwan Syazli Saidin

LONDON AND NEW YORK

First published 2020
by Routledge
2 Park Square, Milton Park, Abingdon, Oxon OX14 4RN

and by Routledge
52 Vanderbilt Avenue, New York, NY 10017

Routledge is an imprint of the Taylor & Francis Group, an informa business

© 2020 Mohd Irwan Syazli Saidin

The right of Mohd Irwan Syazli Saidin to be identified as author of this work has been asserted by him in accordance with sections 77 and 78 of the Copyright, Designs and Patents Act 1988.

All rights reserved. No part of this book may be reprinted or reproduced or utilised in any form or by any electronic, mechanical, or other means, now known or hereafter invented, including photocopying and recording, or in any information storage or retrieval system, without permission in writing from the publishers.

Trademark notice: Product or corporate names may be trademarks or registered trademarks, and are used only for identification and explanation without intent to infringe.

British Library Cataloguing-in-Publication Data
A catalogue record for this book is available from the British Library

Library of Congress Cataloging-in-Publication Data
A catalog record has been requested for this book

ISBN: 978-0-367-42355-1 (hbk)
ISBN: 978-0-367-85403-4 (ebk)

Typeset in Times New Roman
by codeMantra

In loving memory of my grandmother, Sepiah Ibrahim (1919–2016).
   I love you with all my heart, body and soul.

Contents

	List of tables	ix
	Preface	xi
	List of acronyms and abbreviations	xiii
	Acknowledgements	xv
	Glossary of non-English terms	xvii
1	Introduction	1
2	The development of the Islamist movements in Malaysia	13
3	Knowledge and perceptions of the Islamist movements in Malaysia towards the Arab Uprisings	40
4	The influences and impacts of the Arab Uprisings on the Islamist movements in Malaysia	71
5	Revolution or political stability? Malaysia's Islamist movements and lessons from the Arab Uprisings	104
6	Concluding remarks and perspectives	140
	Bibliography	147
	Index	165

Tables

2.1	Summary of popular civil protests in Malaysia	35
2.2	Summary of selected cases of Islamist movements in Malaysia	37
3.1	Respondents' age	41
3.2	Respondents' gender	42
3.3	Respondents' level of education	43
3.4	Respondents' last place of education	43
3.5	Respondents' occupational sector	44
3.6	Type of Islamist movement membership	44
3.7	Respondents' knowledge of the Arab Uprisings events	45
3.8	Respondents' knowledge of the Arab Uprisings events based on level of education	46
3.9	Respondents' reasons for not knowing about the Arab Uprisings	47
3.10	Respondents' source of information regarding the Arab Uprisings events	49
3.11	Respondents' perceptions that the Arab Uprisings were a non-violent resistance movement	53
3.12	Respondents' perceptions that the Arab Uprisings were sparked in Tunisia by Mohamed Bouazizi	54
3.13	Perceptions that economic downturn contributed to the Arab Uprisings	56
3.14	Perceptions that autocratic leadership contributed to the Arab Uprisings	57
3.15	Respondents' perceptions that the Arab Uprisings were a phenomenon of Islamist Uprising and the rise of political Islam in the Arab world	61
3.16	Respondents' views that the Islamist parties are capable of governing Arab countries	65
3.17	Respondents' views that the post-Arab Uprisings events have shown the relevance of the Islamist movement as an agent of societal change	66
4.1	Respondents' perceptions that the post-Arab Uprisings have had a destructive impact based on the political and economic context	73

4.2	Respondents' perceptions that the post-Arab Uprisings have supported the democratisation process in the countries involved	74
4.3	Respondents' perceptions that the failure of the post-Arab Uprisings in Syria has led to the emergence of Daesh and the humanitarian crisis	75
4.4	Respondents' perceptions on Tunisia as the 'success story' of the Arab Uprisings	78
4.5	Respondents' perceptions that the Arab world was more stable before the start of the Arab Uprisings	80
4.6	Respondents' views on whether civil disobedience during the Arab Uprisings has given inspiration to Malaysia's Islamist movements	84
4.7	Respondents' views that the role of new social media (Facebook, YouTube, Twitter) during the Arab Uprisings influenced the activism of Malaysia's Islamist movements	88
4.8	Respondents' views that the rise of Islamist parties in the post-Arab Uprisings has given political inspiration to the Islamist movements in Malaysia	90
4.9	Respondents' views that post-Arab Uprisings events have influenced the ideology of Islamist movements in Malaysia	92
4.10	Respondents' views that post-Arab Uprisings events have strengthened cooperation between Islamist movements in Malaysia and Islamist movements in the Middle East and North Africa	97
5.1	Respondents' views that the development of Islamist parties after the Arab Uprisings have taught some valuable lessons to Islamist movements in Malaysia	108
5.2	Respondents' attitudes towards the importance of political cooperation between Islamist and non-Islamist parties or groups in Malaysia	114
5.3	Respondents' views that political stability is valued above a regime change through street protest	116
5.4	Respondents' views that Malaysia does not need any Arab Uprisings-style revolution in the future (based on lessons learned after the Arab Uprisings in the MENA)	119
5.5	Respondents' views on whether acts of civil disobedience and street protest suggest a positive political transition (based on the lessons learned after the Arab Uprisings in the MENA)	121
5.6	Respondents' views on whether democracy and elections are the best medium for political change in Malaysia (based on lessons learned following the Arab Uprisings in the MENA)	124
5.7	Respondents' views on whether the series of protest events organised by the Bersih were an indirect effort to create a 'Malaysian Spring'	126

Preface

The Arab Uprisings and Malaysia's Islamist Movements

The Arab Uprisings and Malaysia's Islamist Movements examines the attitude of Malaysia's Islamist movements – (1) The Pan-Malaysian Islamic Party (PAS), (2) The National Trust Party (AMANAH), (3) The Muslim Youth Movement of Malaysia (ABIM) and (4) the Malaysian Muslim Solidarity Front (ISMA) – towards the 2011 Arab Uprisings events. In particular, it explores the knowledge and perceptions of selected Islamist movement activists, politicians and members in Malaysia regarding these protests, also considering how the events impacted their activism, political approach and attitudes towards the issues of regime change, civil disobedience, political revolution, democracy, Islamism and political stability. This book identifies a number of lessons learned by the Malaysian Islamists from the development of post-Arab Uprisings in the MENA.

The tendency of Malaysian Islamists to be influenced by the development in the Middle East and global political Islam is not new, as shown by the 1979 Iranian Islamic Revolution. This popular event was known for its indirect impact on the political activism and approaches of PAS and ABIM in Malaysia in the 1980s and 1990s as well as for inspiring many Malaysian Islamists to uphold the struggle of establishing an Islamic state in their country. Following the recent Arab Uprisings, which also witness the rise of Islamist parties as a ruling power, these events have also been followed by the Malaysian Islamists with great interest. Furthermore, the major involvement of Malaysian Islamists in a series of mass protests, circa 2011–2016, against the regime were perceived by numerous local and foreign journalists as an attempt to create a Malaysian Spring', inspired by the 'Arab Spring' phenomenon. However, some Malaysian authorities have suggested that there is no basis for presuming that the Arab Uprisings had an impact on the Malaysian experience. This raises questions about the relationship between the Arab Uprisings and Malaysian Islamists. Nevertheless, before jumping to any conclusions about the 'Malaysian Spring' polemics, it must be understood to what extent Malaysian Islamists grasp the fundamental issues of the Arab Uprisings.

xii *Preface*

Speaking of the global impact of the Arab Uprisings, some elements of political repression, coupled with corruption and power abuse (which some claimed had been practised by the previous Malaysian regime), led to a number of Malaysian Islamists' believing that they were inspired by the acts of mass street protests during the Arab Uprisings. This inspiration came when they witnessed the ousting of several long-serving autocratic Arab rulers from their respective positions by the Arab protesters. However, the fear of insecurity and political instability which is currently evident following the Arab Uprisings in Egypt, Libya, Syria and Yemen led to many respondents' favouring political stability rather than regime change. Most of them were quite sceptical about the polemics of the 'Malaysian Spring' as most neither disagreed nor agreed that the series of local political rallies were an indirect effort to topple the government. Overall, this empirical study found that the majority of Malaysian Islamists from PAS, ABIM, ISMA and AMANAH are supportive of free and democratic elections as a relevant medium for political change and less supportive of overthrowing the BN-led regime via civil disobedience, street demonstration or 'revolution'.

Written in a clear manner, this book sheds new light on widespread assumptions regarding 'Malaysian Spring' polemics in the post-Arab Uprisings period and contributes to the literature on the Arab Uprisings, political Islam and beyond, making it a very valuable resource to students and researchers interested in Islamism and contemporary politics in Malaysia.

Acronyms and abbreviations

1MDB	One Malaysia Development Berhad
ABIM	*Angkatan Belia Islam Malaysia* (Muslim Youth Movement of Malaysia)
ACT	Adjustment to Change Theory
AD	*Anno Domini* (In the year of our lord)
AKP	*Adalet ve Kalkınma Partisi* (Justice and Development Party)
AMANAH	*Parti Amanah Negara* (The National Trust Party)
BBC	British Broadcasting Corporation
BC	Before Christ
BCL	Basic civil liberties
BERSIH	*Gabungan Pilihanraya Bersih dan Adil* (The Coalition of Free and Fair Election)
BN	*Barisan Nasional* (Party of National Front)
CEC	Central Executive Committee
CIA	Central Intelligent Agency
CNCD	National Coordination for Change and Democracy
DAESH	*Ad-Dawla Al-Islamiyya fil Iraq Wa Al-Sham* (Islamic State of Iraq and al-Sham)
DAP	Democratic Action Party
GCC	Gulf Cooperation Council
GE	General Election
GNP	Gross national product
EP	Effective power to govern
EU	European Union
FIS	*Front Islamique du Salut* (Islamic Salvation Front)
FLN	*Front de Libération Nationale* (National Liberation Front)
IGP	Inspector General of Police
IKRAM	*Pertubuhan Ikram Malaysia* (Malaysia Ikram Movement)
IS	Islamic state
ISA	Internal Security Act
ISIL	Islamic State of Iraq and Levant
ISIS	Islamic State of Iraq and Syria/Islamic State of Iraq and al-Sham

ISMA	*Ikatan Muslimin Malaysia* (Malaysian Muslim Solidarity Front)
JIM	*Jemaah Islah Malaysia* (Malaysia Congregation Reform)
JMP	Joint Meeting Parties
MCA	Malaysian Chinese Association
MENA	Middle East and North Africa
MIC	Malaysian Indian Congress
NATO	The North Atlantic Treaty Organization
NGO	Non-Governmental Organisation
NGOs	Non-Governmental Organisations
NVIVO	Software for qualitative data analysis
OIC	Organisation of Islamic Cooperation
PAS	*Parti Islam Se-Tanah Melayu* (Pan-Malaysian Islamic Party)
PJD	*Parti de la Justice et du Développement* (Party of Justice and Development)
PKR	*Parti Keadilan Rakyat* (People's Justice Party)
PKS	*Partai Keadilan Sejahtera* (Prosperous Justice Party)
PSC	Parliamentary Selection Committee on Electoral Reform
RCE	Reasonably competitive election
RM	*Ringgit Malaysia* (Malaysian Ringgit)
RP	*Refah Partisi* (Party of National Salvation)
SAVAK	*Sāzemān-e Ettelā'āt va Amniyat-e Keshvar* (Organisation of National Security and Information of Iran)
SCAF	Supreme Council of Army Forces
SMs	Social movements
SMOs	Social movement organisations
SOSMA	Special Offences and Security Measures Act
SPSS	Statistical package for social sciences
UAE	United Arab Emirates
UK	United Kingdom
UKM	*Universiti Kebangsaan Malaysia* (National University of Malaysia)
UMNO	United Malays National Organisation
UN	United Nations
UNSC	United Nations Security Council
US/USA	United States
USD	United States Dollar
VIP	Very important person
WTO	World Trade Organisation

Acknowledgements

This book is dedicated to my wonderful family, especially my mother, Zakirah, and my father, Saidin, for their limitless support, love and prayers. Not to forget my queen and loving wife, Azyati, for her great patience, understanding and sacrifice over the past few years when we were blessed with two beautiful princes, Adam and Daniel, after I started to embark on this journey. My sincere apologies must go to my eldest son, Adam, for not being able to be with him on the day he saw the world for the first time, until he finally crawled towards me at the Heathrow Terminal. I firmly believe every success needs sacrifice, and that was the biggest sacrifice of my life.

My special thanks and warmest gratitude must go to a very significant person at the Institute of Arab and Islamic Studies, Dr Lise Storm. Thank you very much for great supervision, dedication and commitment; for good friendship, laughter and concern; for valuable advice, counselling and shared experience; and for encouragement, hope and support whenever I was about to give up. Thank you also to her two wonderful little princesses, Amélie and Alice, who from an early age regularly and cheerily joined the supervision meetings. I am eternally indebted to my supervisor for everything, up to this moment of writing the acknowledgements.

While I dedicate the book to my family and express my deep gratitude to my former mentor, others also played a major role. At the Institute of Arabic and Islamic Studies (IAIS), I would like to thank Dr Eleanor Gao for the outstanding support and assistance that she provided during my first year as a PhD student in Exeter and for introducing me to her beautiful daughter, Lucia. To Associate Professor William Gallois, Dr Katie Natanel, Dr Marc Owen, Dr Billie Jeanne Brownlee, Dr Ross Porter, Dr Claire Beugrand, Mr Ali Mossadegh, Mrs Fatima Rawan and Mrs Sarah Roberts – thank you very much for always having time for a chat, laugh and smile, and for making me feel blessed and welcomed into the IAIS family. To my fellow seniors, who have already graduated their Doctorate with flying colours – Dr Yusuf Bennaji, Dr Abdulrahman Alebrahim, Dr Tayfun Ustun, Dr Sophia Zeschitz and Dr Davide Pettinato – thank you for the much-needed inspiration. Thanks also go to my former PhD colleagues – Stéphane Hlaimi, Enrica Fei, Hamad Aladwani, Zaynab Sayid Zahid, Abdullah Alobaid, Jaber

Alahmari, Karwan Osman, Olivia Jones, Sumeyra Yakar, Enise Yakar, Manami Goto and others. Thank you for the positive 'competition', constructive discussion and encouragement when I was feeling too stressed to finish the study.

In Exeter, I thank my beautiful neighbours, especially Mr Jerry Bird and Mrs Dawn Bird, for their true multi-cultural friendship and neighbourhood spirit, and for insisting that my family join them for sightseeing visits during summer, when we would otherwise have been inclined to stay at home. Not to forget my second family, the Malaysian community, Exeter Mosque and Saudi society, for the traditional foods, enjoyable Eid celebrations and football sessions.

In Malaysia, I would like to thank several people who have indirectly helped my PhD journey – Professor Wan Kamal Mujani, Professor Hazita Azman, Professor Nordin Hussin, Professor Mohammad Agus Yusoff and Associate Professor Dr Sity Daud – for believing in me by approving my precious scholarship and Mr Abdul Muein Abadi (my best friend since our bachelor's degrees) for his outstanding motivation. To all my respondents, 'informants' and interviewees from PAS, ABIM, ISMA and AMANAH – thank you for your cooperation and willingness to participate in the survey. Without your involvement, I certainly could not have contributed any relevant and original research findings.

In Tunisia, I owe sincere thanks to the Tunisia Language Centre, particularly to Mrs Intissar Ghannouchi, who made initial contact with the centre, and Miss Takwa Kheriji, who arranged my meetings with members of the Ennahda party. My special thanks go to Sheikh Rached Ghannouchi, who sacrificed his time during my intensive interview with him.

Elsewhere, I would like to thank Dr Sophie Lemière and Dr Stéphane Valter in France, and Dr James Dorsey and Dr Teresita Cruz in Singapore for their ideas, feedback and valuable comments on my early proposal. Dr John Glenn in Southampton, Associate Professor Dr Kartini Khalid and Professor Rashila Ramli in Malaysia deserve many thanks for providing me with references that enabled me to obtain a place as a PhD student at IAIS Exeter. To all my family and friends in Malaysia and abroad, many thanks for your prayer, encouragement and support. Thanks must also go to Mrs Elaine Davies for checking, proofreading and editing my English language. I owe thanks to her for her outstanding commitment and the impressive quality of her work.

Finally, this book is the result of sponsorship and financial support. I would like to thank the Ministry of Higher Education of Malaysia and the National University of Malaysia for their valuable scholarship; the funding enabled me to enjoy the experience of my memorable years as a PhD student in Europe. Thank you also to the Prince Al-Waleed Awards, the Zarith Sofiah Foundation and the Leche Trust for the fieldwork research grant and additional monetary support.

Thank you, Tak, Terima kasih, Merci, Tesekkurler, Syukran Jazilan

Glossary of non-English terms

Ad-Din   Religion
Ad-da'wah al Islamiyyah   Islamic propagation/the call for Islam
Coup/ Coup d'état   Unexpected military takeover
Demos   Common people
Demokratia   Direct democracy
Din Wa Dawla   Religion and the state
Haj   The compulsory pilgrimage to Mecca
Harakah   Islamiyyah Islamist movement
Hejaz   The holy land of Islam
Hudud   Islamic law for capital punishment
Islah   Reform
Khilafah   Islamiyyah Islamic Caliphate
Mazhab   Schools of Sunni Islamic law
Madrasah   School
Quran   Islamic sacred book
Rahmatan lil Alamin   Blessing for the whole world
Reformasi   Reformation
Shafi'i Imam   Shafi'i School of Law
Sharia   Islamic law
Syura   Consultation
Tajdid   Renewal
Ummah   Muslim community
Umrah   The sacred visitation to Mecca
Usrah   Family/group gathering
Waqi'   Context

1 Introduction

This book discusses the Islamist movements in Malaysia in order to explore questions about the global impact of the Arab Uprisings phenomenon beyond the Middle East and North Africa (MENA). In particular, it will examine the connection between the 2011 Arab Uprisings and the Islamist movements in Malaysia from the perspective of Malaysian Islamists, considering how the phenomenon impacts and influences the movements' ideology and activism. This book will look at the post-2011 Arab Uprisings to determine how these events played a decisive role in influencing the Islamist movements in Malaysia; it will also contribute useful insights into the Malaysian Islamist experience. However, there have been strong opinions voiced by the Malaysian authorities and various scholars, claiming that there was no basis for presuming that the Arab Uprisings have had an impact on Malaysian politics. The involvement of several Islamist movements in a series of mass protests against the government, popularly known in Malaysia as *'BERSIH'*, along with strong relationships with Islamist parties in the countries involved in the Arab Uprisings, might suggest a link with the Malaysian experience. Moreover, the Malaysian public has followed the events of the Arab Uprisings with deep concern since the beginning. This raises the question of whether the previously 'semi-democratic' state of Malaysia will follow the same paths of regime change witnessed in Tunisia, Egypt and Libya in 2011, and topple their respective autocratic rulers.

Furthermore, the rise of Islamist parties in Tunisia, Egypt and Morocco in the aftermath of the Arab Uprisings is suggestive of the potential future of Malaysia's Islamist movements. The central concern that should be highlighted is the extent to which the Islamist movements in Malaysia are influenced by the Arab Uprisings or the 'Arab Spring' before coming to any conclusions about the polemics and possible future of the 'Malaysian Spring'. This brings us to the core questions of this book, regarding the influence and impact of the Arab Uprisings, which can be gauged through the reactions of selected Islamist parties – the Pan-Malaysian Islamic Party (PAS) and the National Trust Party (AMANAH) – and civil society organisations – the Muslim Youth Movement of Malaysia (ABIM) and the Malaysian Muslim Solidarity Front (ISMA) in Malaysia.

Background and context

During the late 1970s and 1980s, several Islamist movements in Malaysia, particularly the PAS and the ABIM, were greatly influenced by the Iranian Revolution of 1979 (Mohamed Osman & Saleem 2016: 2). This transnational influence on Islamism and Islamist politics in Malaysia took a further turn with the downfall, after 58 years, of Shah Pahlavi's monarchy in Iran (Liow 2009: 35). The impact of the revolution, although primarily indirect, stimulated Islamic political ideas and ideology, and led to an increased emotional attraction to a greater degree of Islamist political activism for Muslim communities in Malaysia (Esposito & Piscatori 1990: 11–33; Bramsen 2012: 197; Müller 2014: 55–56). Following the 1979 Revolution in Iran, a number of other Islamist movements such as *Jemaah Islah Malaysia* (JIM) were formed in Malaysia to embrace the success of the new so-called 'Islamic Republic'. The efforts of the Iranian Islamic community to overthrow the Shah were also found to resonate with the views of many Islamist activists in Malaysia, compelled to struggle to achieve a stronger Islamic society (Von Der Mehden 1990: 249).

Nearly four decades after the 1979 Revolution, which influenced the development of Islamist movements in Malaysia, the world has witnessed a new dramatic political scenario in the MENA, with the fall of several long-serving autocratic rulers in Tunisia, Egypt, Libya and Yemen via a massive revolution known as the 'Arab Spring'. In a domino effect, popular uprisings became widespread across the region, from one country to another, until a huge part of the Arab region was involved. 2011 was undoubtedly a turning point in the history of modern Middle Eastern politics.

Malaysia and the Arab-Muslim world

In the meantime, as a moderate Muslim state in Southeast Asia, Malaysia has significant economic, political and diplomatic ties, as well as social relationships, with the MENA nations, given their shared 'Islamic values', which indirectly unite the countries. Long-established and strong relationships between Malaysia and the Arab world are undeniable. Historically, the penetration of religious thought from the Middle East is part of a centuries-long legacy of relations between Muslims in Southeast Asia and the Middle East (Von Der Mehden 1990: 235). Malaysia has developed and cultivated multi-dimensional relationships with the Arab world for more than 500 years, and these can be traced to the establishment of the first Muslim state in the Malay-Archipelago in the thirteenth century. These 'bilateral' relationships subsequently led to published news and information regarding the uprisings in Tunisia, Egypt, Libya, Bahrain, Algeria, Yemen and Syria flooding into Malaysia and being widely discussed by Malaysians via social media platforms such as Facebook, YouTube and Twitter. As pointed out by Osman Bakar (2012: 743), the Malaysian public in general, and political observers and academics in particular, have been observing the unfolding of events in the Arab world with great interest, if not with deep concern. Osman's statement is supported by Abdul Hadi Awang (PAS president), who admitted that even Malaysians with no season called 'spring' were passionately following the 'Arab Spring' development. There was great interest among Malaysians because the phenomenon was unexpected and extraordinary. They felt that the Arabs deserved a real change for the better, especially in the political sphere. On the other hand, civil groups and academics, as well as the majority of Internet users at that time, were debating whether Malaysia would be the next victim of regime change and democratic transition after they witnessed Tunisia, Egypt and Libya toppling their respective autocratic governments.

For Abdul Malek, the Arab Uprisings, specifically the 2011 Egyptian uprising, were significant for Malaysians for two major reasons. First, the majority of Muslims in Malaysia held Egypt in high regard as the sanctuary for Arabic and Islamic knowledge. Thousands of Malaysian school leavers flocked to Egypt every year to enrol in numerous Egyptian higher education institutions, with Al-Azhar, Mansoura, Zaqaziq and Cairo Universities their most popular destination. Second, the majority of Malaysian Muslims were concerned by the role of Islam within the revolution because they knew that the Muslim Brotherhood was a dominant force in the Egyptian opposition. Thus, they were interested in whether political Islam and the Egyptian Islamists would triumph over the autocratic rule of president Hosni Mubarak (Abdul Malek 2011: 75–76). The rise of Islamist parties, Tunisia's Ennahda Party and Egypt's Freedom and Justice Party shortly after the collapse of the incumbent regimes in Tunisia and Egypt seemed like a beacon of hope and provided an early direction for the future of Islamist movements in Malaysia. According to Peter Mandaville (2014: 369):

> The success of Islamists in the wake of the 2010–2011 Arab Uprisings seemed to confirm the dominance of political Islam as a socio-political force in the Middle East. Combined with the rise of Turkey's AKP and routinized participation of Islamist parties in electoral politics across Southeast Asia, there seems to be strong evidence that religiously based parties have become a firm fixture in Muslim politics.

The thinking of Rachid Ghannouchi (the leader of the Ennahda Movement) and Mohamed Morsi (Egypt's former president) have inspired majority of the Islamist movements across Malaysia. Many academic discourses and student forums were held to discuss their political philosophy and strategy. Rachid Ghannouchi was well known in Malaysia by members of the Islamist movements. His thoughts, speeches and writings on the issues of political Islam, social justice and governance were widely viewed and read.[1] According to Muhammad Najib, Ghannouchi's concept of '*Faraghat for ijtihad*' heavily influenced the Malaysian Islamists.[2] Many Muslim activists

4 Introduction

expressed support for Tunisia's Jasmine Revolution and the new Ennahda-led government, merely because they were associated with al-Ghannouchi (Bakar 2012: 745). The PAS delegation, led by their president Hadi Awang, had gone to Tunisia in July 2012 and February 2015 to pay a visit to Rachid Ghannouchi and several members of the Ennahda Movement; in August 2014, Ghannouchi's daughter, Intissar Kherigi, and a number of representatives from Ennahda came to Kuala Lumpur to join an event organised by the PAS Youth Wing and Asian Federation of Muslim Youth entitled 'Survival of the Ennahda Party After Revolution in Tunisia'.[3] Speaking about the political relationship between Malaysia and the Arab world, particularly Tunisia, Naoufel Eljammali,[4] a former Tunisian Minister of Employment and Vocational Training, and member of the Ennahda Political Bureau, further commented that:

> I think the Malaysian (political) experience is also near to us . . . and I think the Muslim world in Asia is much better compared to the (development of) political parties in the Middle East for instance, which are still stuck in the old mindset and practice of the 50s and 60s of the last century. That is why we feel ourselves to be nearer to Malaysian politicians than for instance Egyptian ones. So, I think Tunisia in this way finds itself as a Muslim political party with a lot more affinity with the Asian Muslim ones than many other Arab Muslim political parties.

The 'Malaysian Spring' polemics

During the post-2011 Arab Uprisings, the Malaysian authority strongly believed that there would be no basis for Arab Uprisings protests in Malaysia.[5] However, a series of large-scale mass protests had taken place in the capital (Kuala Lumpur) prior to the 2013 general election, during which the protesters and opposition parties (including PAS and several other Islamist movements and NGOs) had mainly demanded political and electoral reforms from the government. Nevertheless, the demonstrations were a far cry from what had been seen in the MENA, where there had been a countless number of violent incidents as well as intimidation and brutality as a result of government action to suppress and undermine protesters. Quite a few Malaysian political observers interviewed by the Malaysian National News Agency (BERNAMA) established that Malaysians would reject the possibility of an Arab Spring-style Revolution because there were no concrete justifications for them to imitate it, especially after seeing its terrible and appalling repercussions. As Kaisan Abdul Rahman (2013) emphasised, the reason for people's rejection of such an idea was Malaysia's proven track record of democratic practice: general elections had been held every five years without fail, and this had ensured the nation's progress and well-being.[6] Another reason was that people could choose their government, and the voice of the majority was always respected, as proven by the three states

(Selangor, Penang and Kelantan) currently under opposition rule. Furthermore, Kaisan believed the National Front Party (*Barisan Nasional* or BN)-led government to be transparent and constant in making efforts to enhance the welfare of its people through various programmes.

Similarly, Abdullah (2013) was of the opinion that the Arab Spring phenomenon would not spread to Malaysia because the government was constantly making changes for the better. Meanwhile, in an interview with the BBC in London, Malaysia's Prime Minister Najib Razak (2013) believed that there was no reason for his country to mount a protest similar to the Arab Uprisings because the country had enjoyed 55 years of peace and stability, and witnessed good economic progress. From these statements, it was clear that the Malaysian authority rejected the possibility of an Arab Uprisings phenomenon among its citizens (including any Islamist movements in the country). However, these debatable statements were only subjective views, either from the authority or from individuals. On the other hand, Larry Diamond, a leading contemporary scholar in the field of democracy studies, claimed that the effect of the Arab Uprisings might spread to East Asian countries, including Malaysia. According to him:

> With the eruption of mass movements for regime change across the Arab nations, scholars and analysts of democratic prospects have focused attention on the Middle East and North Africa. But if a new regional wave of transitions to democracy unfolds in the next five to ten years, it is more likely to come from East Asia since this region has been strangely neglected in recent thinking about the near-term prospect for expansion of democracy.
>
> (Diamond 2012: 5)

Diamond's views are also in line with those of Welsh (2011), who points out that[7]

> Largely driven by ordinary citizens, often connected through the social media, Southeast Asia is experiencing important and substantive political change. In this year of the Arab Spring, attention has centered on developments in the Middle East. With street protests and elections, amidst violence, there is no question that the region has experienced a profound political upheaval. Yet, 2011 has been extremely significant in Southeast Asia as well. The ripples of change are here. Largely driven by ordinary citizens, often connected through the social media, Southeast Asia is experiencing important and substantive political change, with the balance clearly in favour of greater empowerment of citizens, human dignity and promise.

Shedding light on the performance of the previous government under the leadership of Najib Razak, many issues concerning financial crises, corruption, power abuse and the implementation of unnecessary taxes, as well as internal conflicts among the ruling party members, had tarnished the regime's reputation. These issues have ultimately affected the legitimacy of the administration. According to Case (1993, 2007), Means (1996), Abbott (2009, 2011) and Diamond (2012), Malaysia is considered as a semi-democratic state or 'quasi-democracy', and some elements of a 'soft, competitive and electoral authoritarian' regime remains due to issues relating to human rights, news and media censorship, and certain laws/acts that limit the freedom of political activity as well as the movement of opposition parties. Levitsky and Way (2002: 52) explained the concept of competitive authoritarianism:

> In a competitive authoritarian regime, formal democratic institutions are widely viewed as the principal means of obtaining and exercising political authority. However, incumbents violate those rules so often and to such extent, the regime fails to meet conventional minimum standards for democracy.

As Jiří Holík (2011: 4) demonstrates, the opposition in Malaysia is generally allowed to compete in elections and operate in the parliament, but only under the condition that it accepts the rules of the game set by the government and does not threaten the dominant position of the ruling coalition. This statement is also supported by Freedom House ratings for political rights and civil liberties, which state that Malaysia has assumed the relatively average position of 'partly free'.[8] The political and economic struggles facing Malaysians today, although on a different scale, are almost the same factors that have contributed to the Arab Uprisings. Economic crises, which led to rising food prices, endemic poverty and chronic unemployment as well as systematic political repression and corruption at various levels, also led Tunisian, Egyptian, Libyan, Syrian and Yemeni revolutionaries to take to the streets (Achy 2011: 5; Bishara 2011: 5; Driss 2011: 21–22; Korotayev & Zinkina 2011: 167; Arieff 2012a: 34; Gelvin 2012: 21–44).

Aspirations and desires for a more accountable and democratic government have permeated into the country, and for years to come Southeast Asia will be a contested terrain of possibilities for regime change. Hence, with regard to the current political situation in Malaysia, it is plausible and not too much of an exaggeration to propose that 'revolution' and mass mobilisation, with the assistance of new social media, could possibly occur if the government continuously fails to fulfil the people's demand for political, economic and social reforms. Indeed, Musa Hassan (2013), a former Malaysian Inspector General of Police (IGP), advised that an 'Arab Spring' style protest could happen in Malaysia if any losing parties in the general election (the 13th general election) are dissatisfied with the result.[9] He also lamented the fact that several politicians are willing to gamble on the nation's dignity and religion in order to achieve their political ambitions.

Additionally, as a political parties or an NGOs, the Islamist movements in Malaysia are undeniably capable of playing a significant role in mobilising such uprisings against the ruling government, as was seen during the 1998 'Reformation Movement' (*Reformasi*), in response to the demotion of Anwar Ibrahim from his Deputy Prime Minister position.[10] Nonetheless, before jumping to any conclusion about the possible future of the 'Malaysian Spring', the most crucial issue that needs to be clarified is the extent to which the Islamist movements in Malaysia – both political parties and NGOs – really understand the Arab Uprisings. This brings us to the core question of this book: the influence and impact of the Arab Uprisings through reactions of Islamist politicians, Muslim organisations and activists in Malaysia.

Despite its challenges and difficulties, it is fair to describe Malaysia as potentially able to maintain its political stability, although there has been strong and consistent pressure for a transparent and accountable government at the grass roots level. According to Joseph Liow, since the end of the Second World War, Malaysia's admirable record of social and political stability was, to a great extent, made possible by its economic growth, although the 'economic graph' has shown fluctuations in terms of progress. With its stable conditions, developing economy and relative social and political stability, Malaysia is widely celebrated as the epitome of progressive, moderate Islam by the international media and major Western European states (Liow 2009).

Writing in 1993, 2007 and 2013, William Case suggested that Malaysia's semi-democracy is stable at present, although in a limited form, and may persist unchanged for a considerable period. This 'stable-tension' situation, as described by Baharuddin (2009), has fabricated the landscape of Malaysia's politics since the 13 May 1969 Ethnic Riot. An alternative view is that the emergence of numerous political parties and civil society groups from various backgrounds, including religious and Islamist backgrounds, has generally supported the democratisation process via the check and balance mechanism. Diamond (2012: 6) claims that there are now significant prospects for democratic change in Malaysia as it shows signs of entering a period of early democratic transition. Alarmed by the upheavals and regime change that began sweeping in from the MENA at the end of 2010, the Malaysian government has pledged to appoint a broad committee to review the state's electoral system and subsequently vowed to repeal the Internal Security Act in order to improve the future of national politics (Diamond 2012: 9). Nevertheless, in Malaysia the following questions remain unclear and unanswered;

1   To what extent did the Malaysian Islamists really know about the Arab Uprisings?
2   What are the general perceptions and views of Islamists movements in Malaysia of the Arab Uprisings?
3   How important was the Tunisian case to the Malaysian Islamists, particularly with regard to the Ennahda's development in the post-Jasmine Revolution? How have the Tunisian Islamists responded to Malaysian Islamists' views on the Arab Uprisings and the Tunisian case in particular?

8 *Introduction*

4   While Malaysian Islamist movements were inspired by the Iranian Revolution of 1979 in the past, have the Arab Uprisings influenced Malaysian Islamist movements in the same way?
5   To what extent have the 2011 Arab Uprisings phenomenon and the post-Arab Uprisings development influenced and shaped the ideology, political activism and approach of Islamist movements in Malaysia?
6   How have the Islamist activists and politicians in Malaysia greeted and responded to the post-Arab Uprisings development? What lessons can Malaysian Islamists learn from this development?

These core questions are the issues discussed in this book in order to draw some useful insights on the Arab Uprisings from Malaysia's experience.

Academic shortcomings

From the time this research was originally conducted up to the present day, there has been a paucity of publications and specific studies that discuss in detail the Arab Uprisings phenomenon in the Southeast Asian context, particularly in the framework of Islamist movements in Malaysia. The review of the literature suggests that limited studies have explored the impact of the Arab Uprisings events on the political views of Islamist movements in Malaysia.[11] Therefore, in order to fill a knowledge gap, as mentioned above, this book aims to identify the perceptions and influences of the Arab Uprisings phenomenon on the Islamist movements in Malaysia. The impact of the Arab Uprisings is assessed within the setting of the Islamist political party and civil society, focussing on several established Islamist movements in Malaysia. The selected case studies examine the truths and realities of the 2011 Arab Uprisings' influence, from the MENA to the Southeast Asia context. This book also attempts to address the question of how and why the Islamist movements in Malaysia have dynamic approaches, policies and principles with regard to issues of civil disobedience, Arab world affairs and political Islam. To sum up, the main objectives of this study can be summarised as follows:

1   To identify the knowledge, perceptions and views of the different Islamist movements in Malaysia – (1) the PAS, (2) the ABIM, (3) the ISMA and (4) the AMANAH – towards the Arab Uprisings phenomenon in the MENA.
2   To examine the extent of the influences and impacts of the 2011 Arab Uprisings phenomenon and the post-Arab Uprisings development on the political approach and activism of different Islamist movements in Malaysia.
3   To identify the lessons that can be learned by the Malaysian Islamists as well as explain how and why the selected Islamist movements in

Malaysia have dynamic views, approaches and principles with regard to issues of civil disobedience, Arab world affairs and political Islam.

The focus of this study

The study is intended to offer a significant and original contribution to the body of knowledge in the field of Islamist movements in Malaysia, as well as modern Middle Eastern Politics, with specific attention to the issue of the 2011 Arab Uprisings and their wider impact on the global Muslim community. The findings of the study are also expected to reveal new information about the perceptions and influences of the Arab Uprisings phenomenon amongst the Islamist movements in Malaysia, especially in the period following the post-2011 Arab Revolutions. Although a number of studies and publications have examined the relations between the Arab Uprisings and worldwide responses, as well as implications outside of Middle Eastern countries, there has been a lack of comprehensive study on the influence and impact on Southeast Asian countries, in particular as regards the Islamist movements in Malaysia. Therefore, the aim of this study is to fill this gap. Data collection for this study occurred from 2016 to April 2018 – meaning that recent political developments in the MENA and Malaysia, for instance the 14th Malaysian General Election in May 2018 and any subsequent events, were not discussed or included in any part of the thesis.

The main aim in carrying out this research in Malaysia is to explore the opinions of local Islamist movement members and Islamist politicians on global issues (such as the Arab Uprisings) that relate to their Islamic world views and political values. Since the objective of this research is to identify the perceptions and influences of the Arab Uprisings phenomenon on the Islamist movements in Malaysia, a set of questionnaires was developed based on the highlighted research objectives, as indicated above. This method is appropriate for this research because the goal is to focus on understanding human perceptions regarding specific social and political matters. Non-probability (purposive) sampling and the use of target respondents were employed. The latter was determined according to the composition of selected Islamist movement organisations. Before starting the process of field work, the questionnaire was prepared in English and then translated into Malay. The sample covered in this study consists of members of several Islamist movements in Malaysia. Four main established Islamist movements were selected as units of analysis (for a number of reasons). The organisations are as follows:

1 The Pan-Malaysian Islamic Party/*Parti Islam Se-Malaysia* (PAS).
2 The Muslim Youth Movement of Malaysia/*Angkatan Belia Islam Malaysia* (ABIM).

10 Introduction

3 The Malaysian Muslim Solidarity Front/*Ikatan Muslimin Malaysia* (ISMA).
4 The National Trust Party/*Parti Amanah Negara* (AMANAH).

Significance of PAS, ABIM, ISMA and AMANAH as a sample

The case studies examined in this book represent four of the most well-known and often discussed Islamist movements operating in the Malaysian political landscape. For example, the PAS, developed in the mould of the Muslim Brotherhood, has been around since Malaysian independence from Britain in the mid-1950s and even served as part of a coalition government in the 1970s. Its current membership is estimated to be around 800,000, making it the biggest and strongest opposition party in Malaysia.[12] Meanwhile, the ABIM played a key role in instigating the Islamisation trend at the grass roots level in the 1970s, during which the effect of the Iranian Revolution spread to the majority of the Muslim world (Mandaville 2014: 238–239). It has been estimated that ABIM has recruited approximately 50,000 members, and it has more than 150 branches throughout the country, including overseas branches in the United Kingdom, the United States, Egypt, Pakistan, Australia and New Zealand (Monutty 1990: 88–97). As noted by Saodah Abd Rahman and Abu Sadat Nurullah (2012), the PAS and ABIM are the prominent Islamic parties and movements, and can be regarded as the driving forces behind the Islamic awakening in Malaysia.

Meanwhile, the ISMA is popularly involved with politics and Islamic propagation activities in Malaysia under the banner of 'United Malay and Supreme Islam'. Although ISMA has declared that it is purely an NGO, its leaders acting as electoral candidates in the previous general election (2013) showed its effort to strengthen the movement via political channels. Its more than 23 local branches as well as nine international bases seem more than sufficient to indicate its strength and progress as a movement. The AMANAH, however, is a newly registered political party in Malaysia that claims to promote progressive and moderate political Islam. Most of its members were a part of PAS before the party's internal conflicts resulted in a split amongst its leadership. As the party currently has more than 20,000 new members across the country, it is a necessary case study for researchers who are dealing with Islamist movements in Malaysia.[13] Overall, these case studies undoubtedly provided a variety of contexts and presented their own unique view of the presuppositions regarding the global impact of the Arab Uprisings. Thus, to summarise, PAS, ISMA, ABIM and AMANAH were included in the research sample due to their large number of supporters as well as their presence in the current Malaysian political scenario and their concern with Arab world affairs.

Outline of the book

This book is divided into six chapters. The first chapter is an introductory chapter, which states the background and context of the book. Chapter 2 highlights the historical background of the four case studies of Islamist movements in Malaysia – the PAS, the AMANAH, the ABIM and the ISMA. There is also a snapshot of popular civil protests in Malaysia – the *BERSIH* and a brief description of Arab Uprisings events. Chapter 3 examines the perceptions and attitudes of the different Islamist movements in Malaysia towards the Arab Uprisings phenomenon. Chapter 4 explores the influence and impact of the Arab Uprisings on the Islamist movements in Malaysia using a number of key questions. Chapter 5 establishes lessons learned from the post-Arab Uprisings development on the Malaysian Islamists. Finally, Chapter 6 summarises the main findings of the book, along with a final discussion, and provides tentative perspectives for future development of political Islam in Malaysia.

Notes

1 An example would be a recent book on Ghannouchi's thought, written and published in the Malay language by several Islamist movement members in Malaysia. See also Hassan, Zulkifli, ed. (2016). *Rashid Al-Ghannouchi: Intelektual – Reformis Politikal Islam.* Kuala Lumpur: ABIM.
2 Personal interview with the AMANAH Youth Leader, Muhammad Najib. Kuala Lumpur, Malaysia. September 2016. What Ghannouchi meant by the concept of *Faraghat* is that, in terms of politics or question of governance, Islam left some space for humans to fill (in their own way) in accordance with the respective needs and exigencies of time and place. See Tamimi, A.S. (2001). *Rachid Ghannouchi: A Democrat within Islamism.* New York: Oxford University Press, p. 187.
3 Personal interview with the Amanah Central Committee (former PAS Chief Youth), Suhaizan Kayat. AMANAH Headquarters, Kuala Lumpur, Malaysia. 19 October 2016.
4 Personal interview with the former Minister of Employment and Vocational Training of Tunisia, and member of Ennahda Political Bureau, Naoufel Eljammali. Tunis, Tunisia. January 2018.
5 See, for example, The Star. (2013). 'Najib: No Basis for Arab Spring after 55 years of Peace, Stability'. www.thestar.com.my/news/nation/2013/07/03/najib-tun-razak-arab-spring-bbc.
6 Sinar Harian (2013). 'Pemerhati Politik: Rakyat Malaysia Tolak Revolusi ala-Arab Spring' (Political Observer: Malaysians would reject an Arab Spring-style Revolution/Uprisings). www.sinarharian.com.my/mobile/pemerhati-politik-rakyat-malaysia-tolak-revolusi-ala-arab-springs-1.120389.
7 Bridget Welsh is an Associate Professor at John Cabot University, a Senior Research Associate at NTU, a Senior Associate Fellow of THC and a University Fellow of CDU. She analyses Southeast Asian politics, especially Malaysia, Myanmar, Singapore and Indonesia. See also http://bridgetwelsh.com/2011/12/democracy-is-shining-in-the-dark/ [23 July 2015].
8 Freedom House (2017). Malaysia. Available at https://freedomhouse.org/country/malaysia.

9 Astro Awani (2013). 'Musa Hassan: "Arab Spring" boleh berlaku di negara ini' (Musa Hassan: 'Arab Spring' Could Happen in this country). www.astroawani.com/berita-malaysia/musa-hassan-arab-spring-boleh-berlaku-di-negara-ini-6913.
10 In 1998, under the iron rule of Mahathir Mohamad, Anwar Ibrahim was dismissed as the Deputy Prime Minister of Malaysia after being charged with several instances of misconduct, including sodomy and corruption. Many international observers, including Amnesty International, Human Rights Watch and opposition parties, condemned the acts of the Malaysian government, specifically those of Mahathir, as they strongly believed that all the accusations towards Anwar were made up to strengthen Mahathir's position. As a result, many protests were held in Kuala Lumpur against the ruling government and to show solidarity with Anwar Ibrahim.
11 With regard to the 2011 Arab Uprising and its connection with Malaysia, several materials have been published in Malay and English that stand out: specifically those by Joseph Liow (2015) on Islamist activism in Southeast Asia (Malaysia and Indonesia) in the post-Arab Spring events, Osman Bakar (2012) on Malaysian responses to the Arab Uprising, Mohd Safar Hashim (2015) on the views of the National University of Malaysia's post-graduate students about Arab Spring events, Syed Abdul Razak Al-Sagoff (2015) on the reaction of Malaysia's government and its society towards the Arab Upheavals, Alan Chong (2014) and Sulaiman and Khalid (2017) on the question of the 'Malaysian Spring', Salmi Edward and Wan Kamal Mujani (2015) on the influence of the Arab Uprisings in Malaysian society, Ahmad Al-Battat et al. (2013) on the effect of the Arab Revolution on the Malaysian Hospitality Industry and Kelley Currie (2012) on how the Arab Uprisings inspired the popular protest movement – the *BERSIH* in Malaysia. Nevertheless, the views of Malaysia's Islamist movements towards the Arab Uprisings have not been explored along with the impact of the phenomenon on their ideology and activism.
12 Personal interview with the Secretary General of the Kuala Lumpur PAS Youth Branch, Ubaid Hj. Abd Akla. Puchong, Malaysia. 3 September 2016.
13 The decision to include AMANAH as one of the case studies was originally based on Sophie Lemière's suggestion during the researcher's presentation at a conference in Le Havre University, France, in 2015. Lemière is a French researcher who is currently a Postdoctoral Fellow at Harvard University, specialising in the development of Malaysian politics comprising local political parties, civil society, political Islam and the role of Muslim women democrats.

2 The development of the Islamist movements in Malaysia

This chapter highlights the development of political Islam and the emergence of Malaysia's Islamist movements – the Pan-Malaysian Islamic Party (PAS), the Muslim Youth Movement of Malaysia (ABIM), the Malaysian Muslim Solidarity Front (ISMA) and the National Trust Party (AMANAH) – and provides 'snapshots' of the political protests in Malaysia. Before examining all of the selected cases of Islamist movements in Malaysia, it is vitally important to understand the context and nature in which these movements operate under the former *Barisan Nasional* (BN)-led regime. The chapter will focus on the historical background, ideology, political approach and connection to global political Islam of selected Islamist movements in Malaysia – the PAS and AMANAH Islamist parties as well as the ABIM and ISMA Islamist NGOs. It is essential to review these fundamental aspects of each Islamist movement before investigating and analysing their members' attitudes towards the development of the Arab Uprisings in the Middle East.

The emergence of Islamist movements in Malaysia

According to Von Der Mehden (1986: 177), Islam in Malaysia has developed in a religious environment significantly different from that in those Middle Eastern states where it is the faith of the vast majority of the population. It is important to note that even though Malaysia is a multi-racial and multi-religious country, Islam is dominant politically and culturally amongst its adherents and the majority of its citizens. Given the growing popularity of Islamic activism across the Muslim world, popular perspectives on the direction of Islam, as represented by alternative voices, caught the attention of Islamists and Islamic movements in Malaysia.[1] In fact, the increasing visibility of Islam in Malaysian politics is driven by the established Islamist opposition party, the PAS. In addition, alternative actors, such as NGOs and civil society groups (e.g. ABIM and ISMA), are increasingly 'weighing in' due to the discursive nature of Islamisation and its politicisation in Malaysia today (Liow 2009: 4–10).

14 *The development of the Islamist movements*

Although the government never acknowledges Malaysia as an 'Islamic state', Islam somehow constitutionally 'enjoys' the privileged status of the official religion of the Federation; still, other religions may be practised in peace and harmony in any part of the Federation (Federal Constitution of Malaysia 2015: Article 3 [1]). According to Yuki Shiozaki (2007: 100), this has an impact on the legitimacy of the Malaysian state from an Islamic viewpoint and on debates about an Islamic state. In addition, recent trends in Malaysian Islamisation have been quite striking, and a number of political leaders have raised the question (repeated in public discourse) as to whether Malaysia is essentially a secular or essentially an Islamic country (Liow 2009). Moreover, along with the recent upheavals that took place in the Middle East and North Africa (which led to the growth of several Arab Islamist parties), these circumstances inevitably caught the attention of many Malaysians (especially Muslims and Islamists) – who considered the way in which these Arab Islamist parties would work in the new spectrum of leadership as well as the prospect for democratic consolidation.

Undoubtedly, the upsurge in local Islamist movements and parties in Malaysia has been an essential force in creating the landscape of current Malay-Muslim politics.[2] One of the reasons for this Islamisation trend was the nature of Islamic political discourse, which became the focus of many debates between the ruling government and the Islamists about influencing the state's policy and decision making process. Furthermore, Von Der Mehden (1986) pointed out that past decades have seen a resurgence of Islam throughout the world, including in Malaysia. Events in Iran and the Middle East have also kindled interest in the new ideas and approaches of the Islamist movement. As acknowledged by Jomo and Cheek (1992: 79):

> The beginning of an Islamic revival was in the early seventies among the young Malaysian Muslims, especially with the first oil shock in 1973. The apparent alliance between PAS, ABIM and Iran's Islamic Revolution in the late seventies drew renewed interest to the phenomenon (of Islamic revivalism) and its implications for the wider Muslim world.

The apparent increased power of Muslim countries following the 1979 Iranian Revolution has reinforced pride in religion (Islam) amongst the majority Malay-Muslims in Malaysia (Mutalib 2008: 27). Since then, the country has witnessed what has come to be known as the 'revival' of Islam amongst the Islamists and the Muslim population. Due to the increased mobility of young Malaysian Muslims, the old-fashioned quality of Islam in Malaysia is being infused and filled with concepts from the outside, particularly from the Arab Muslim world (Von der Mehden 1986: 193). This trend has indirectly led to an Islamic awakening or revivalism in Malaysia, which started to emerge through ethnic Malays[3] (as the majority Muslims in Malaysia) and Islamist political parties and organisations.

The development of the Islamist movements 15

Historically, as identified by Suzalie Mohamad Antang (2007), there were two Islamist movements that shaped Islamic political discourse in Malaysia. The first movement, in the 1920s and 1930s, was The Young Faction, also known in Malay as the *Kaum Muda*.[4] The vast majority of its members received religious education in the Middle East and were instilled with the spirit of 'Pan-Islamism' advocated by prominent Muslim reformers, such as Jamaluddin al-Afghani (1839–1897), Muhammad Abduh (1849–1905) and Muhammad Rashid Rida (1865–1935). Due to these transnational interactions, references to and translations of text written by these Muslim reformers were disseminated for the first time into the Malay world. This led to the influence of new streams of thought amongst the Islamists, which further encouraged the local Malay Nationalists and leftists to struggle against colonialism.

The second movement was composed of Muslim youths, mainly from the PAS, the Society for Islamic Reform of Malaysia (JIM) and the ABIM. They received conventional education, both from local and overseas institutions, but with strong influences from the global Islamic resurgence of the 1970s and 1980s. These groups were trying to influence local politics by promoting 'Islam as the way of life', calling for an all-encompassing Islamic macro- and micro-order of state and society in Malaysia (Müller 2014: 16). For Müller, the emergence of a new generation of Muslim students during this period became a crucial agent of change within the Malaysian political landscape as these students introduced a previously unseen and intense emphasis on Islamist ideologies. Müller's claim was supported by Suzalie's accounts that since the first election in post-independence Malaysia, Islamic political discourse was oriented towards the identity of Malaysian Muslims who recognised themselves within Islam and were prepared to place religion as a reference point in all socio-economic and political affairs within their community.[5] However, this orientation has gradually changed to cover a wide range of domestic as well as global Islamic issues, such as the status of Malaysia as an Islamic state; the role of Islam in Malaysia's foreign policy; debate on Sharia law; and consideration of external humanitarian conflicts, such as the Middle East and Palestinian issues, and the Balkans' civil conflict.

Current Islamist movements in Malaysia have changed in line with the development of global Islamic resurgence.[6] Since the 1979 Islamic Revolution, the pattern of increased Islamist involvement in political life has continued in Malaysia. However, as a result of new movements and parties that were formed in the 1990s and 2000s, the expansion of the Islamist movement is no longer reliant on PAS and ABIM for developments. The new parties include the ISMA, the *Pertubuhan Ikram Malaysia* (IKRAM) (formerly JIM) and the new 'progressive' Muslim party – the AMANAH. All of these are very politically committed in order to gain support within the Muslim population as well as from the non-Muslims in Malaysia. Although their movements might be diverse in terms of ideology, political approach and political activism, these new actors within the Islamist movement and Muslim organisations in Malaysia have made a great contribution to the dynamic of Islamic political discourse.

The next section will discuss in further detail the selected cases of Islamist movements in Malaysia – (1) the PAS, (2) the ABIM, (3) the ISMA and (4) the AMANAH. There will be a focus upon their ideology and organisational structure, followed by consideration of the influence of the 1979 Iranian Islamic Revolution on the movements as well as the nature of transnational relations with global Islamist movements, specifically regarding affiliation with the Egyptian Muslim Brotherhood (MB).

The Pan-Malaysian Islamic Party (PAS)

The PAS, also known in Malay as *Parti Islam Se-Malaysia*, is a particularly insightful example of the complexity, cultural creativity and diversification of contemporary Islamist movements in the twenty-first-century Muslim world (Müller 2014: 5). For nearly six decades, the party has been prominent in the Malaysian political arena. It was officially established prior to Malaysian independence on 24 November 1951. Since its establishment, it has dominated the discourse on political Islam in the country (Wan Jan 2017: 1). Its current membership is unofficially estimated at around 800,000, making it one of the largest and strongest opposition parties in Malaysia. According to Mohd Izani Mohd Zain (2014: 39), PAS is the only opposition party that has remained in political rivalry in Malaysia since the first general election in 1955. Politically sophisticated, PAS has evolved to meet new challenges and excelled in playing the 'democratic game'. It has done this not by winning overwhelming electoral victories but by remaining a viable political force for over 55 years, despite the challenges posed to opposition parties by Malaysia's semi-democratic system (Miller 2006: 83).

Ideology and organisational structure

Broadly speaking, Islamist movements vary in terms of the ways in which they achieve their objectives and strategic goals (Bayat 2013: 5). As an ideological party, PAS believes strongly in Islam or political Islam as its basis and doctrine, and in this way the party differentiates itself from other non-Islamic- oriented parties in Malaysia. PAS leaders have often stressed the idea that Islam is not only about ritual, prayer and worshipping Allah – it should be perceived as a way of life (Mohamed 1990). The writing by Nasharudin Mat Isa (2001) – a former Secretary General of PAS – further explained that within the party, any (political) action or decision must be justified by the doctrine of Islam. Any response to political changes must also be viewed and studied from and within the Islamic perspective, and guided by the strong and deep-rooted PAS Islamic Council of Ulama. PAS is of the view that the life of human beings, especially the Muslim Ummah themselves, will be valuable only if utilised for the 'service' of Allah, society and state in accordance with the injunctions of Islam. For PAS, Islam is not merely a system of beliefs and dogmas to which to strictly adhere but also a programme for action with a definite purpose and an objective for all Muslims. Thus, since its formation, PAS has seen Islam as an embodiment of every principle of life – be this politics, economics or social matters (Mat Isa 2001: 8). Apart from its political agenda, PAS also considers the party as *Harakah Islamiyyah* (an Islamist movement which stresses Islamic preaching): the propagation of ad-Da'wah al-Islamiyah or the call for Islam has become part and parcel of its main activities. In this respect and in accordance with the aim of establishing an Islamic State, PAS also considers itself as an Islamist movement and party that represents the Muslim community in Malaysia. PAS also works hand in hand with other Islamist movements in the country for the sake of a common goal – to preach on the road towards Islam (Mat Isa 2001: 10).

According to Mohammad Nor Monutty (1990: 114), PAS's leadership is mainly controlled by religiously oriented figures as well as a significant number of Malay-Muslim intellectuals and professionals. However, the recent selection of the 2015 PAS Central Executive Committee (CEC) has seemed to alter the composition of PAS committees (the balance between religious and professional members). Primarily 'pious individuals' were selected by party members, leaving the 'progressive camp', otherwise known as the professional group (members whose professions and academic backgrounds were mainly based in fields of non-Arabic Islamic studies), deeply frustrated. Monutty further explained that since the presidency of Mohamad Asri Muda (de facto president from 1964 to 1969 and president from 1969 to 1983), PAS has witnessed the growing power of the Muslim cleric or Ulama as the highest authority in party policies through the effective role of the Council of Syura.[7] Thus, it makes sense that Abdul Hadi (current president of PAS and Muslim cleric) has managed to successfully maintain his position since 2002, despite being hampered by scores of controversial issues and internal conflicts within the party.

In terms of party structure, there are three wings in the PAS organisational hierarchy: (1) the Religious Scholars' Wing, (2) the Youth Wing and (3) the Women's Wing. A fourth wing, the PAS non-Muslim Supporters' Wing, was launched in 2010 but does not receive the same status as the other wings. PAS is structured in four organisational layers: (1) national, (2) state, (3) district branch and (4) sub-district branch. At each organisational layer, it maintains the CEC, which executes PAS policies. It is headed by the PAS president, and other committees run their specific portfolios under designated bureaus and departments (Müller 2014: 46).

PAS and the connection with global Islamist movements

The relationship of PAS with other global Islamist movements is, for example, reflected by the role of the Egyptian MB in shaping and influencing the party's ideology and activism. Amongst PAS members, the MB is often regarded as one of the most important political organisations in the

18 *The development of the Islamist movements*

Arab Muslim world. In Wan Saiful Wan Jan's opinion (as reported by *Al Jazeera*), PAS is also held up by the MB as a model of a successful Islamist party that can win elections and rule.[8] In fact, the MB often invites PAS to speak in foreign countries about its experiences. For instance, in 2005, the current president of PAS, Abdul Hadi Awang, was invited by the Brotherhood to speak alongside renowned Islamic scholars, including Sheikh Yusuf al-Qaradawi (one of the world's most influential Muslim clerics and a supporter of the MB).

PAS also maintains well-established contacts and an international agenda through links with other MB affiliates and Islamist parties, such as the Freedom and Justice Party (FJP) in Egypt, the Islamic Action Front (IAF) in Jordan, Hamas in Gaza, The Prosperous Justice Party (PKS) in Indonesia, Jamaat-e-Islami in Pakistan, the Islamic Salvation Front (FIS) in Algeria, the Party for Justice and Development (PJD) in Morocco and Ennahda Party in Tunisia. Several PAS official events, such as the General Assembly, have included members from these movements as overseas 'VIP' guests.

The Muslim Youth Movement of Malaysia (ABIM)

The most prominent, influential and widely studied Islamist civil society movement in Malaysia, after PAS, is Malaysia's Muslim Youth Movement or, in Malay, *Angkatan Belia Islam Malaysia*. This popular movement is possibly the largest and most organised NGO and civil society movement in Malaysia. It was officially formed in August 1971, established by youth organisations, in particular university students, throughout the country.[9] From its founding, ABIM steadily rose in the ranks of Malaysia's sociopolitical arena as a popular and influential youth movement for the Malaysian Muslim majority (Abdul Malek 2011).

According to Liow (2009: 115), the arrival of ABIM on the Malaysian political landscape was profoundly significant as it signalled the beginning of a shift in the pattern of Malay-Muslim politics. Throughout the 1970s ABIM proved dominant amongst the educated Malay-Muslim population, which found itself in the throes of a global Islamic revival. The movement grew rapidly, with branches spreading across the nation (Bahari and Saat 2014: 14–17). As an Islamist civil society organisation, ABIM often acts as a 'check and balance' entity to the ruling government. The group often debated and challenged the state on key issues, such as the character of an Islamic state and leadership, education and the Islamic way of life, as well as Malaysia's involvement in international politics as part of global Muslim solidarity (Saliha Hassan 2003: 105).

Ideology and organisational structure

Since its establishment, ABIM, via its former president (Ahmad Azam Abdul Rahman), has considered the ideology, approach and activism of the movement to be in line with the principle of *Harakah Islamiyyah*, which distinguishes it from other apolitical Islamic movements in Malaysia: for instance the Jama'a hat-Tabligh Malaysia.[10] Observers such as John Funston (1985) and Zulkifly Abdul Malek (2011) suggest that the ideology of ABIM is greatly influenced by the Egyptian MB. This statement was also supported by Monutty (1990), who stated that ABIM officials learned from and referred to literature written by the MB of Egypt as a source of their early Islamic activism. Moreover, ABIM's primary source of influence draws from the ideas and experience of Hasan Al-Banna, the famed Egyptian scholar who founded the MB in 1928 (Mohd Rumaizuddin 2003; Abdul Malek 2011). Funston also points out that ABIM takes seriously the bonds with the international MB, asserting that the role of Islam in Malaysia cannot be separated from the fate of Muslims around the world (Funston 1985: 172).

As a result of MB ideological influences, ABIM's philosophy in Malaysia appears to be distinct in that it mixes socialism and capitalism, but this is done within a distinctively Islamic framework (Abdul Malek 2011: 37). The motto of ABIM is 'striving towards building a society which is based on the principles of Islam' and presenting Islam as *ad-din* (a way of life). ABIM's constitution reveals the idealism of its leadership in reforming the mind and spirit of Muslim society using every possible means (Monutty 1989: 76–77). Some of its major objectives include the establishment and propagation of Islamic beliefs and principles (as enshrined in the Quran and Hadith) as well as the mobilisation of Muslim youth. Since its establishment, ABIM has received tremendous support from the majority of Muslim students in Malaysian universities. According to Rahman and Nurullah (2012: 106), it has several core objectives, which are derived from its main ideology:

i   To increase religious activity among people in Malaysia and its neighbourhood.
ii To struggle for the establishment of a Muslim society, which adopts a way of life based on the principles of Islam.
iii To form a faithful group of human beings who have a strong commitment to the Islamic struggle.
iv To bring about the consciousness of Islam in the society through publications, religious talks, forums, seminars, etc.
v   To nurture the Islamic mission within the organisation, in the country and abroad.

As a long-term objective, ABIM is believed to be committed to the establishment of a democratic Muslim state in Malaysia that highlights the importance of integrity, is corruption free and has good governance. Its leaders also acknowledge the benefits of political power in speeding the agenda of Islamisation in the country.[11] Its organisational structure can be classified as formal since it is officially registered with the government's Registrar of Society. Within ABIM, the CEC, led by the president, followed by the deputy president, two vice presidents, the secretary general, the treasurer and several other chief representatives in specific bureaus, constitutes the highest body in the movement, responsible for articulating and implementing its policies and activities. The CEC itself reports to the Council of Syura and the General Assembly. The Council of Syura is empowered to nominate ABIM's leadership, including the CEC. The Council also has liberty to give opinions to ABIM's leadership at all levels.

In terms of ABIM's general policies, the Council can determine the policies, strategies and activities of the movement, and then evaluate them from time to time. It is also worth mentioning that the leading role in ABIM's early years was taken by Anwar Ibrahim, Deputy Prime Minister of Malaysia from 1993 to 1998. Many observers have called him a popular and charismatic leader, who boosted the image of ABIM as a truly Islamist civil society movement. The members of ABIM come from many different walks of life. University students (local and overseas); lecturers in higher education institutions; teachers in primary and secondary schools; civil servants; and other professionals, such as doctors and lawyers, constitute the bulk of its members. Over the last few decades, it has been estimated that ABIM has recruited approximately 50,000 members, and it has more than 150 branches, including overseas branches in the United Kingdom, the United States, Egypt, Pakistan, Australia and New Zealand (Monutty 1989: 88–97).

Involvement in Malay-Muslim politics

The resurgence of ABIM's political activism extended to its increasingly vocal defence of Malay-Muslim primacy in the wake of activism by non-Muslim groups that sought to question the supremacy of Islam in Malaysia's legal and political constellations (Liow 2009: 117). Although initially ABIM specifically forbade its members from participating in political activities so that it would remain a non-partisan movement, this changed when its former president joined UMNO in 1982, followed by a vast majority of its members, who became PAS sympathisers (Weiss 2004: 151). For John Funston, the stress on Islam as 'the way of life' makes ABIM the most directly political of all Islamic civil society groups in Malaysia at that time. This politicisation is expressed particularly in calls for the introduction of Islamic legal, educational and economic systems, and for economic reform that would end corruption and the misuse of power, and guarantee basic political freedom. Indeed, the two major issues that were politically touched upon by ABIM were corruption and lack of political freedom. Its leaders continued to allege that corruption amongst Malaysia's top political leaders remained one of the most profound problems facing society and one which undermined the economic and political stability of the country (Funston 1985: 172).

As pointed out by Liow, ABIM was, for a time, regarded as the youth wing of PAS, and some of its members even openly campaigned for the party in the 1978 and 1999 elections. According to Abdul Rahman (2003: 5), the severe political crisis between the former Malaysian Prime Minister (Mahathir Mohamad) and his Deputy Prime Minister (Anwar Ibrahim) led ABIM to launch the 'Reformation Movement' on 6 September 1998 as a response to Anwar Ibrahim's demotion. Consequently, three of ABIM's top ranked leaders (including their president) were detained by the regime authority and charged under the Internal Security Act (ISA). This incident marked a turning point in ABIM's history as it openly chose a confrontational political approach against the regime. As ABIM introduced modern reforms in political strategy, it managed to get support from Malaysian Muslims and introduced the 'Islamic economy' as an alternative to capitalism and socialism.

Several former leaders of ABIM are now prominent politicians in Malaysia, including former Deputy Prime Minister and current People's Justice Party (PKR) leader Anwar Ibrahim as well as former PAS president, the late Fadzil Noor (1937–2002). Against the backdrop of a determinedly 'secular government' (led by UMNO and BN) and an increasingly Islamist opposition political party (PAS), ABIM sought to fill a gap by providing an avenue for the expression of Islamic ideals amongst Malaysian Muslims. Globally speaking, ABIM also managed to enhance its international recognition by maintaining excellent relations with Islamic countries all over the world – both Sunni and Shiite blocs. Domestically, ABIM became one of the most significant religious and political pressure groups – this indirectly meant that their members and leaders were seen as Islamists (Liow 2013).

The Malaysian Muslim Solidarity Front (ISMA)

The ISMA is an Islamist NGO. According to the CIA World Factbook, ISMA is considered a political pressure group, along with the *Bersih* movement. It was first established in 1997 under the banner of Malaysian Muslim Students Solidarity (Ikatan Siswazah Muslim Malaysia), which was changed to the Malaysian Muslim Solidarity Front in 2005. Like ABIM, ISMA is mainly involved in Islamic propagation activities – particularly focussing on the ethnic Malay and Muslim populations in Malaysia, based on their slogan (in Malay) *Melayu Sepakat, Islam Berdaulat*, which literally means 'Malay Consensus, Islam Sovereign'. As the popularity of ISMA spread, aided by controversial issues and speeches made by its leader,[12] its membership increased. It has more than 23 branches nationwide and nine international branches located in Egypt, Jordan, Australia, New Zealand, the United Kingdom, India, South Korea, Japan, Canada and the United States.[13] Most of these global branches are organised and maintained by Malaysian university students studying overseas.

22 The development of the Islamist movements

Ideology and organisational structure

In terms of stated objectives and ideology, ISMA does not differ much from ABIM as its ultimate vision and goal is to make Islam the 'ultimate way of life' for the Muslim population in Malaysia. However, ISMA's views on issues involving non-Muslim affairs have often trapped it in radicalism, absolutism and extremism. It is also seen as holding an exclusivist view when it comes to dealing with non-Muslim politicians, believing that major policy decisions affecting Islam – whether at party or government level – must be mainly, if not solely, in the hands of Muslims. The movement was also labelled by the media and journalists as a new far-right Malay-Muslim group.[14] It has repeatedly courted controversy, with statements critical of the country's non-Malay and non-Muslim communities, as part of its professed defence of Islam against a multitude of 'perceived threats'.

As reported by the *Malay Mail*, in July 2014, Abdullah Zaik, the ISMA president, was charged under the Sedition Act for calling the Chinese community in Malaysia 'intruders' and labelling their arrival in pre-Independence Malaysia a 'mistake' that must be rectified. Earlier in February 2014, ISMA vice president Muhammad Fauzi Asmuni was also investigated under the Sedition Act after he was reported calling on Muslims nationwide to be aggressive when defending Islam. The critical views of ISMA, as well as their anachronistically xenophobic and ethnocentric world view on issues involving the interests of Malaysian and international Muslims, have often placed this Islamist civil society movement in line with other far-right Malay-Muslim groups in the country (Abdul Hamid & Che Mohd Razali 2016). Unlike PAS and ABIM, ISMA does not have an equivalent of the Syura Council to act as a 'supreme advisor' or 'spiritual leader' within the organisation. Although the Ulama body (Majlis Ulama ISMA) exists within the movement, its role is rather less formal. Basically, ISMA is organised by a small executive body, which runs its activities and policies. Apart from the Islamic educated members, ISMA's membership is largely made up of professionals, including wealthy businessmen, academics, doctors, engineers and scientists, along with a strong student cohort that makes up its largest support base.[15]

Connection with global Islamist movements

ISMA traces its foundation to guidance given by the MB activists to Malay-Muslim student groups overseas. This took place directly in Egypt and indirectly in the United Kingdom via members of the MB British diaspora. Links with MB are understood to have had an electrifying effect on Malay-Muslim students, who were determined to translate their idealism into practice upon their eventual return to Malaysia (Abdul Hamid & Che Mohd Razali 2016). While ISMA may appear to be just another Islamist movement inspired by the Brotherhood, it is radically different because it aggressively promotes its affiliation and loyalty to the Brotherhood in Egypt (Abdul Malek 2011: 72–73). For instance, in February 2010, ISMA organised a convention to discuss the thoughts of Hassan Al-Banna; this was perceived as the first official convention on Al-Banna ever organised in Malaysia. Moreover, Mohd Syafiq (an ISMA activist) acknowledges that 'The ISMA office has various books related to Ikhwanul Muslimin (The Muslim Brotherhood). Although the relationship with Ikhwan is not clear on the surface, we do have a connection emotionally'.

According to Amar Yasier, a registered and active member of ISMA since 2006, there was an indirect 'competition' amongst Islamist movements in Malaysia in terms of expressing their support for (and recognition of the influence from) the Egyptian MB.[16] During the 2010 Egyptian Parliamentary Election, ISMA released an official statement about the MB's involvement in the polls, suggesting that the whole electoral process was a fraud, which led the Brotherhood to boycott the second round of voting (Abdul Malek 2011). Interestingly, it was also testified that ISMA's president, Abdullah Zaik Abdul Rahman, formally congratulated Dr Mohammed Badie Abdul Majid Sami on his appointment as the eighth Supreme Guide of the Egyptian MB.

Since ISMA's members were mostly educated in the field of religious studies (Arab and Islamic studies) in Egypt, particularly at Cairo and Al-Azhar Universities, admiration for the Egyptian MB seemed inevitable, which led to the infusion of Al-Banna's and Sayid Qutb's thoughts into the movement. ISMA also justifies its political agenda by referring to the original thoughts of Hassan al-Banna, in particular his idea of integral nationalism (an Islamic version of nationalism that stresses the important position of Islam (religion) and Muslims (citizens) in the country). His 'Arab nationalism' idea was made on the basis of ISMA's embrace of Malay nationalism and applied on the grounds of their Islamic activism (Abdul Hamid & Che Mohd Razali 2016). Speaking about the relationship with other Islamist movements, Abdullah Zaik, the president, mentions that[17]:

> We have a good relationship and practise an open policy with all (legal) Islamist movements and parties, whether in the direction of Salafi, moderate and so on. For instance, ISMA may not be that close to the Ennahda in Tunisia, but I am personally close to Ghannouchi and I know him well, from the outcome of several series of meetings.

Involvement in Malaysia's domestic politics

In 2013, ISMA entered the Malaysian electoral skirmish by contesting seven parliamentary and two state seats in the 13th general election. However, it declared that it was not a full political party and still an Islamist NGO while participating in the election. The involvement of its members as electoral candidates was based on the ticket of the newly rebranded Islamic Congregation Front of Malaysia Party or, in Malay, *Parti Barisan Jemaah Islamiyyah se-Malaysia* (BERJASA). However, none of the candidates secured any parliamentary seats, although the movement claimed that people supported their motives for joining the general election. ISMA claimed that its first ever participation in electoral politics was intended to reassert and strengthen Malay and Muslim political dominance in 'affected' areas, where the position of Islam had faded. Although it maintains its distinctiveness as an Islamist NGO within the spectrum of Malaysia's Islamism by adopting electoral politics, it continues to disavow pluralist politics that might not be appropriate for political success in the context of the multi-ethnic and multi-religious society in Malaysia. This peculiar practice is somehow based upon its ethnocentric world view, which sees the supremacy of Islam and the interest of the Muslim community in Malaysia as the movement's highest priorities in terms of its operational base and political activism (Abdul Hamid & Che Mohd Razali 2016).

The National Trust Party (AMANAH)

The National Trust Party, commonly and officially known in Malay as *Parti Amanah Negara* or 'AMANAH', is a newly registered Islamist political party promoting the approach of moderate and progressive political Islam. The party was originally founded as the Malaysia Workers' Party before it was handed over in August 2015 to a group of Islamists who had been members of the PAS. As reported by the party's official website (as well as by mainstream media in Malaysia), due to internal conflict within PAS and the split between the professional and conservative groups, along with the frustration of not being re-elected as the party's executive committee, the group led by former PAS deputy president, Mohamad Sabu, finally decided to leave PAS in order to be a party mainly dominated by conservative Islamists. This group, who dubbed themselves as 'progressive and professional' Islamists, officially redefined the Malaysia Worker's Party as a newly Islamist democratic party on 16 September 2015. This scenario was also confirmed by Damien Kingsbury (2017: 75), a prominent Australian professor of Southeast Asian politics, who stated that:

> Following the removal of moderates from the party in 2015 in response to discontent over the party's increasingly hardline position, thousands of moderates and progressive PAS members split from the party to form the National Trust Party (Parti Amanah Negara or AMANAH), which was previously the leftist National Workers' Party.

According to Wan Saiful Wan Jan (2017: 3), the main reason for the internal split within PAS was due to a long-standing ideological battle between the progressive and conservative factions.

The conservative faction in PAS has often been labelled the Ulama or 'religious scholars camp' – although there are also members who are not religiously educated. The Islamists within this camp generally adhere to a conservative interpretation of how Islam should be applied to public policy, especially on the issues of implementing Sharia – which often leads to the practice of exclusivity towards non-Muslims. The progressive faction, on the other hand, is widely known as the 'professional camp' – implying that they come from professional and non-religious backgrounds (e.g. doctors, engineers, lawyers). Leaders and members within this camp emphasise good governance, inclusivity towards non-Muslims and human rights, instead of being narrowly focussed on the immediate implementation of Sharia. They acknowledge that it is necessary to respect all views, regardless of whether they come from Muslims or non-Muslims, and that all these ideas need to be negotiated within a liberal democratic framework (Wan Jan 2017: 4–5). According to Muhammad Najib, the party currently has six elected Members of Parliament (previously PAS MPs) and receives support from approximately 20,000 members throughout the country. The involvement of other Islamist civil society organisations, like IKRAM Malaysia (formerly JIM), is also known to provide extensive support to this new brand of Malaysian Islamist party.[18]

Ideology and organisational structure

The party's main ideology, as stated by its president, Mohamad Sabu, reflects progressive and moderate political Islam, which emphasises the importance of openness, tolerance and inclusiveness in all layers of society and amongst the multi-religious citizens in Malaysia – as long as Islam is respected as the party's core value. The party acknowledges that it is necessary to respect all views, regardless of religion, and that there is a need to negotiate different political ideas and approaches within a liberal democratic framework (Wan Jan 2017: 4–5). Although its efforts to attract more non-Muslim supporters seem pragmatic, the party managed to differentiate itself from PAS in terms of reform and renewal (*islah* and *tajdid*) since its ultimate goal is no longer focussed on the issue of Sharia law or the creation of an Islamic state. Leaders within AMANAH have stressed that defence of basic civil liberties and political rights in a multi-cultural and multi-religious country is the new party's top priority. As its strategy director, Dzulkefly Ahmad[19], points out:

> AMANAH affirms our commitment to establish Islam as the basis of human well-being and good governance in a civil state instead of advocating Islamic Criminal Law (*Hudud*) and the other punitive aspects of Islam. Where narrow nationalism divides, Islam unites. Where religious bigotry excludes and decriminalises, Islam embraces and enriches. Where corruption wounds and destroys, Islam heals and redeems. Where tyranny represses, Islam liberates.

26 The development of the Islamist movements

According to the party's official website, the purpose of its establishment as a new Islamist party in Malaysia can be summarised as follows:

i   To uphold Islam as the basis for the party's struggle.
ii To establish a state and civil society in line with the principle 'Islam is a blessing for all' (*Islam Rahmatan Lil' Alamin*).
iii To implement a rule based on good governance in line with the principles of trust, fairness, impartiality, competence and transparency.
iv To support the approach of moderation, openness and democracy, and to operate within the framework of democracy guided by the Federal Constitution of Malaysia.
v   To mobilise all segments of citizens in an inclusive political struggle, no matter what their races, cultures and beliefs are, throughout the Federation.

Unlike the other Islamist movements being studied, AMANAH's organisational structure is slightly different as the party (at the time this thesis was being written) does not have any official Syura or Ulama Council to serve as an 'absolute or supreme religious advisor'. However, it decided to retain a position for a general advisor, and this is now held by the former president of the Malaysian Ulama Society (1981–1999), Ahmad Awang. The party leadership consists of ten executive committees, which run the party's activities and programmes, and are led by its president, Mohamad Sabu. As a new contender in the Malaysian 'political game', the AMANAH appears to be a rival for PAS and UMNO, and is gaining support from the Muslim population.

Connection with global Islamist movements

In terms of the connections between AMANAH and other Islamist movements in the Middle East and the Arab world, Muhammad Najib (an AMANAH Youth Leader) claims that the party has recently established a progressive relationship with the Ennahda Party in Tunisia and the Justice and Development Party (AKP) in Turkey. PAS, ABIM and ISMA were infused with the Egyptian MB's ideas on *Harakah Islamiyyah* – however, as a new Islamist party, AMANAH seems to be trying not to emulate any foreign model of political Islamism, aiming instead to establish its own model of modern political Islam in Malaysia. According to Najib[20]:

> AMANAH builds relationships with all (overseas) Islamist movements, with Ennahda in Tunisia, AKP in Turkey and various others. But AMANAH does not reach the point of making their approaches the sole source of our guidance. During the founding of AMANAH, it is true that we tried to think of a model that we were going to use. We

also tried to learn some lessons. We take all these great things about the Islamist movements and at the same time we try not to imitate their approach 100 percent. So, finally AMANAH decides to establish an Islamist party in Malaysia with our own mould.

Malaysian Islamists and impacts of the 1979 Iranian Revolution

Dominik Müller (2014: 55) has stressed that during the 1970s and 1980s, Iran and its popular revolution played a decisive role in the development of PAS. The trajectory of Iranians in forming a modern Islamic republic electrified idealistic Muslim youth in Malaysia who wanted to bring fundamental politics towards the 'government of Allah' (Farish Noor 2004: 331). There are obvious doctrinal and theological differences between PAS and Iran. For example, Malaysian Muslims are almost entirely Sunni in practical orientation and follow the Shafi'i school of Islamic jurisprudence (*mazhab*), while the Iranian Revolution was viewed by many observers as a Shiite phenomenon (Durac & Cavatorta 2015: 144). However, such differences did not stop the revolution from serving as a source of inspiration for PAS leaders and members. One key actor in PAS during this period of global Islamic resurgence was Yusof Rawa, the former president of PAS and the Malaysian ambassador to Iran, Turkey and Afghanistan. His tour of duty in Iran in the mid-1970s – a period when popular protest against the Shah was building at an alarming pace – gave the Islamist party critical first-hand experience of the formation of an 'Islamic state' as well as the build-up towards an Islamic Revolution (Liow 2009: 34).

Liow (2009: 34) and Müller (2014: 55) note that in the aftermath of the revolution, in addition to celebrating and admiring the new Islamic state post-Shah regime, several PAS members accepted invitations issued by the Islamic republic and visited Tehran. This was for the purpose of learning and experiencing the revolution, and many participated in educational programmes organised by the Iranian government. In addition, the youth wing of PAS, which stood at the forefront of party reform, sent students and study groups to Iran as a way of improving the 'bilateral' relationship with the new Iranian government and studying its model of rule (Liow 2009). Furthermore, as a result of the Iranian Revolution, PAS's leadership re-emphasised the special role of Ulama in the party's organisation. The Ulama served as the spiritual leader of the party and PAS's 'internal advisor' (Monutty 1990: 117; Noor 2014: 118).

Ahmad Uzair claims that there are some spiritual songs and prayers within PAS which stress the importance of Muslim unity and the struggle to achieve a greater Muslim Ummah. These were composed by PAS members influenced by the 'soul' of the Iranian Revolution.[21] In terms of mass mobilisation, PAS involvement in the 1998 'reformation' rally and the series of Bersih protests indicates that they tried to follow what was done in Iran in the 1970s and 1980s, although not with the same objective (to aggressively overthrow the ruling government). The situation is discussed by Farish Noor (2014: 117), who states:

> Soon after the revolution (1979 Iranian Revolution), the younger generation of PAS leaders like Mohamad Sabu began using the Ayatollah's revolutionary rhetoric in their (political) speeches…(which resulted in) the thought that thousands of Malay-Muslim students might take to the streets in violent demonstrations against the government.

This claim seems too controversial and would probably be denied by PAS. However, the experiences witnessed during the global Islamic resurgence might well have offered PAS members new ideas and strategies to remain relevant as a strong Islamist opposition in the Malaysian political game.

For ABIM, and as a youth organisation that had been established in the early 1970s, at the height of global Islamic resurgence, the movement was very much an Islamist (*Harakah Islamiyyah*) product of its time. Like PAS in the aftermath of the Iranian Revolution, ABIM did not want to miss an opportunity to strengthen its international agenda by supporting the formation of a new Islamic republic in Iran. Farish Noor (2003: 204–205) claimed that the leadership of ABIM, in particular Anwar Ibrahim (its first secretary general and second president from 1974 to 1982), praised the Iranian revolutionaries for their commitment to Islam. Ahmad Azam (former president of ABIM) acknowledged that the movement was inspired by the Iranian Revolution and viewed as a new symbol of the Muslim struggle against Western Hegemony, following the fall of the Ottoman Empire in 1924. Many books and publications on Iran (post-1979 Iranian Revolution), particularly concerning the thoughts of Khomeini, were imported for reference by ABIM members. At one time, the ABIM leadership was also encouraged to memorise the full name of Khomeini ('Ayatollah Sayyed Ruhollah Mostafavi Moosavi Khomeini') as a way of showing the movement's solidarity with him as a new political and Islamic leader in Iran and the Muslim world.[22]

According to Mohamad Mazuki (an active member of ABIM since the 1970s), in 1979 Anwar Ibrahim and other ABIM members decided to visit Tehran, and they met Ayatollah Khomeini to celebrate the success of the Iranian people in forming a new Islamic republic. Upon his return from Iran, Anwar called for an 'Iranian Liberation and Solidarity Day' to be held on 16 March 1979.[23] Nevertheless, although ABIM was a strong supporter of the Iranian Revolution, Funston argues that the movement did not endorse all Iranian developments as ABIM leaders, such as Anwar Ibrahim, recognised that the situation in Malaysia was unique and thus rejected the possibility of completely transplanting a foreign model (Funston 1985: 173).

Semi-democratic Malaysia: between the regime and the Islamists

In the context of the semi-democratic Malaysian political setting, PAS, ABIM, ISMA and AMANAH are generally allowed to involve themselves in politics and participate in any local or national election in Malaysia. However, many of their members had been politically repressed by the UMNO-BN ruling regime over the past decades, mostly through the notorious ISA – which put a number of Malaysian Islamists from those movements behind bars for several years without any chances to be tried in court. Among the allegation claimed by the regime (to justify their actions) was the existence of a connection between several Malaysian Islamist leaders and global terrorist networks. Using terrorism's 'card', the country has witnessed scores of members of PAS Youth being detained under the ISA and accused of being associated with Islamist militant groups, such as the Jemaah Islamiyah and Al-Qaeda, between the 1980s and the 2000s. Without substantial evidence, the regime's desire to make allegations that PAS Islamists and terrorism were linked (by also implying that PAS's brand of Islam lent itself to some sort of extremist ideology) was perceived as part of its 'systematic' efforts to suppress and undermine support for the Islamist party among the Malay-Muslim majority. In the words of Liow (2009: 159),

> ...Not surprisingly, the basis of government allegations against these (Islamist) groups has also been contested by a broad spectrum of critics including human rights groups, opposition parties, and many quarters in the academic community (both secular and Islamic). Chief among these criticism is the fact that the government has yet to provide sufficient evidence of the existence of connections to international terrorist networks. This in turn has fed suspicions that the charges were manufactured toward political ends.

Several ABIM leaders were also detained under the ISA for various reasons and periods, especially at the height of *Reformasi* protests against the regime in the late 1990s. These included then-president Ahmad Azam Abdul Rahman, deputies Abdul Halim Ismail and Mukhtar Redhuan, and secretary general Shaharudin Badarudin (Liow 2009: 117). The occasional use of ISA by the regime, since 1960, undoubtedly had a devastating effect on the relationship between the Islamist opposition parties and NGOs, and the UMNO-BN ruling government. The active involvement of PAS, ABIM and AMANAH members in the past street protests (i.e. Bersih rallies) against the ruling regime clearly expressed the uncomfortable relationship between the Islamist oppositions and the state. For some observers, such as Weiss (2004) and Ufen (2009), the deployment of such policies against the former appeared to be politically motivated so that the regime can retain its status quo, power and position in Putrajaya – even though the Islamists posed no realistic threat to the government. Despite being repressed, those Islamist parties and movements in Malaysia never once being clandestine. Inspired by the agenda of global Islamism, they remain committed to taking power from the government through ballot boxes, as shown in the past series of elections (though the results were already expected not to favour Islamists) – making them one of the oldest and strongest opposition groups in the country.

The Arab Uprisings, Islamists and popular civil protests in Malaysia

Within the Malaysian 'semi-democratic' setting, it is understandable why the opposition politicians, political activists and ordinary citizens who yearned for political change were inflamed by resentment, which led them to 'occupy' the streets of Kuala Lumpur to express their frustration. This section will briefly highlight the development of popular political protest and mass mobilisation in Malaysia – the *Reformasi* and the series of Bersih movements. According to William Case (2017), excessive corruption and the practice of political repression by autocratic leaders can be challenged by people's resentments, and this trajectory recently began to unfold in Malaysia via a series of civil resistance actions. For instance, Malaysia's Bersih Movement 3.0 was established in 2013 in the spirit of 'contentious politics' in order to fight political injustice and for free and fair elections as well as to voice the campaign of anti-corruption. The movement reportedly managed to gather nearly 200,000 Malaysians in the capital – Kuala Lumpur – for the purpose of expressing their frustration towards the ruling regime.

The Bersih movement is also viewed as the most notable attempt to improve Malaysia's democratic practice through its aggressive demand for electoral reform. This wave of protests in Malaysia, which originally started in 2007, was dubbed Bersih 1.0 and was followed by Bersih 2.0; Bersih 3.0; Bersih 4.0; and the latest, Bersih 5.0, which was held in November 2016. According to Saravanamuttu (2016: 255), the Bersih movement is symbolic of the role of civil society in its constant resistance to the authoritarian regime and repressive politics in the country. However, since the last rally, the government has intensified its crackdown on the movement by raiding the offices of the organisers and arresting leaders and participants (Freedom House 2017). In 2011–2012, the Arab nations' struggle – dubbed the Arab Uprisings – inspired others around the world, and perhaps this included Malaysia, whether in a direct or an indirect way (Currie 2012). Members and supporters of the Islamist opposition parties and civil society organisations, such as PAS, AMANAH and ABIM, committedly joined all these rallies. In the words of John Bradley (2012: 161–162),

The local and Western press were quick to describe the (Bersih 2011) event as marking the beginning of the country's own version of the Arab Spring, and there were indeed striking parallels... the protesters were fed up with the decades-old domination of the ruling UMNO and the crony economy that had grown up around it...they had gathered under the banner of greater freedom and a more equitable distribution of profits from the country's burgeoning economy. Again, as in the Middle East, the state's reaction was as brutal as it was disproportionate. No fewer than 1600 of them were bundled off to jail.

Although this polemic was denied by the movement's leaders, the strong relation that has been established between Islamist movements in Malaysia and the Middle East could possibly suggest a link or influence to the Arab Uprisings. The answer to this question will be discussed in Chapters 4 and 5, which focus solely on the findings most strongly related to the above issues. In the meantime, it is worth considering the background of the existence of civil protests and mass demonstrations in Malaysia. Historically, mass mobilisation and political protests have been common in the Malaysian political landscape (Hooi 2014: 86; Smeltzer & Paré 2015: 121). In 1998 Anwar Ibrahim's defamation crisis led to several protests known as *Reformasi*, followed by the emergence of the Coalition for Clean and Fair Elections or the Bersih movement (in Malay, the word *Bersih* literally means 'clean'). This was perceived as Malaysia's first mass movement on electoral reform. Such events have triggered a sentiment of 'people power' amongst Malaysians and served as a catalyst for reviving protest actions in Malaysia. Since then, mass mobilisations and protests have become a defining aspect of Malaysian politics and, to an extent, instigated intense political reactions. According to Andreas Ufen (2009), mass mobilisation in Malaysia, such as the 1998 *Reformasi* protest and the series of Bersih rallies, has the potential to be a catalyst of the democratisation process in the country. The increasing number of participants in protests and rallies has indirectly reflected Malaysian awareness of improvements in the quality of democracy and instigated increased political openness and democratic maturity (these aspects will be discussed in further detail in Chapter 5). The following section briefly reviews the series of protest events or mass mobilisations that have taken place in Malaysia over the past few years.

The 1998 Reformasi

Many observers and analysts of Malaysian politics agree that the 1998 Reformation movement was a turning point towards a new era of Malaysian politics in terms of street demonstrations and political protest. The protest was originally ignited by a concrete political event – the sacking of former Deputy Prime Minister, Anwar Ibrahim, during the reign of former Prime

32 *The development of the Islamist movements*

Minister Mahathir Mohamad (1981–2003). It was estimated that on 20 September 1998, more than 30,000 people took to the streets of Kuala Lumpur to express their solidarity with Anwar Ibrahim. This was viewed as a 'movement from the street' – made up of participants from different classes, backgrounds and ethnic groups, including the influential Islamist party and groups such as PAS, ABIM and Jemaah Islah Malaysia (Nair 2007: 351). After the emergence of the movement, an element of 'pro-reform' commenced which eventually brought a significant change to Malaysian politics: for instance in the formation of a new opposition political bloc comprised of PAS, DAP, the Socialist Party (PRM) and the PKR (Hooi 2014: 87). This extraordinary turn of events triggered an explosion of support for Anwar, alongside anti-Mahathir and anti-UMNO sentiment that led to Malaysia's 'first organised large-scale protest movement', which came to be known as the reform movement or *Reformasi* (Nair 2007: 339).

Coalition for Clean and Fair Election 2007 (Bersih 1.0)

The Bersih movement, dubbed the 'Yellow Wave', is arguably an influential symbol of electoral and governance reform, and is iconic as a pro-democracy movement in Malaysia. Yellow was chosen by the committee to signify democracy. It emerged as a coalition consisting of five opposition political parties (including PAS) and 26 other civil society groups campaigning for electoral reform. In particular, the movement can be seen as a 'platform calling for genuinely free and fair elections, including an end to Malaysia's notorious gerrymandering system and other forms of electoral corruption' (Kingsbury 2017: 75). Steered by its motivational banner 'Save Malaysia: Restore Our Rights', the rally, which was held on 10 November 2007, managed to attract nearly 40,000 protesters, mainly members from opposition parties and activists (including those from PAS and ABIM). They poured into the streets of Kuala Lumpur and reached the final 'battle camp': Independence Square (Dataran Merdeka). There are arguably many factors which triggered the emergence of Bersih 1.0. As testified by the Asia Report (2012: 7), when Anwar Ibrahim was released from prison in 2004, he still held momentous influence over the nation, especially among his loyal followers. Grievances against the ruling government quickly escalated, ranging from Islamisation issues to widespread power abuses and corruption cases. Hooi (2014: 90) also argues that it was within this context that civil society and opposition politicians began organising Bersih 1.0, with the goal of changing the 'game' in the upcoming 2008 General Election.

Coalition for Clean and Fair Election 2011 (Bersih 2.0)

The Bersih 2.0 event, dubbed the 'Walk for Democracy' protest, also aimed to construct an atmosphere of fairness in the elections. This rally was organised on 9 July 2011 with the primary aim of pressuring the ruling government to carry out electoral and political reforms before the next general election (Hooi 2014: 98). The first rally had received encouraging support from most opposition parties and supporters as well as a number of NGOs and civil society groups (including the Islamist parties and PAS and ABIM). Bersih 2.0 managed to attract a larger turn-out than the first rally and expanded its demands to eight specific points: (1) to clean up the electoral roll, (2) to reform the postal ballot, (3) to use indelible ink, (4) to limit the campaign period to a minimum of 21 days, (5) to freely and fairly access media, (6) to strengthen public institutions, (7) to end all forms of corruption and (8) to stop dirty politics.[24]

Coalition for Clean and Fair Election 2012 (Bersih 3.0)

Following the Bersih 2.0 demonstration, the Bersih's committee decided to organise a third rally known as Bersih 3.0 to continuously pressurise the ruling government for electoral reform. This decision was made after the Parliamentary Selection Committee (PSC) on Electoral Reform failed to address fundamental electoral issues in their 22-point electoral reforms report (Hooi 2014: 99). As reported by the Malaysian Bar (2012) and Jonah Fisher (2012), it was estimated that more than 200,000 'yellow-shirt' people took to the streets on 28 April 2012 to call for substantial change to the voting system. PAS and ABIM called upon their thousands of national members to mobilise for the purpose of attending the rally. Interestingly, to this day the Bersih 3.0 event is perceived as the largest mass mobilisation and political protest in Malaysian political history.

Despite the violent nature of the demonstration, with the authorities trying to enforce restrictions on entering Independence Square, and with scores of protesters reportedly beaten and detained by the police, the protesters in Bersih 3.0 were nevertheless determined to voice their discontent with the ruling government. Aided by rumours about the next general election, which was to be held in 2013, there was a sense of excitement amongst the protesters, and the sentiment to topple the regime seemed 'convincing' as the protesters felt that reform was not only possible but also inevitable (Hooi 2014). For many young Malaysians, participation in a mass protest of this magnitude was extraordinary. Bersih 3.0 took place amidst an upsurge of dissent within civil society in the Middle East – which led to comparisons to the 'Arab Spring'. As demonstrated by Smeltzer and Paré (2015: 126),

> A key struggle for Bersih, and one that it shares with other social movements around the world (e.g., the Arab Spring and Occupy movements), is to transform public places like Dataran Merdeka into spaces where citizens can engage in diverse political activities, including those that challenge the established political order.

34 *The development of the Islamist movements*

Prime Minister Najib Razak accused the protesters of the Bersih 3.0 movement of trying to overthrow the government, like Egypt's Tahrir Square protest in 2011.[25] However, the opposition leaders, in turn, dismissed the accusation as an overreaction to the people's protests (Yee 2012).

Coalition for a Clean and Fair Election 2015 (Bersih 4.0)

Bersih 4.0 is the fourth rally. It was held on 29–30 August 2015 in Kuala Lumpur and in several other major cities around the world to call for an immediate resignation of Prime Minister Najib Razak and institutional reforms to prevent prime ministerial corruption (Saravanamuttu 2016: 255). As reported by *The Straits Times*, the rally came amidst allegations in the *Wall Street Journal* and *Sarawak Report* that US$700 million in state funds had been deposited into the Prime Minister's personal bank accounts and regarding the mismanagement of debt-ridden state investor 1Malaysia Development Berhad (1MDB).[26] Other controversial events in Malaysia, for instance the removal of Abdul Gani Patail as Attorney-General and those of ministers who had spoken out about the 1MDB scandal, also triggered the call for the rally (Saravanamuttu 2016). A few influential Islamist movements and civil society groups, such as AMANAH and ABIM, played a significant role in mobilising their members to join the protest for a 'better future for Malaysia'.[27] PAS, however, decided not to mobilise its members and supporters for Bersih 4.0 (due to post-internal conflict with former PAS members, who left the party and formed AMANAH). The party instead sent unofficial representatives to show their support for a clean and fair electoral system, and did not bar its members from participating in the two-day protest event. During the demonstrations, the Malaysian regime deemed the rally to be illegal but failed to prevent more than a hundred thousand Malaysians from flooding into the area around Independence Square. Overall, there were five issues that were targeted by Bersih 4.0: (1) a free and fair election, (2) a transparent government, (3) the right to demonstrate, (4) strengthening the parliamentary democratic system and (5) saving the national economy.[28]

Considering the nature of Malaysia's semi-democratic practices, all requests outlined in the series of Bersih protests were highly relevant and would potentially improve the quality of democracy, if the regime proved responsive to the demands. It is also clear that members of Malaysia's Islamist parties and NGOs actively participated in the mass protests to voice citizens' frustration with the Malaysian ruling regime. The thousands of activists and registered members, largely comprised of the majority Malay-Muslims in the country, show that the role of Islamist movements in the Malaysian political game is undeniably significant. Table 2.1 summarises the popular political protest events in Malaysia, as previously discussed.

Table 2.1 Summary of popular civil protests in Malaysia

Major Civil Protest Events	Motives	Involvement of Islamist movements
Reformasi (1998)	Frustration against the regime of Mahathir Mohamad as a result of Anwar Ibrahim's ousting, arrest and detention under the Internal Security Act (ISA). Protesters demand the immediate resignation of Mahathir Mohamad from the government.	PAS and ABIM
Bersih 1.0 (2007)	Grievances against widespread corruption and power abuses. Demand for electoral reform before the 2008 General Election as well as free and fair access to the mass media for opposition parties.	PAS and ABIM
Bersih 2.0 (2011)	Pressure against the regime and Electoral Commission of Malaysia for electoral reform and academic freedom for university graduates.	PAS and ABIM
Bersih 3.0 (2012)	Calls for drastic electoral reform and substantial change to the voting system. Fairness and transparency in the upcoming election (the 13th General Election in 2013).	PAS and ABIM
Bersih 4.0 (2015)	Request the immediate resignation of Najib Razak due to allegations of corruption and mismanagement of national funds (1MDB). To pressure the government towards a reformed Malaysia through institutional changes and electoral reform ahead of the 14th General Election in 2018.	AMANAH and ABIM

Source: Prepared by the author.

Conclusion and summary

As pointed out by Von Der Mehden (1986: 184–186), events in contemporary Malaysia have exacerbated differences within Islamist parties and movements. Even beyond Malaysia, Samer Shehata (2012: 4) claims, Islamist movements (in general) indeed differ in many respects: for instance their ideology, mobilisation tactics and strategies, attitudes towards proper political participation, use of violence and acceptance of the nation-state as the foundation for political community. Although Von Der Mehden's opinion is from about 30 years ago it remains relevant as the progress of Islamist movements in Malaysia currently presents further dynamics and diversity as regards ideology, organisational structure, political approach and ground activism. The values and policies promoted by Islamists in Malaysia may of course differ across parties and movements. However, there is a single set of values that seems to be central to any Islamist movement in Malaysia. This relates to the significance of Islam (or religion) in political and social life. On politico-religious grounds, it is possible to divide Islamist movements in Malaysia into four categories:

i   Politically Conservative: The ISMA. This Islamist movement is often labelled by alternative media in Malaysia as a far-right Malay-Muslim group since its views towards non-Muslims, especially the minority Chinese and Christian groups, seem 'strong' and sometimes racist and controversial.
ii Politically Traditionalist: The PAS. This Islamist group seems consistently focussed on Islamic roots and terminologies, in line with championing the Islamic state agenda and the implementation of Sharia as a political ambition within the framework of democracy and election.
iii Politically Fundamentalist: The ABIM. Its role as an 'Islah (reform) and Tajdid (renewal)' civil society movement has undergone significant changes, which led it to become relatively more moderate in its outlook and activism.
iv Politically Accommodationist: The AMANAH. As a new self-proclaimed Islamist democratic party, it pragmatically recognises major elements of democracy and individual freedom within the Islamic perspective as the basis of party struggle. This can be seen by its political strategy, which emphasises universal issues such as democracy, justice, good governance and multi-ethnic and religious interests without rhetorical expressions of Islam and Sharia.

PAS, ABIM, ISMA and AMANAH are unquestionably regarded as the main Islamist movements in Malaysia, comprising dynamic ideologies, objectives, political approaches, organisational structures and connections with global Islamism. In their early stages, most of the Islamist movements in Malaysia were clearly influenced by ideas and forms of organisation that originated outside the region – most notably the MB in Egypt. In addition, events like the Iranian Revolution of 1979 provided initial inspiration to many Malaysian Islamists – they became increasingly focussed not just on the Islamisation of society but also on the political context in which they operated. The structure and historical process of Malaysian politics and Islamist movements have been sketched in this chapter and emphasise the fact that Islam has become a firm fixture in today's Malaysian political landscape. A summary of the selected Malaysian Islamist movements is provided in Table 2.2.

Table 2.2 Summary of selected cases of Islamist movements in Malaysia

Islamist Movement	Ideology, Position and Political Approach	Goals and Involvement in Politics	Involvement in Political Protest Against the Regime	Influenced by External Political Islamism
The Pan Malaysian Islamic Party (PAS)	Conservative Islamism. *Harakah Islamiyyah* – Islamist political party.	To establish an 'Islamic state' and the implementation of Sharia law. Participated in all general elections as opposition party.	*Reformasi* 1998, Bersih 1.0 (2007), Bersih 2.0 (2011), Bersih 3.0 (2013)	Egyptian Muslim Brotherhood. The 1979 Iranian Revolution.
The National Trust Party (AMANAH)	Moderate and Progressive Neo-Islamism. Islamist Democratic political party.	To defend basic civil liberties and political pluralism through moderation and inclusiveness. Participated in two district elections in 2016. Join a new opposition coalition in 2017 for the next 2018 general election.	Bersih 4.0 (2015), Bersih 5.0 (2016)	AKP Party in Turkey. Ennahda Party in Tunisia.
The Muslim Youth Movement of Malaysia (ABIM)	Fundamental *Harakah Islamiyyah*. Non-governmental organisation (NGO).	To improve the Islamisation agenda and da'wah in society. Future establishment of an 'ideal Muslim society'. Never participate in any election as a political party. However, several members of ABIM have participated in the previous general election as electoral candidates via the PAS and UMNO platforms.	*Reformasi* 1998, Bersih 1.0 (2007), Bersih 2.0 (2011), Bersih 3.0 (2013), Bersih 4.0 (2015), Bersih 5.0 (2016)	Egyptian Muslim Brotherhood. The 1979 Iranian Revolution. AKP Party in Turkey. Ennahda Party in Tunisia.
The Malaysian Muslim Solidarity Front (ISMA)	Conservative Islamism. Nationalist Islamism. *Harakah Islamiyyah*. NGO.	Contended in 2013 General Election under the name of the BERJASA Party.	None	Egyptian Muslim Brotherhood.

Source: Prepared by the author.

Notes

1 Since the Islamic revival that swept the Muslim world, including Malaysia, which took place in the 1970s and later in the 1980s, Muslim politics has demonstrated political rivalry between the ruling elite and the Islamists. As in the case of Malaysia, the obvious rivalry was between PAS and UMNO. See Mohd Izani Mohd Zain. (2014). From Islamist to Muslim Democrat: The Present Phenomenon of Muslim Politics in Malaysia. *International Journal of Islamic Thought*, 6 (December): 37–45.
2 Note that the term 'Islamist' covers those parties, movements, organisations and individuals who have a religious and clear-cut political agenda (e.g. PAS, ABIM, ISMA and AMANAH), whereas the term 'Islamic' refers to those with a religious interest but apolitical outlook (e.g. Jama'a at-Tabligh).
3 Malays are constitutionally required to be Muslims. The constitutional definition of the relationship between Malays and Islam was allocated in Article 160 (2) of the Constitution, stating that a Malay 'professes the religion of Islam, habitually speaks the Malay language and conforms to the Malay custom'. In other words, all Malays in Malaysia are Muslims by birth. To understand the relationship between Islam and the racial-political setting in Malaysia the Malay-Muslim community should be analysed according to this pretext.
4 For more on the history of the Young Faction, see Mohammad Redzuan Othman & Abu Hanifah Haris (2015) The Role of Egyptian Influences on the Religious Dynamics and the Idea of Progress of Malaya's Kaum Muda (Young Faction) before the Second World War. *British Journal of Middle Eastern Studies*, 42 (4): 465–480.
5 According to Erica Miller (2006: 23), after PAS achieved only one parliamentary seat in the first federal elections in July 1955, its leaders concentrated on creating a more robust organisational structure, expanding the geographic reach of the party, increasing the number of members, exploiting new means of disseminating the party's message and better integrating Ulama into the largely professional party.
6 For more details on the crucial events during the global Islamic resurgence, see Durac, Vincent & Cavatorta, Francesco (2015). Politics and Governance in the Middle East. London: Palgrave. pp. 136-153.
7 The highest and most powerful institution within PAS is the Syura Council, a consultative guidance committee comprising the party's leading religious scholars. Its main function is to control the policies of PAS and ensure that they are in line with the principle of Islam (Müller 2014: 49).
8 Chew, Amy (2013) The rising force in Malaysia's opposition: The Pan-Malaysian Islamic Party is gaining the upper hand within the coalition headed by Anwar Ibrahim. *Al Jazeera*. Available at www.aljazeera.com/indepth/features/2013/02/201321092433869462.html [16 October 2015].
9 According to Zulkifly Abdul Malek, in 1969, a group of graduating Malay-Muslim students from the University of Malaya gathered to ponder post-university life. The group consisted of high ranking members of the National Association of Muslim Students Malaysia – commonly known in Malay as Persatuan Kebangsaan Pelajar Islam Malaysia (PKPIM) – and they were apprehensive about their future. As student activists, they were prominently identified as the prime mobilisers of an 'Islamisation effort' on campus and beyond, with the goal of reviving Islam as a way of life. Graduation would effectively put an end to the momentum they had built as they had no means of continuing their activities as post-graduates. Yet they believed that their noble mission was not over. A member and leader of the group, Anwar Ibrahim, eventually suggested that they form a new Islamic civil society movement for university graduates, and the idea

for the Muslim Youth Movement of Malaysia (ABIM) finally crystallised (Abdul Malek 2011).
10 Fieldwork at the 'Seminar on the Future of Islamic Awakening', in conjunction with ABIM's 45th Annual Meeting. Shah Alam, Malaysia. 29 October 2016. The statements were originally recorded from Ahmad Azzam's presentation on the 'Lessons from Global Islamist Movements' Experiences' at the event.
11 Personal interview with ABIM senior member, Mohamad Mazuki Ariffin, London, December 2015.
12 See, for example, Murad, Dina (2014). 'Abdullah Zaik: The Man Behind ISMA'. *The Stars*. Available online at www.thestar.com.my/news/nation/2014/05/22/abdullah-zaik-man-behind-isma/ [13 June 2015].
13 Ikatan Muslim Malaysia (The Malaysian Muslim Solidarity Front) official website. Available online at http://isma.org.my/v2/ [13 June 2015].
14 See, for example, (1) Tan, Julian (2014). A Malaysian Neo-Nazism? Available online at http://www.huffingtonpost.co.uk/julian-tan/a-malaysian-neonazism_b_5300721.html [11 January 2015] and (2) Weng, Hew Wai (2016). A rise in anti-Chinese rhetoric. Available online at http://www.newmandala.org/rise-anti-chinese-politics-malaysia-indonesia/ [27 November 2016].
15 Personal interview with Amar Yasier, London, June 2016.
16 Ibid.
17 Personal interview with the ISMA president, Abdullah Zaik Abdul Rahman. Bangi, Malaysia. 5 November 2016.
18 Personal interview with the AMANAH national youth leader, Muhammad Najib. Kuala Lumpur, Malaysia. September 2016.
19 Personal interview with Dzulkefly Ahmad, Cyberjaya, August 2016.
20 Ibid.
21 Personal interview with PAS member, Ahmad Uzair Mazlan, Southampton, June 2016.
22 Ahmad Azam's presentation on 'Lessons from Global Islamist Movements' during the 'Seminar on the Future of Islamic Awakening', in conjunction with ABIM's 45th Annual Meeting. Shah Alam, Malaysia. 29 October 2016.
23 Personal interview with Mohamad Mazuki Ariffin, London, December 2015.
24 For more information about Bersih 2.0 see the official website for Bersih 2.0 – 'About Bersih 2.0'. Available at www.bersih.org/about-bersih-2-0/ [10 October 2015].
25 Polemics regarding the Arab Uprisings' influence on the Bersih movement protesters will be fully discussed in Chapter 5.
26 *The Straits Times* (2015) 'What you need to know about Malaysia's Bersih movement'. Available at www.straitstimes.com/asia/se-asia/what-you-need-to-know-about-malaysias-bersih-movement [20 October 2015].
27 ABIM (2015) 'We want a better future for Malaysia'. Available at www.abim.org.my/berita-program/abim-pusat/item/878-bersih-4-0-kami-mahukan-masa-depan-yang-lebih-baik-untuk-malaysia- presiden-abim.html [20 October 2015].
28 Astro Awani (2015) 'Bersih 4: Four things you need to know'. Available at http://english.astroawani.com/malaysia-news/bersih-4-four-things-you-need-know-71003 [20October 2015].

3 Knowledge and perceptions of the Islamist movements in Malaysia towards the Arab Uprisings

This chapter examines the awareness and perceptions of selected Islamist movements in Malaysia – the Pan-Malaysian Islamic Party (PAS), the Muslim Youth Movement of Malaysia (ABIM), the Malaysian Muslim Solidarity Front (ISMA) and the National Trust Party (AMANAH) towards the Arab Uprisings phenomenon. It is based on the empirical findings of a questionnaire-based survey that was conducted in Malaysia, with 643 respondents, primarily from among the members of the named movements.[1] The survey involved a Likert-scale type questionnaire, which was composed of 18 main questions/statements relating to basic facts about the Arab Uprisings, Islamism and political Islamic issues, and the role of Islamist movements. Respondents were provided with five selections for their answers: strongly agree, agree, neutral/neither disagree nor agree, disagree and strongly disagree. The questions/statements were developed based on established typologies and scholars' definitions of the Arab Uprisings as well as on intensive reviews of the factors that contributed to the 2011 Arab Uprisings and the Islamist debates.[2]

The first section deals with the respondents' basic demographic backgrounds. The second section deals with their knowledge of the Arab Uprisings, including their sources of information and any reasons for which they did not know about the events. The third section presents research findings and data analysis. Eighteen questions are covered, divided into three main themes: (1) understanding the general issues of the Arab Uprisings phenomenon, (2) understanding the factors that led to the Arab Uprisings and (3) attitudes towards Islamist movements within the Arab Uprisings context. In order to explain the trends and patterns in the statistical data, the author uses additional information from a number of face-to-face interviews with selected respondents from each movement. Some findings were also supported with theories and concepts, as discussed in Chapter 2. The final section concludes the findings and summarises the degree of understanding and perception of PAS, ABIM, ISMA and AMANAH Islamist activists towards the Arab Uprisings events.

The initial questions: respondents' backgrounds

In the early section of the questionnaire, there were several questions regarding the background of the research sample – for example age, gender, level of education, last place of education, occupational sector and type of Islamist movement membership. All these aspects provide added value to analyse any differences in the trend of responses as well as the patterns in the statistical data. Table 3.1 shows the respondents' age ranges.

As can be seen from Table 3.1, the majority of the respondents (493) were aged between 16 and 25, and 26 and 35. This is due to the current composition of each movement, whereby youths represent approximately one-third of overall membership. Thus, it was no surprise for the author (during his field trip in Malaysia) to see that many attendees of the events (i.e. gatherings, annual meetings, political speeches) organised by PAS, ABIM, ISMA and AMANAH were youth members. These circumstances indirectly reflect the data presented in Table 3.1 regarding why a majority of the participants in the survey were aged between 16 and 35. Within these ages, respondents were normally considered as part of their respective movement's Youth Wing or Division. For example, in 2016 the PAS Youth Movement operated at approximately 180 branches nationwide and primarily worked towards the party's succession planning and providing ground support for its political activism, especially during a pre-election period.[3] The remaining respondents (23.3 per cent) were aged between 36 and 45 (58 respondents), 46 and 55 (51 respondents) and 56 and above (41 respondents).

Table 3.2 shows details of the gender distribution of the sample (i.e. male and female respondents) from each movement. Of the 643 respondents, 451 are male Islamists, which constitutes 70.1 per cent of the total, while 192

Table 3.1 Respondents' age

Type of Islamist Movement	Age (Frequency)					Total
	16–25	26–35	36–45	46–55	56 and above	
The Pan Malaysian Islamic Party (PAS)	257	87	25	11	7	387
The National Trust Party (AMANAH)	16	32	13	19	15	95
The Muslim Youth Movement of Malaysia (ABIM)	17	18	13	17	16	81
The Malaysian Muslim Solidarity Front (ISMA)	47	19	7	4	3	80
Total	337	156	58	51	41	643

Source: Field Research 2016.

Table 3.2 Respondents' gender

Type of Islamist Movement	Gender (Frequency) Male	Female	Total
The Pan Malaysian Islamic Party (PAS)	274	113	387
The National Trust Party (AMANAH)	75	20	95
The Muslim Youth Movement of Malaysia (ABIM)	48	33	81
The Malaysian Muslim Solidarity Front (ISMA)	54	26	80
Total	451	192	643

Source: Field Research 2016.

(30.9 per cent) are female. The author believes that the reason behind this visible gender gap reflects the current actual membership of PAS, ABIM, ISMA and AMANAH at the national level, where the ratio between male members and female members has been around 70:30 since the 2000s.[4]

Table 3.3 provides details on the respondents' levels of education. The majority of respondents have a Bachelor's Degree (354), followed by those with a Diploma (147), Secondary School Education (84), a Master's Degree (52) and a PhD (6). With regard to the last place of education, Table 3.4 highlights respondents' last place of study by specific country. 88.3 per cent graduated from or finished their education at local institutions, while the remaining 11.7 per cent are overseas educated respondents. There were a number of overseas graduates who studied Arabic and Islamic studies in the Middle East and North Africa (MENA) (particularly in Egypt, Morocco and Jordan). Other fields, such as Medicine, Education, Engineering and Law, were also reportedly studied by respondents in the United Kingdom, the United States, the Republic of Ireland, India and Indonesia.

The last aspect of the respondents' backgrounds to be revealed is their working sectors. The majority of respondents (248) were local university students,[5] followed by 169 respondents who were involved in the private sector. Ninety-three worked in the public sector, mostly as school teachers, university lecturers and government officers. There were also a number of respondents (84) who considered themselves to be self-employed. These respondents reportedly run small-scale businesses, such as grocery shops, or worked within sectors such as food or tourism services (including umrah and haj tour packages), or in the education field (for example in the establishment of private religious schools and madrasah). An interview with the Secretary General of Kuala Lumpur PAS Youth revealed that the party's top leaders have encouraged their members to own a personal business, so they can maximise their contribution and dedication to the party in terms of time, energy and monetary remuneration.[6] The author has also been told that there are a few wealthy members in the other movements who own a private company that indirectly benefits the movement via financial and material contribution.[7] Only 41 respondents were not working at the time

Table 3.3 Respondents' level of education

Type of Islamist Movement	Secondary School	Diploma	Bachelor's Degree	Master	PhD	Total
The Pan Malaysian Islamic Party (PAS)	42	98	227	17	3	387
The National Trust Party (AMANAH)	8	20	48	19	0	95
The Muslim Youth Movement of Malaysia (ABIM)	31	23	15	10	2	81
The Malaysian Muslim Solidarity Front (ISMA)	3	6	64	6	1	80
Total	84	147	354	52	6	643

Level of Education (Frequency)

Source: Field Research 2016.

Table 3.4 Respondents' last place of education

Location (country)	Percentage
Malaysia	88.3
Egypt	3.0
Morocco	1.4
Jordan	0.5
United Kingdom	1.6
United States	0.6
Republic of Ireland	0.2
India	0.5
Indonesia	0.6
Other	2.5
Total	100.0

Source: Field Research 2016.

the survey was conducted. Table 3.5 provides details of the respondents' working sector.

To ensure that the selected respondents were relevant for the study, the author decided to ask a question about the type and status of their membership within PAS, ABIM, ISMA and AMANAH. Table 3.6 gives details of each movement's membership status.

Overall, 477 respondents (74.3 per cent) were registered and active members of PAS, ABIM, ISMA and AMANAH, followed by 58 respondents (9 per cent) who considered themselves as registered and non-active. Some of these active members reportedly are a part of the parties' organisation – for example the national, state (county), district branch and sub-district branch.

Table 3.5 Respondents' occupational sector

Type of Islamist Movement	Private	Public Sector	Self-Employed	Not Working/ Not Yet working	Student (Higher Education)	Retired/ Pensioner	Total
The Pan Malaysian Islamic Party (PAS)	68	54	35	35	194	1	387
The National Trust Party (AMANAH)	36	11	32	1	14	1	95
The Muslim Youth Movement of Malaysia (ABIM)	43	13	7	0	12	6	81
The Malaysian Muslim Solidarity Front (ISMA)	22	15	10	5	28	0	80
Total	169	93	84	41	248	8	643

Source: Field Research 2016.

Table 3.6 Type of Islamist movement membership

Type of Islamist Movement	Registered and Active	Registered and Non-Active	Non-Registered and Active (Volunteer)	Non-Registered and Non-Active (Passive Supporter)	Total
The Pan Malaysian Islamic Party (PAS)	271	30	68	18	387
The National Trust Party (AMANAH)	86	4	2	3	95
The Muslim Youth Movement of Malaysia (ABIM)	50	15	15	1	81
The Malaysian Muslim Solidarity Front (ISMA)	70	9	1	0	80
Total	477	58	86	22	643

Source: Field Research 2016.
Pearson Chi Square Test (*P* Value): 0.00.

Knowledge of the Islamist movements 45

There were also 86 respondents who were voluntarily involved in their movement's political activity without having official membership status, while 21 believed that they were ordinary supporters of PAS (18), AMANAH (3) and ABIM (1) due to their infrequent participation in any programmes and their not being registered within the party's official membership.

Knowledge of the Arab Uprisings in the Middle East and North Africa

In order to identify the awareness of respondents towards Arab Uprisings events, the following question was asked in the questionnaire: 'Do you know anything about the people's upheaval in the Middle East and North African countries (the Arab Uprisings or the "Arab Spring") that started in the year 2011?' Of the 643 sample, 532 respondents (82.7 per cent) answered 'yes', while 111 respondents (17.3 per cent) believed that they had never heard of such uprisings occurring in the Arab world.

Table 3.7 presents the results of the respondents' knowledge of the Arab Uprisings based on the different Islamist movements. Interestingly, there is no single respondent from ABIM who did not know or hear anything about the Arab Uprisings. This result somewhat reflects the movement's tradition (since its establishment in the 1970s) as being consistently engaged with global political issues which relate to Muslim matters (Mohd Azhar Bahari & Ishak Saat 2014: 8–9). For ISMA and AMANAH, it seems that the large majority of members were very aware of the Arab Uprisings. Only 2.1 per cent of respondents from AMANAH and 13.8 per cent from ISMA had never heard about the Arab Uprisings in the Middle East.

The responses received from PAS were quite different from those above as the movement recorded 25.3 per cent of respondents (98) having no

Table 3.7 Respondents' knowledge of the Arab Uprisings events

Type of Islamist Movement	Knowledge of the 2011 Arab Uprisings Events in the Middle East and North Africa (Frequency)		Total
	Yes	No	
The Pan Malaysian Islamic Party (PAS)	289	98	387
The National Trust Party (AMANAH)	93	2	95
The Muslim Youth Movement of Malaysia (ABIM)	81	0	81
The Malaysian Muslim Solidarity Front (ISMA)	69	11	80
Total	532	111	643

Source: Field Research 2016.

46 *Knowledge of the Islamist movements*

knowledge about the Arab Uprisings – although they were involved in one of the oldest and most influential Islamist movements in Malaysia and the Southeast Asian region.[8] Regarding the respondents' levels of education, this research found that the majority (99 per cent) of those with a post-graduate qualification (Master's and PhD) acknowledged the existence of Arab Uprisings events in the MENA. Out of 354 respondents who had a Bachelor's degree, 84.7 per cent were aware of the events, as were respondents with a diploma (72.8 per cent) and those educated at the High School level (81 per cent). Thus, this research finding, as indicated in Table 3.8, shows that level of education might partially help determine the Malaysian Islamists' knowledge of the Arab Uprisings phenomenon.[9]

In terms of a gender perspective, there was no significant difference between male and female respondents as 86.5 per cent of male respondents (390) and 74 per cent of female respondents (142) knew about the Arab Uprisings (of the total 82.7 per cent who said 'yes').[10] Out of 17.3 per cent of respondents who did not know about the events, 9.5 per cent were male, and 7.8 were female. Thus, the ratio between male and female respondents regarding knowledge about the Arab Uprisings (either 'yes' or 'no') seems quite balanced, which strongly suggests that gender has no impact on the Malaysian Islamists' responses to that specific question.

With regard to the respondents' membership status, the analysis of cross tabulation between respondents' types of membership and knowledge or awareness of the Arab Uprisings phenomenon in the MENA shows that those who were registered and actively participated in the programme organised by their respective movements were more likely to pay close attention to the events. Of the 532 respondents who observed the Arab Uprisings, 78.9 per cent (420) came from the 'registered and active' category. Only 11.9 per cent of respondents (57) from the same category did not know anything about the Arab Uprisings.[11] Hence, from the previous discussion, which involved some of the respondents' demographic aspects and their impact on

Table 3.8 Respondents' knowledge of the Arab Uprisings events based on level of education

Level of Education	Knowledge of the 2011 Arab Uprisings Events in the Middle East and North Africa		Percentages (Yes/ No)
	Yes	No	
SRP/PMR/SPM (Malaysian High School)	68	16	81/19
STPM/STAM/Diploma	107	40	72.8/27.2
Bachelor's Degree	300	54	84.7/15.3
Master's	51	1	98.1/1.9
PhD	6	0	100/0

Source: Field Research 2016.

knowledge about the Arab Uprisings, it is obvious that level of education and membership status somehow played a significant role. Although the number of respondents with a High School certificate, diploma and degree qualification who were not aware of the popular events was fairly low, this still leads to the question – why did some people, especially those who were educated and actively involved in a movement or political party which has a history of transnational relations with the Arab world (in general), not know anything about the Arab Uprisings? Details of the respondents' answers will be discussed in the following section.

Reasons for not knowing about the Arab Uprisings

Those respondents who did not know about the Arab Uprisings were asked why they had never heard or known about the events. As can be seen from Table 3.9, the main reasons for which 111 respondents did not know about the Arab Uprisings related to their lack of knowledge – as a result of seldom reading, hearing or watching global news, either through mainstream mass media (television, radio, newspaper) or through newer social media (Internet). There were 50 respondents who mentioned that they did not have the opportunity or 'free time' to find any printed sources relating to the Arab Uprisings. Fifty-eight respondents admitted that they had not been exposed to any of the Arab Uprisings facts over the past few years.

There were also a few written comments left by respondents in the questionnaire which might reveal more about why some Islamist activists

Table 3.9 Respondents' reasons for not knowing about the Arab Uprisings

Reasons for Not Knowing about the Arab Uprisings	The Pan Malaysian Islamic Party (PAS)	The National Trust Party (AMANAH)	The Malaysian Muslim Solidarity Front (ISMA)
Lack of/absence of information	59	1	9
Not finding relevant printed materials	42	1	7
Lack of time for reading local/international news	63	1	5
Lack of opportunity to watch local/international TV	44	1	4
Lack of opportunity to surf the Internet/social media	37	0	3
Have never been exposed to the Arab Uprisings	47	0	11

Source: Field Research 2016.
Notes: There are no responses from ABIM respondents since all of those involved in the survey had knowledge of the Arab Uprisings.

48 *Knowledge of the Islamist movements*

had no knowledge of the Arab Uprisings. Among the random comments received were:

- 'Been busy with the "*jemaah*" (movement's) works, thus I did not have enough time to know more about the Arab Uprisings' – PAS activist.
- 'Did not notice about this issue and have never been told that there was an "Arab Spring" in the Middle East' – PAS activist.
- 'Too many unreliable and non-credible sources. In Malaysia, there is a lack of reliable news and reports from the media, especially in the Malay language regarding the Arab Uprisings events' – AMANAH activist.
- 'Not interested in politics, chaos and instability' – AMANAH supporter.
- 'Never attempted to find out any information on the Arab Uprisings' – PAS supporter.
- 'Previously not interested to learn anything about current issues' – PAS supporter.

From the above comments, it is clear that there was a respondent from AMANAH who simply was not interested in global politics and the Arab Uprisings events due to the state of political instability which occurred in some Arab countries after the Arab Uprisings. However, one of the respondents (a female AMANAH member) seems to not agree with all the excuses given, stating:

> The reason people might not know about the 'Arab Spring' is because they are just not interested in paying attention to what happens around the world. Information does exist actually. From my observation, they (the Islamists) watch TV every day, read newspapers, surf the internet and yet they do not have any idea about the Arab Uprisings phenomenon.[12]

Her opinion was supported by another AMANAH member, Ahmad Zubaimi, who believes that:

> Ignorance is one of the reasons why some Malaysians were not aware of the 'Arab Spring' in the MENA region. It seems that the Malaysian people need coherent, reliable and accurate information in order to stay alert to local and international politics.[13]

Some respondents from PAS seem to 'blame' themselves for their tight schedules and lack of effort to be more aware about the Arab Uprisings in the Middle East. There was also an issue raised by one of the AMANAH activists about the abundance of unreliable sources on the Arab Uprisings[14] – which could explain why some people refused to engage with developments. Again, those excuses were condemned by a senior AMANAH member, who argued that:

> There was no awareness and understanding of the real meaning of the 'Arab Spring' among (some of) the Islamists in Malaysia. They were too

lazy to read, research and participate in any seminar or lecture. Some of them received information about the Arab Uprisings from untrustworthy sources. Only a few put some effort into understanding the 'Arab Spring'.[15]

Nevertheless, the issues of 'unreliable' and inadequate sources seem not to impact the majority of respondents who gave a positive response regarding their knowledge of the Arab Uprisings. The author believes that this category of respondents might have referred to credible sources, which enabled them to fully participate in the survey. Details of their sources of information regarding the Arab Uprisings are presented in the following section.

Sources of information regarding the Arab Uprisings events

For those 532 respondents who knew about the Arab Uprisings, their sources of information were varied, as can be viewed in Table 3.10. In particular, 475 respondents considered social media and the Internet (for instance Facebook and Twitter) as the most resource-rich mediums through which to stream information on the Arab Uprisings. Three hundred and seventy-six respondents watched television, particularly certain world news channels, to obtain information about the Arab Uprisings, while 81 respondents heard similar news on the radio. Three hundred and fifty-four respondents attended a seminar, forum or lecture (in various locations), mostly during their years as university students, to learn more about the uprisings, while 301 respondents simply read a newspaper for the same purpose. Academic books (140 respondents) and journal articles (113 respondents) were also treated as a foundation for knowledge of the Arab Uprisings, while 297 respondents noted the role of lecturers, teachers, friends (via *usrah* – commonly known among Malaysian Islamist activists as discourse gathering) and family in providing them with information. Fourteen respondents referred to their personal experience whilst staying in Egypt during the launch of the January 25 Revolution, including a series of announcements made by the Malaysian Embassy in Egypt (Table 3.10).

Table 3.10 Respondents' source of information regarding the Arab Uprisings events

Source	Frequency
Television	376
Newspaper	301
Internet/Social Media	475
Radio	81
Book	140
Journal Article	113
Forum/Seminar/Talk/Lecture	354
Lecturer/Teacher/Friends/Family	297
Self-Experience	13

Source: Field Research 2016.

50 *Knowledge of the Islamist movements*

These various sources made respondents more open to understanding the Arab Uprisings phenomenon from different angles and perspectives. The next section will examine the opinions and attitudes of the different Islamist movements' respondents towards the Arab Uprisings, specifically how they understand the general facts about the events, including contributing factors, as well as the present phenomenon of neo-Islamism,[16] specifically the role of Islamist movements during the anti-government protests, as well as the prospects for Islamist parties in the MENA after the Arab Uprisings.

Understanding the general issues about the Arab Uprisings phenomenon

This section of the chapter presents the results of the study's first objective, which was to explore the opinions and understanding of selected Malaysian Islamist movements (PAS, ABIM, ISMA and AMANAH) about the Arab Uprisings. It was based on selected fundamental issues that closely related to the 2011 Arab Uprisings – (1) the nature of anti-government protests, (2) the Arab Uprisings as a modern form of political revolution and (3) the Arab Uprisings as an act of non-violent civil resistance. The respondents were asked whether these issues should be considered within the basic description of the Arab Uprisings. The following section will discuss in further detail the questions and the respondents' responses.

Anti-government protests

The Arab Uprisings can be traced back to January 2011, when the so-called 'Tunisian Jasmine Revolution' led to the unexpected removal of Ben Ali's regime, triggering a region-wide protest effect that soon brought down Mubarak's regime in Egypt, Ali Abdullah Saleh in Yemen and Gaddafi in Libya, also destabilising the position of Assad in Syria, which led to wider political repercussions across the MENA (Whitehead 2014: 17). Prior to the launch of the Arab Uprisings, there was no doubt that most of the Arab states had long been ruled by autocratic rulers (Gelvin 2012; Owen 2012). Authoritarian rule had been the reality for so long in the region that some considered it to be, if not the 'normal' form of ruling among Arab citizens, at least the expected political reality (Esposito et al. 2016).

For the majority of Malaysian Islamist members in this study (84.4 per cent), the genesis of the Arab Uprisings protests was certainly deemed a large-scale civil resistance, with anti-government protests against previously oppressive leaders: specifically Ben Ali in Tunisia, Mubarak in Egypt, Gaddafi in Libya, Ali Abdullah Saleh in Yemen and Bashar al-Assad in Syria. The responses received from the specific movements show a similar pattern; respondents from PAS (82.9 per cent), AMANAH (92.5 per cent), ABIM (91.3 per cent) and ISMA (71 per cent) all agreed that the Arab Uprisings were the people's upheaval against autocratic rulers. Meanwhile,

12.3 per cent of respondents, with a higher percentage from ISMA and PAS, preferred to remain neutral in viewing the Arab Uprisings as the citizens' disapproval of their so-called 'undemocratic' leaders. Only 3.4 per cent of respondents disagreed with the question being asked.

One of the respondents from PAS who disagreed with the question claimed that the Arab Uprisings issues in the Middle East should be viewed as the people's manifestations towards state leaders who refused to implement Sharia and thus failed to serve the interest of citizens.[17] However, his single opinion did not reflect that of the majority of PAS members, who largely viewed the Arab Uprisings as a clear sign of the rejection of dictatorship rule by Arab citizens. According to the PAS president, the Arab Uprisings were unquestionably a situation whereby Arab citizens took to the streets to protest against Arab dictators for the sake of democracy and fair election as well as to promote anti-corruption efforts.[18] His opinion seems to line up with that of Abdullah Zaik, the president of ISMA, who agreed that the Arab Uprisings were the inevitable result of 'political cruelty' which had been practised for several decades by some Arab leaders. Thus, for him, there was no conflict as regards accepting the common facts about the popular anti-government protests during the Arab Uprisings.[19] Overall, respondents from all the four Malaysian Islamist movements generally agree that the Arab Uprisings or the 'Arab Spring' is the popular terminology used to describe the anti-government protests that occurred throughout the MENA in 2011.

Political revolution

In general, revolution in the political context can be defined as a change in the way a state is governed, usually a change to a different and better political system (Kimmel 1990). Political revolution often involves mass mobilisation and sometimes uses violence or war to achieve the means for political change. Several major revolutions have occurred throughout world history: for instance the famous American Revolution (1783), French Revolution (1789), Bolshevik Revolution (1917) and Iranian Revolution (1979). All these revolutions successfully transformed their national political landscapes into new governing systems. Regarding the 2011 Arab Uprisings, Abdul Hadi Awang (PAS president) believes that a similar revolution occurred 100 years earlier, when the so-called 'great 1916 Arab-revolt' was launched by Arab Nationalists to liberate the land of *hejaz* (a region in the west of present-day Saudi Arabia) from the Ottoman Empire. As a result (following several agreements made with colonial powers: for instance the Sykes-Picot Agreement), a few Arab nations (Jordan, Iraq, Syria, the Gulf countries) were established with a different style of rule, including the monarchic system of government.[20]

Although the outcome of the recent Arab Uprisings varies from one country to another, some scholars and observers describe the events as political revolutions or 'The Arab Revolutions' – referring to the struggle of Arab nations against their former regimes and ruling systems via massive street protests. The label also accounts for the radical transformation in politics and values that the Arab world is undergoing (Pierre-Filiu 2011; Hanafi 2012; Noueihed & Warren 2012; Milton-Edwards 2012; Lawson 2015). The majority of members of PAS, ABIM, ISMA and AMANAH (76.4 per cent) perceived the Arab Uprisings to be a national revolution in terms of its objectives to achieve social, economic and political reform. Only 6.4 per cent of the respondents disagreed with the statement, believing that the Arab Uprisings were just a normal protest, similar to those that had occurred in other countries in the world. 17.2 per cent remained neutral in associating the Arab Uprisings with political revolution.

The number of respondents who viewed the Arab Uprisings as an event of political revolution (both agree and strongly agree answers) dominates the reaction for each Islamist movements. This research also found that respondents' perceptions on this issue could be shaped by their sources of information. Among the nine sources (as previously stated), books recorded the highest percentage (82.2 per cent) for respondents who agreed that the Arab Uprisings were a modern political revolution in the Arab world, followed by television (80.8 per cent), newspaper (79.6 per cent), forum or lecture (79.3 per cent), Internet (77.8 per cent), journal article (77 per cent), lecturer or friends (76.8 per cent), radio (74 per cent) and self-experience (53.9 per cent). Thus, this finding indicates that the majority of Islamist movements in Malaysia understand the Arab Uprisings as political revolution based on their members' interpretation of books as well as other secondary information sources.

Non-violent resistance movements

The concept of non-violent civil resistance was popularised by Mahatma Gandhi as a psychological method to counter the British occupation in India circa the 1940s (Horsburgh 1968). According to Nepstad (2011), non-violent resistance movements are qualitatively different from violent revolutions, although they generally arise from the same factors – widespread grievances against the state regime. As a result, long-standing grievances are often transformed into moral outrage, which may make citizens willing to act and 'occupy' the streets. Regarding the case of the 2011 Arab Uprisings, the protests started with a peaceful demonstration, wherein the protesters were seen utilising strategic non-violent tactics: for example 'sit and protest', inspiring military defections,[21] influencing support from political elites, creating structures of a parallel civil society and using social media to coordinate and mobilise the protest (Batstone 2014). However, the protests turned violent when the regimes of Mubarak, Qaddafi and Assad deployed military force to crack down on protesters, which later resulted in casualties. Do the Islamists from PAS, ABIM, ISMA and AMANAH in Malaysia perceive the Arab Uprisings or the 'Arab Spring' as a violent protest?

Table 3.11 Respondents' perceptions that the Arab Uprisings were a non-violent resistance movement

Type of Islamist Movement	\multicolumn{5}{c	}{Perceptions that the Arab Uprisings Were a Non-Violent Resistance Movement (Frequency and Percentages)}	Total
	Strongly Disagree	Disagree	Neutral	Agree	Strongly Agree	
The Pan Malaysian Islamic Party (PAS)	25 −8.70%	42 −14.60%	77 −26.80%	93 −32.40%	50 −17.40%	287 −100%
The National Trust Party (AMANAH)	5 −5.40%	6 −6.50%	16 −17.20%	31 −33.30%	35 −37.60%	93 −100%
The Muslim Youth Movement of Malaysia (ABIM)	4 −4.90%	4 −4.90%	19 −23.50%	22 −27.20%	32 −39.50%	81 −100%
The Malaysian Muslim Solidarity Front (ISMA)	7 −10.10%	21 −30.40%	7 −10.10%	23 −33.30%	11 −15.90%	69 −100%
Total	41 −7.70%	73 −13.80%	119 −22.50%	169 −31.90%	128 −24.20%	530 −100%

Source: Field Research 2016.

As shown in Table 3.11, 128 respondents (24.2 per cent) strongly agreed that the Arab Uprisings should be seen as a non-violent resistance movement. One hundred and sixty-nine respondents (32.9 per cent) moderately supported the statement. Most of these respondents' arguments relied on the fact that the Arab Uprisings protests were joined by all layers of society – the elderly, women, children, civil servants, students and general workers. All of them took to the streets unarmed and in a peaceful way, without any intention to cause harm or chaos. Thus, for them it is definitely unfair to consider the demonstrations during the Arab Uprisings as violent acts. The question was relatively subjective, and 22.5 per cent of respondents seemed uncertain of whether the Arab Uprisings were violent or non-violent protests, while the remaining 21.5 per cent disagreed that the protests were peaceful events.

Among the four Islamist groups being studied, ISMA showed quite balanced responses compared to PAS, ABIM and AMANAH. As explained by the ISMA president, the Arab Uprisings undoubtedly had elements of violence, most notable in Egypt, Libya and Syria, where the 'revolutionaries' threw stones and Molotov cocktails, and set government buildings ablaze. Thus, for him, as a leader of ISMA, the Arab Uprisings could not be classified as a non-violent resistance movement, although he agreed that the protesters showed resilience and succeeded in toppling several key Arab leaders using non-violent means.[22] The next section will explore the attitudes of respondents towards several key factors that contributed to the Arab Uprisings in 2011.

Understanding the factors that led to the Arab Uprisings

The respondents' understanding of fundamental facts concerning the Arab Uprisings was examined by asking them whether Bouazizi's death ignited the anti-regime protests in Tunisia, which later spread and quickly evolved into political revolution throughout the MENA. As pointed out by several prominent academics, the recent trend of uprisings in the Arab world is broadly believed to have started in December 2010, in the wake of the self-immolation of the street vegetable seller (Bouazizi) in front of government municipals in Sidi Bouzid (Milton-Edwards 2012: 219; Alcinda 2013: 1; Storm 2014: 112; Esposito et al. 2016: 2; Volpi 2017: 74). The day after the suicide, a large crowd of fellow Tunisians made up of youths, political activists, lawyers, workers and some opposition politicians began protesting against the Ben Ali regime (Gelvin 2012: 42). This action later sparked an upheaval in Sidi Bouzid and ignited a massive uprising in Tunisia that rapidly spread to the rest of the MENA (Ghanem 2016a: 63).

So, how did the Islamist movements in Malaysia react to this popular 'story'? As can be seen in Table 3.12, more than half of the respondents (53.5 per cent) agreed that the death of Bouazizi undoubtedly sparked the Arab Uprisings events. The PAS president, in his official statement, also agreed with this statement and further added that Bouazizi's desperate condition was due to decades of unresolved unemployment crises in Tunisia.[23] However, there were a considerable number of Malaysian Islamists who did not share this view. One hundred and seventy-four respondents (32.8 per cent),

Table 3.12 Respondents' perceptions that the Arab Uprisings were sparked in Tunisia by Mohamed Bouazizi

Type of Islamist Movement	Strongly Disagree	Disagree	Neutral	Agree	Strongly Agree	Total
The Pan Malaysian Islamic Party (PAS)	10 −3.50%	33 −11.50%	106 −36.90%	82 −28.60%	56 −19.50%	287 −100%
The National Trust Party (AMANAH)	5 −3.20%	6 −7.50%	16 −28.00%	31 −21.50%	35 −39.80%	93 −100%
The Muslim Youth Movement of Malaysia (ABIM)	4 −4.90%	4 −2.50%	19 −12.30%	22 −34.60%	32 −45.70%	81 −100%
The Malaysian Muslim Solidarity Front (ISMA)	7 −4.30%	21 −14.50%	7 −46.40%	23 −24.60%	11 −10.10%	69 −100%
Total	41 −3.80%	73 −9.80%	119 −32.50%	169 −27.70%	128 −25.80%	530 −100%

Source: Field Research 2016.

mainly from PAS (60.9 per cent) and ISMA (18.4 per cent), were not certain about the tragedy in Sidi Bouzid due to lack of knowledge and a focus on Tunisia's Jasmine Revolution. The rest of the respondents (14.8 per cent) disagreed with the question being asked – unfortunately, with no clear reason.

The research also examines the attitudes of respondents towards the other underlying causes of the Arab Uprisings. As discussed above, it is known among a number of Malaysian Islamists that the tragedy of Bouazizi's death sparked the outraged protests in Tunisia, which later spread to neighbouring countries, starting with Egypt, Libya, Yemen and Syria. However, it is worth mentioning that deep inside the nature of the uprisings, protesters were actually trying to tell their respective ruling regimes that people were fed up with the increasing unemployment crisis due to economic instability as well as the practice of dictatorship amongst the authorities (Anderson 2011; Arieff 2012b; Owen 2012). According to Gelvin (2012), the repressive nature of the Arab regimes and their suppression of citizen's rights, coupled with on-going corruption and the worsening economy, were the major causes leading to the Arab revolutions. The development of social media (Facebook and Twitter) also played an important role in assisting Arab activists during the Arab Uprisings (Howard and Hussain 2013). Thus, this research highlights three crucial factors that triggered the emergence of the people's revolts in a large part of the Arab world in 2011–2012, namely: (1) economic downturn, (2) political dictatorship and (3) media technology. The following section reveals the reactions of PAS, ABIM, AMANAH and ISMA members towards these three major factors.

Perception that economic downturn, autocratic leadership and the role of social media contributed to the Arab Uprisings

This section is based on the survey questions that asked respondents about the factors that caused the Arab Uprisings. First, the findings show that almost 74.9 per cent of PAS, ABIM, ISMA and AMANAH Islamists generally agreed (combination of agree and strongly agree categories) that weak economic development, which gave birth to the chronic unemployment crisis among Arab youth, was the main reason for the uprisings. Their view seems to align with the survey conducted by the Arab Barometer, in which 63 per cent of Tunisian respondents believed that the weak economy was the major reason for the revolt against the Ben Ali regime.[24] Only 5.5 per cent of respondents disagreed with the statement, while 19.6 per cent preferred to remain neutral. In terms of feedback from specific movements, AMANAH showed the highest percentage of positive responses (93.4 per cent), followed by ABIM (91.4 per cent) and PAS (71.3 per cent). ISMA, on the other hand, seemed quite sceptical about the economic problem being one of the contributing factors in the Arab Uprisings. 40.6 per cent of ISMA respondents had no idea about the statement (neutral response), whilst 8.6 per cent totally disagreed. Details about the number of respondents' opinions can be seen in Table 3.13.

Table 3.13 Perceptions that economic downturn contributed to the Arab Uprisings

Type of Islamist Movement	Strongly Disagree	Disagree	Neutral	Agree	Strongly Agree	Total
The Pan Malaysian Islamic Party (PAS)	7 −2.40%	9 −3.10%	67 −23.30%	120 −41.80%	84 −29.30%	287 −100%
The National Trust Party (AMANAH)	2 −2.20%	1 −1.10%	6 −6.50%	34 −36.60%	50 −56.80%	93 −100%
The Muslim Youth Movement of Malaysia (ABIM)	0 0.00%	4 −4.90%	3 −3.70%	28 −34.60%	46 −56.80%	81 −100%
The Malaysian Muslim Solidarity Front (ISMA)	1 −1.40%	5 −7.20%	28 −40.60%	24 −34.80%	11 −15.90%	69 −100%
Total	10 −1.90%	19 −3.60%	104 −19.60%	206 −38.90%	191 −36.00%	530 −100%

Source: Field Research 2016.

Second, regarding the issue of political repression, there were 177 respondents (33.4 per cent) who strongly agreed that the Arab Uprisings were the result of several decades of dictatorship in Tunisia, Egypt, Syria, Libya and Yemen, followed by 202 respondents (38.1 per cent) who moderately shared the same view. One hundred and six respondents (20 per cent) were not certain whether political dictatorship caused the launch of the Arab Uprisings, while 45 (8.5 per cent) simply rejected the claim of 'iron fist' leadership by Arab rulers and the absence of political freedom as a reason for the protests. Table 3.14 presents the respondents' perceptions of the relationship between authoritarianism and the emergence of the Arab Uprisings protests.

Third, concerning the role of social media, it is worth mentioning that online social media products (Facebook and Twitter) have grown rapidly over the last 10 years in the Middle East region, though their expansion certainly varies from state to state (Seib 2007). Throughout the series of Arab Uprisings street protests, social media platforms were instrumental in constructing alternative news and mobilising citizens to take to the streets; most importantly they cascaded messages about political freedom, civil rights and positive hope from the uprisings. In other words, digital media had a causal role in the Arab Uprisings in that it provided the infrastructure that created deep communication ties and organisational capacity in groups of activists before the major protests took place and while street protests were being formalised (Howard and Hussein 2013: 120).

When respondents were asked about their opinion regarding the effectiveness of social media during the Arab Uprisings events, 84.2 per cent (446) agreed that Facebook, Twitter, the YouTube channel and web blogs, as

Table 3.14 Perceptions that autocratic leadership contributed to the Arab Uprisings

Type of Islamist Movement	Strongly Disagree	Disagree	Neutral	Agree	Strongly Agree	Total
The Pan Malaysian Islamic Party (PAS)	5	23	67	111	81	287
	−1.70%	−8.00%	−23.30%	−38.70%	−28.20%	−100%
The National Trust Party (AMANAH)	3	2	12	31	45	93
	−3.20%	−2.20%	−12.90%	−33.30%	−48.40%	−100%
The Muslim Youth Movement of Malaysia (ABIM)	0	4	8	30	39	81
	0.00%	−4.90%	−9.90%	−37.00%	−48.10%	−100%
The Malaysian Muslim Solidarity Front (ISMA)	4	4	19	30	12	69
	−5.80%	−5.80%	−27.50%	−43.50%	−17.40%	−100%
Total	12	33	106	202	177	530
	−2.30%	−6.20%	−20.00%	−38.10%	−33.40%	−100%

Source: Field Research 2016.

well as foreign media's online portals, were extremely useful in helping the protesters to 'secure' the success of the revolutions. 12.3 per cent of respondents (65) seemed uncertain whether the social media factor was associated with the success of the Arab Uprisings, while the remaining 3.6 per cent (14) disagreed with the statement. Additionally, the Islamist movements which the respondents represented did not make any significant difference since the pattern of reaction was similar for PAS, ABIM, ISMA and AMANAH. Based on the major findings in this section, it seems that PAS, ABIM, ISMA and AMANAH agreed that the three factors mentioned (economic downturn, political repression and the role of social media) were valid reasons why thousands of Arab citizens took to the streets against their former regimes. According to ISMA, activist Amar Yasier[25]:

> The Arab Spring was a process of revolution and political reformation in the Middle East. The worsening economic problems and widespread political mercilessness contributed to what was triggered as the 'Arab Spring'. The people were no longer seen to be capable of facing various corrupted systems, even the garbage collection system in housing areas. The people felt as if they were taken advantage of by the authorities. Thus, the final method was to rise and fight by taking it to the streets.

Nevertheless, the ISMA movement, via its president and several members interviewed by the author, believed that the Arab Uprising events were also triggered by another factor – the role of 'invisible hands' – which they specifically referred to as external powers: for instance the United States and

58 *Knowledge of the Islamist movements*

its Western allies through 'confidential or secret plans'. The movement 'accused' these foreign powers of having personal political agendas and economic interests within the MENA and thus supporting Arab revolutionaries to overthrow leaders of Muslim nations. Central to these claims, the ISMA president believes that[26]:

> It was true, the 'Arab Spring' was indeed an effort to fight against the cruelty of Arabic dictatorial regimes. The ruling of the Arab world prior to the Arab Spring had reached a hiatus, where there was no agenda that benefitted the people and there was a separation or a big gap between the people and the government. But the 'Arab Spring' was not only an effort to fight against the cruelty of the leaders; there were some back 'hands' that took advantage of what was called the 'Arab Spring' or people's uprising. The Arab Uprisings were also spurred by an external influence through campaigns to re-energize the civil society, or in other words, a movement from the outside coming to take advantage of the Arab Uprisings situation by using the civil society as a tool to overthrow the government. The external influence implied was from the West, where they were seen to use a new format to change the government through the role of the civil society. In Syria for instance, Mossad-Israel, CIA-America and FSB-Russia undoubtedly want the future of the country to be determined according to the respective countries interest. Thus, in talking about the 'Arab Spring', it is not something easy as we would normally understand it, which is a people's uprising to overthrow a regime. It is far from that.

An ISMA activist, Mohd Syafiq, seems to support his 'President', saying that[27]:

> In general, we can see that the Arab Uprisings were a concerted effort by the people to unite and collaborate in rejecting any leaders that they felt did not benefit the people. So, they tried to change the leaders. But at the same time, if we were to look at it more deeply, actually there were efforts from outsiders, for example from the US, where they tried to take advantage of the chaos of the Arab Spring Revolution to destroy the administration in Arab countries.

Asyraf Farique, an independent researcher within ISMA, further explains what the movement thinks about the 'relationship' between the West and the Arab Uprisings[28]:

> I think the Arab Spring is not something that happened out of the blue when the self-immolation of Bouazizi took place and there were uprisings amongst the people who rebelled against the rulers and so on. We (ISMA) see the 'Arab Spring' as a properly arranged plan by Western powers like America. If we look at several series of demonstrations

in Tunisia, Libya and Egypt, the agency called the National Endowment for Democracy has given a lot of funds to civil movements to oust their leaders. The same method was used in Europe as was once used in Ukraine. The external factors play a very important role, as well as the internal factors to the point that the people in Arab countries have successfully brought down the regimes in countries involved in the Arab Spring.

These 'prejudicial' sentiments indirectly reflected the movement's ideology and long-term practice of an 'aggressive approach' (discussed in Chapter 4) when it comes to issues of Muslim and non-Muslim relations, be they at the local or the global level. Thus, for the author, it was not a surprise to note that all the interviewees from ISMA responded similarly, by pointing out the role of foreign powers behind the backdrop of the Arab Uprisings.[29] Although the actual involvement of foreign powers in the anti-government protests has not been legitimately proven, Michael Hudson, an American Political Scientist, raised the same issue in his writing: 'I never believed that the sudden explosions of massive popular protest (the Arab Spring) were just coincidental. This is not to say, obviously, that there was a foreign conspiracy behind them, as some people in the Arab world believe' (Hudson 2015: 32).

In comparison, PAS, ABIM and AMANAH seem to share an opinion regarding the factors that contributed to the Arab Uprisings. For ISMA, although the movement generally agreed with the three factors mentioned, the survey results found that quite a number of its members remained sceptical about economic and political factors. The role of foreign powers was mentioned by several ISMA members, including its president, as another factor that should be considered. This scenario is best explained by the theory proposed by Robin Goodwin – the 'Adjustment to Change' theory – which examines how individual or group characteristics (in this case the political approach and ideology of ISMA) affect the views and responses of its members towards rapid and dramatic social change (the Arab Uprisings events). Accordingly, in addition to the demographic aspects and the type of sources of information, the role of an Islamist movement's ideology and political approach can also be considered as a predictor of its attitudes towards the Arab Uprisings phenomenon, as was shown by the feedback of ISMA Islamic activists.

Attitudes towards Islamist movements and the Arab Uprisings

The purpose of this section is to explore the attitudes towards Islamism, political Islam and Islamist movements issues of the Malaysian Islamists, specifically the Ennahda Party in Tunisia and the Muslim Brotherhood in Egypt, within the context of the Arab Uprisings. As stated in Chapter 4, the strong connection between the Islamist movements in Malaysia (PAS, ABIM, ISMA, AMANAH) and transnational Islamist movements is

60 *Knowledge of the Islamist movements*

undeniable. In general, the parties and movements' policies remain firm on supporting the idea of political Islam (though through different approaches) as well as the development of any Muslim Brotherhood-inspired movements all over the world. Hence, it is quite reasonable for one to assume that these movements' strong ties with the global Islamist network will lead to a biased view on any issues relating to Islamism and Islamist movements in the MENA during the Arab Uprisings and post-Arab Uprisings events.

Nevertheless, it is worth mentioning that the events of the 2011 Arab Uprisings, as argued by Olivier Roy (2012), were not a kind of 'Islamic Revolution' and were far from any direct involvement of Islamist movements during the 2011 anti-government protests. In Tunisia, for instance, during the first few weeks of protest that led to the fall of the Ben Ali regime, there was a not much active participation by the Tunisian Islamists as an organised group (Merone and Volpi 2014). Meanwhile in Egypt, prior to the uprising, the role and involvement of the Islamists, particularly the Muslim Brotherhood, were uncertain as members were seen as hesitant to openly protest against the Mubarak regime and remained 'low profile' during the popular January 25 Revolution (Paciello 2011; Kerckhove 2012). In Syria, Yemen and Libya, there was also no concrete evidence of any direct participation by Islamists when the uprisings broke out. From these established facts, it was clear that the Arab Uprisings were not on the agenda of the Islamists in the first place. The question here is – are they (the Malaysian Islamists from PAS, ABIM, ISMA and AMANAH) on the 'same page' as those scholars in viewing the role of Islamist movements during the Arab Uprisings? The following section provides their responses.

The role of Islamist movements

As Islamism and the relationship with Islamist movements in the MENA are significant elements for all four movements (PAS, ABIM, ISMA and AMANAH), the respondents were asked whether Islamist movements in the MENA played a role in assisting protesters during the Arab Uprisings. The results were statistically significant as well as expected. It is not surprising to see that only a minority of respondents (5.1 per cent) agreed with Olivier Roy's argument that Islamists and Islamist movements did not play a significant role in supporting the Tunisian and Egyptian protesters in overthrowing their former regimes (those of Ben Ali and Mubarak). As mentioned by Abdullah Zaik (ISMA president)[30]:

> The Arab Uprisings that happened (in the Middle East) were indeed something that was not on the agenda of the Islamist movements (in the first place) - even the Muslim Brothers in Egypt did not take part in the early phase of the revolution. They were hesitant to take part in the demonstrations, or in other words, they were not sure whether to take advantage of them or not.

Knowledge of the Islamist movements 61

Instead, the majority of Malaysian Islamists (70.3 per cent) believed that their 'Islamist counterparts' in Tunisia and Egypt had somehow assisted the protesters during the Arab Uprisings. Although their opinion seems contradictory to the mainstream notion, there are scholars, such as Masoud (2011: 24), Gelvin (2012: 58) and Ghabra (2015: 209), who argued that the members of the Youth Wing of the Muslim Brotherhood in Egypt had 'secretly' participated (as individuals) in the protests and even played a visible role in defending the protesters against pro-Mubarak supporters during the 'Battle of Camel'. These arguments could soundly justify why these respondents chose to agree with the question. The rest of the respondents (27.4 per cent) remained neutral on this question.

The 'Islamist Winter'

In the aftermath of the Arab Uprisings, several Islamist parties, most notably Tunisia's Ennahda Party and Egypt's Freedom and Justice Party (FJP), gained attention due to their victory in the national elections following the overthrow of their former autocratic regimes (Esposito et al. 2016). As part of the Muslim Brotherhood's global Islamist movements, such news was celebrated among Islamist activists all over Malaysia.[31] When asked whether the Arab Uprisings were a phenomenon resulting from Islamist uprising and the rise of political Islam in the Arab world, 69.6 per cent of the respondents said 'yes', and 9.4 per cent said 'no'. Table 3.15 presents the PAS, ABIM, ISMA and AMANAH Islamists' responses regarding the trend of the 'Islamist Winter'.

Table 3.15 Respondents' perceptions that the Arab Uprisings were a phenomenon of Islamist Uprising and the rise of political Islam in the Arab world

Type of Islamist Movement	Perceptions that the Arab Uprisings Were a Phenomenon of Islamist Uprising (Frequency and Percentages)					Total
	Strongly Disagree	Disagree	Neutral	Agree	Strongly Agree	
The Pan Malaysian Islamic Party (PAS)	4 −1.40%	16 −5.60%	72 −25.10%	127 −44.30%	68 −23.70%	287 −100%
The National Trust Party (AMANAH)	4 −4.30%	11 −11.80%	15 −16.10%	39 −41.90%	24 −25.80%	93 −100%
The Muslim Youth Movement of Malaysia (ABIM)	3 −3.70%	0 0.00%	9 −11.10%	31 −38.30%	38 −46.90%	81 −100%
The Malaysian Muslim Solidarity Front (ISMA)	4 −5.80%	8 −11.60%	15 −21.70%	25 −36.20%	17 −24.60%	69 −100%
Total	15 −2.80%	35 −6.60%	111 −20.90%	222 −41.90%	147 −27.70%	530 −100%

Source: Field Research 2016.

It is undeniable that political Islam gained popularity after Islamist parties successfully 'hijacked' the Middle Eastern Revolts by winning the majority of seats in the parliament (Bradley 2012). This trend led to a naive and misleading perception among the 222 respondents who saw the Arab Uprisings or the 'Arab Spring' as a phenomenon of political Islam's awakening in the MENA. One hundred and forty-seven respondents even strongly perceived the Arab Uprisings as an Islamist uprising. Fifty, however, rationally rejected the statement by arguing that the Arab Uprisings should be viewed as a mass uprising without placing any exclusivity on Islamist groups, while 111 neither disagreed nor agreed. As acknowledged by Muhammad Najib (AMANAH Youth Leader)[32]:

> The 'Arab Spring' was not the phenomenon of Islamist movements uprising. The Islamist movements in the Arab world only took advantage upon the political uncertainty (in the post-Arab Uprisings) to come to power, without any preparation and governing model. Hence, some of them failed to stay in power and govern. The development of AKP in Turkey, with a decade under Erdogan's leadership is the real phenomena of the Islamist uprisings, as the party seems successful in accommodating the country's secular values with political Islam which enables it to continuously gain support in every series of elections.

Speaking of AKP as a 'real' phenomenon of political Islam, Muhammad Najib's view was also supported by another AMANAH activist, who commented[33]:

> Turkey has gradually expanded the value of Islam in public life until it is openly accepted by the majority of Turkish Muslims. I hope that there will be a party in Malaysia - I suggest AMANAH – which will apply the approach of the AKP in Turkey. Long Live Erdogan!

Prospect for Islamist parties

The 2011 Arab Uprisings have undoubtedly given rise to an unprecedented number of political parties in the region, including the Islamists.[34] In Egypt, for instance, before the June 2013 coup, the January 25 Revolution paved the way for the creation of more than 80 new parties (Vannetzel 2017: 211). Given the strong performance of the Ennahda Party in Tunisia's legislative elections in 2011 and of the FJP in the 2012 Egyptian presidential election,[35] respondents were asked whether they saw the Arab Uprisings as a great opportunity for Islamist parties to gain power. The findings show that 49.5 per cent of PAS, ABIM, ISMA and AMANAH Islamists are positive that the post-Arab Uprisings provided a significant chance for Islamist parties to come to power for the first time ever. For these respondents, it became

Knowledge of the Islamist movements 63

apparent that without the Arab Uprisings, the Islamist parties could only dream of achieving political power and ruling their states, given the nature of the previous party systems in both Tunisia and Egypt – the Hegemony and one-party dominant system.[36] As Anani (2012: 466) points out, 'After decades of brutal repression and exclusion, the Arab Spring opened the doors of power for Islamists. From Morocco to Egypt, Islamist parties have fared well in elections held since the eruption of revolts in early 2011'.

However, the trend of the so-called 'Islamist Winter' after the Arab Uprisings did not last long when the Ennahda Party failed to capture the majority of seats in the 2014 legislative election, which led to its becoming an opposition party to the newly rebranded secular party government – the Nidaa Tounes. In Cairo, the June 2013 coup tragically ended the one and only term in Egypt's political history of the Muslim Brotherhood's rule, under Mohamed Morsi. 13.5 per cent of the respondents cited these facts to justify their disagreement that the Arab Uprisings were an opportunity for Islamist parties to come to power. The remaining 33.1 per cent of neither disagreed nor agreed with the question being asked. Interestingly, the number of respondents who were not certain about the prospects for Islamist parties in the aftermath of the Arab Uprisings was relatively high, especially for PAS, ISMA and ABIM, which reflects the subjective nature of the question.

The second part of the question involved asking respondents whether the Arab Islamist parties were capable of governing the Arab countries. In general, the lengths of experience that these Islamist parties had in governing their respective states in the post-Arab Uprisings era were about three and a half years for the Ennahda Party and one year for the FJP. Were they seen as capable of doing such a 'job'? 56.5 per cent of the respondents believed that the mainstream Islamist parties[37] (in the Middle East) are capable of governing due to decades of experience in the opposition camp to most Arab regimes. Furthermore, a number of respondents believe that Arab Islamist movements have increasingly adopted more moderate positions and policies, which suggested a readiness to assume the responsibilities of power. One of the respondents from PAS further stated that:

> The ability of Islamist parties in governing the Arab state are self-evident. As long as there is no act of sabotage from the military, external actors or powers and opposition parties, they (the Islamist parties) can perform their job very well. Nowadays, Islam and democracy have proven to be compatible – thus opportunity should democratically be given to Islamist parties without any prejudice, so that these parties can 'demonstrate' their abilities in ruling Arab countries.[38]

Paradoxically, there were a small number of respondents (12.2 per cent) who doubted the ability of Islamist parties to govern Arab countries, while 31.3

per cent of respondents were not entirely sure about the statement. One of the reasons raised by an AMANAH representative was:

> The Islamist parties (in MENA), especially Egypt's Muslim Brotherhood, seem to lack a proper plan and governing model to rule their states in the post-Arab Uprisings. They (the Islamist parties) should know which one is a priority between the agenda of political Islam and the basic needs (economic aspects) among the people. If they can come out with a practical solution towards the issues of corruption, poverty and unemployment, then people will certainly have confidence in supporting the ability of any Islamist- oriented parties to govern.[39]

If the issue of readiness to assume power, as demonstrated by the case of the FJP under the former Egyptian president Mohamed Morsi, was one of the reasons (for some Malaysian Islamists who doubted the capability of Arab Islamist parties to govern), then it seems that Marc Lynch (2016) had a better opinion to 'harmonize' those two different views within the Malaysian Islamists. According to him, Islamist parties were indeed poorly equipped to deal with any political openings after the Arab Uprisings in 2011, but many have adapted to the aftermath in diverse and pragmatic ways – for example with the introduction of a 'Muslim Democrat' approach by Ennahda Party leader Rachid Ghannouchi. Furthermore, the rise and fall of Egypt's Muslim Brotherhood was critically important across the region, but its experience was not typical among regional Islamist parties. Moreover, Islamist parties have continued to participate successfully in democratic elections, despite domestic and regional pressures. Thus, Lynch (2016) believes that Islamist parties will continue to play an important role in the politics of most Arab states, despite the pressures they have faced in recent years. Overall, Table 3.16 indicates the attitudes of respondents towards the capability of Islamist parties in governing Arab countries.

As Table 3.16 demonstrates, the number of respondents from each movement who are not convinced of the governing capability of Islamist parties in the Arab world is relatively balanced, except for those in ABIM – since more than half of these (77.8 per cent) gave a positive response. There were approximately 46.1 per cent of PAS, 45.2 per cent of AMANAH and 52.1 per cent of ISMA members who did not share the majority view (either by remaining neutral or disagreeing). The final section will continue with a discussion on the nature of Islamist movements as part of the society's agent of change, based on respondents' attitudes.

The Islamist movements as an agent of societal change

This section explores the respondents' views on whether post-Arab Uprisings events have highlighted the relevance of the Islamist movements as a societal agent of change in the context of Malaysia's experience. In 2004,

Table 3.16 Respondents' views that the Islamist parties are capable of governing Arab countries

Type of Islamist Movement	Strongly Disagree	Disagree	Neutral	Agree	Strongly Agree	Total
The Pan Malaysian Islamic Party (PAS)	8 / −2.80%	29 / −10.10%	98 / −34.00%	98 / −34.00%	55 / −19.10%	287 / −100%
The National Trust Party (AMANAH)	2 / −2.20%	11 / −11.80%	29 / −31.20%	33 / −35.50%	18 / −19.40%	93 / −100%
The Muslim Youth Movement of Malaysia (ABIM)	0 / 0.00%	3 / −3.70%	15 / −18.50%	29 / −35.80%	34 / −42.00%	81 / −100%
The Malaysian Muslim Solidarity Front (ISMA)	5 / −7.20%	7 / −10.10%	24 / −34.8	25 / −36.20%	8 / −11.60%	69 / −100%
Total	15 / −2.80%	50 / −9.40%	166 / −31.30%	185 / −34.80%	115 / −21.70%	530 / −100%

Source: Field Research 2016.

Diane Singerman argued that the Islamic movement is not exceptional but rather has elements common to all social movements – purposeful and organised groups which strive towards a common goal via collective identity and behaviour, a range of strategies and so forth.[40] It is seen as quite similar to other social movements in the world, except for the political aim and political context within which it operates, which leads to the distinctive character of the so-called 'Islamist movement'. Although the capacity of social movements to construct a new social order is sometimes limited, they are undoubtedly capable of creating social change, as can be seen in the case of the Arab Uprisings. The Ennahda Party and Muslim Brothers are clear examples of Islamist movements acting as agents of change in their respective civil societies through their adoption of political power.

Throughout the period of Ennahda's rule in the post-2011 Jasmine Revolution, the movement contributed positively to the overall development of Tunisian politics and remains significant within the country's democratic consolidation process (Guazzone 2013: 30). Meanwhile in Egypt, apart from the political aspect, the Muslim Brotherhood's network of social services, in particular schools and medical facilities, served millions of Egyptians, who relied on these services to meet their daily needs before the military regime's crackdown following the coup in June 2013 (Brooke 2015). Despite years of repression and political discrimination by the former regimes, the two examples mentioned above might illustrate the relevance of Islamist movements as agents of societal change in the era of following the Arab Uprisings – as

Table 3.17 Respondents' views that the post-Arab Uprisings events have shown the relevance of the Islamist movement as an agent of societal change

Type of Islamist Movement	\multicolumn{5}{c}{The post-Arab Uprisings Events Have Shown the Relevance of the Islamist Movement as an Agent of Societal Change (Frequency and Percentages)}	Total
	Strongly Disagree	Disagree	Neutral	Agree	Strongly Agree	
The Pan Malaysian Islamic Party (PAS)	9 −3.10%	15 −5.20%	69 −24.00%	135 −46.90%	60 −20.80%	288 −100%
The National Trust Party (AMANAH)	2 −2.20%	8 −8.60%	18 −19.40%	47 −50.50%	18 −19.40%	93 −100%
The Muslim Youth Movement of Malaysia (ABIM)	2 −2.50%	7 −8.60%	9 −11.10%	41 −50.60%	22 −27.20%	81 −100%
The Malaysian Muslim Solidarity Front (ISMA)	0 0.00%	7 −10.10%	19 −27.50%	25 −36.20%	18 −26.10%	69 −100%
Total	13 −2.40%	37 −7.00%	115 −21.70%	248 −46.70%	118 −22.20%	530 −100%

Source: Field Research 2016.

observed by the majority of Malaysian Islamists from PAS, ABIM, ISMA and AMANAH (68.9 per cent) who were involved in the survey. Only 9.4 per cent of respondents disagreed with the view, while 21.7 per cent remained neutral. Table 3.17 shows respondents' reactions to the statement.

Conclusion and summary

The main aim of this chapter was to explore the perceptions of respondents representing the PAS, the ABIM, the ISMA and the AMANAH towards the Arab Uprisings phenomenon. It began with general questions about the respondents' backgrounds, including their membership status within the movements. Most of the respondents came from the age ranges 16–25 and 26–35, which represented 76.7 per cent of the research sample. The majority of respondents were male (70.7 per cent) with a Bachelor's Degree from local institutions and were official members of the PAS, ABIM, ISMA or AMANAH movements. They also actively participated and engaged in their movements' political activism.

The chapter continued with an assessment of respondents' knowledge of the existence of the Arab Uprisings in the MENA. The results indicated that 82.7 per cent of respondents (532) from all movements were highly aware of such events, with the Internet or social media (Facebook and Twitter) as their main sources of information. Of the four movements, ABIM showed the most impressive feedback as all members involved in this study knew about the Arab Uprisings phenomenon. The research also found that level of education and membership status were potential factors determining respondents' general knowledge of the Arab Uprisings. Those who had a higher level of academic qualification and actively participated in their parties' or movements' political activism presented significant knowledge about the Arab Uprisings. On the other hand, there were 111 respondents, mostly from PAS, who did not know about the Arab Uprisings due to lack of time to read or listen to information sources, or watch global news. As a result, these respondents had not been exposed to the Arab Uprisings phenomenon in recent years. The knowledge of those who did know about the protests was highly valuable for this research as it helped the study to examine how the Malaysian Islamists perceive the phenomenon as well as determine whether it affected their attitudes towards certain contemporary issues. The exploration of awareness of the Arab Uprisings among the respondents in terms of their attitudes about the chosen issues generated a number of interesting findings, as summarised in the following paragraphs.

The respondents' perceptions of the general issues concerning the Arab Uprisings were explored through questions which dealt with the issues of dictatorship rule, political revolution, non-violent resistance and the 'sacrifice' of Mohamed Bouazizi. The findings showed that a significant number of PAS, ABIM, ISMA and AMANAH Islamists viewed the Arab Uprisings as the immediate result of Mohamed Bouazizi's tragedy, which led to an Arab political revolution and the people's upheaval against dictatorship via non-violent resistance movements. In general, it appears that all four Islamist movements have genuine knowledge about the Arab Uprisings, which reflects the movements' 'tradition' to constantly maintain focus on Arab Middle Eastern affairs. As regards the factors that led to the Arab Uprisings, the vast majority of respondents agreed that the deteriorating state of economic performance (379) and the long-term practice of political repression (397) triggered the uprisings in Tunisia, Egypt, Syria, Yemen and Libya. They also agreed that social media had been greatly beneficial as a medium to enhance the spread of the protests and later secured the revolutions (446).

In the meantime, ISMA also stressed that the role of foreign powers should be considered as one of the factors that caused popular anti-government protests throughout the MENA. To put it more succinctly, the movement believed that major powers from the West tried to gain advantage from the political uncertainties among the Arab Muslim nations following the Arab Uprisings phenomenon. The consistent view expressed by several ISMA members with regard to this question was due to the movement's ideology and political approaches (of political Islam), which shaped the way of thinking of its members. In other words, individual characteristics might affect the views of members towards any rapid dramatic social change, as in the case of the Arab Uprisings phenomenon – as proposed by Goldwin in his theory of 'Adjustment to Change'.

Next, the attitudes of the respondents towards Islamism and the Arab Uprisings were quite 'one-sided' as 70.3 per cent thought that the Islamist movements played a significant role in assisting the protesters during the Arab Uprisings. This perception led to a deceptive assumption among 69.9 per cent of the Malaysian Islamists in this study that the 2011 Arab Uprisings were a phenomenon of Islamist uprisings and the rise of political Islam in the MENA. Those who came from a movement which strongly favoured Islamism and were very much oriented towards the 'struggle for political Islam' agenda also showed a strong degree of concern about Arab Islamist parties as most of them personally believed that they were capable of governing the Arab states. There was also a small minority of respondents who did not agree or remained neutral about the above statements. Based on the author's observation, those respondents who believed that the Arab Islamists had contributed to the uprisings were quite 'passionate' in their view of the Muslim Brothers' legacy in the Arab world. Another explanation for such differences could be the variety of sources used by these respondents concerning Islamist issues. For instance, mainstream academic writing mostly concluded that Islamism and Islamist movements did not play a prominent role during the revolutions, as can be seen in the work of Roy (2012), Bradley (2012), Willis (2014), Stein and Volpi (2014), and Merone and Volpi (2014). Thus, the information that respondents found in books and journal articles might have helped them to view the relation between Islamism and the Arab Uprisings in a constructive way, despite the positive relationship between PAS, ABIM, ISMA and AMANAH with the Islamist movements in the MENA.

Nevertheless, the findings also reveal one common view among the four named Malaysian Islamist groups: this is that the progressive development of such Arab Islamist parties after the Arab Uprisings might be an indicator of the relevance of the Islamist movements as a powerful agent of societal change. To summarise, one can see that there is not much difference in how the Islamist movements in Malaysia responded to the Arab Uprisings, except for ISMA, whereby the responses to two questions were quite unique compared to those of the other three movements. Most of the respondents' feedback showed a consistent trend of reaction – the 'agree and strongly agree' categories were the most popular answers for the majority of questions and statements in the survey.

Notes

1 In the survey, details of the number of respondents based on their movement/political affiliation are as follows: PAS: ($n = 387$), ABIM: ($n = 81$), ISMA: ($n = 80$) and AMANAH ($n = 95$). Only respondents involved in the selected case studies of Islamist movements in Malaysia were chosen throughout the survey.
2 See Gelvin (2012) for more details on the historical background of the 2011 Arab Uprisings.
3 Personal interview with the Secretary General of the Kuala Lumpur PAS Youth Branch, Ubaid Hj. Abd Akla. Puchong, Malaysia. 3 September 2016. See also

D.M. Müller. (2014). *Islam, Politics and Youth in Malaysia: The Pop-Islamist Reinvention of PAS*. Oxon: Routledge.
4 Personal interview with a PAS activist (name withheld at interviewee's request), Kuala Lumpur, Malaysia. 19 September 2016.
5 PAS was quite popular among Muslim student activists in Malaysia due to the role championed by The Coalition of Malaysian Muslim Students (GAMIS), which indirectly serves as an unofficial PAS recruitment body for local university students. For more information refer to Mohamed Nawab Mohamed Osman. (2014). Muslim Student Activism in Malaysia: A Case Study of GAMIS. In Lemiere, Sophie (ed.), *Misplaced Democracy: Malaysian Politics and People*. Petaling Jaya: SIRD.
6 Personal interview with Ubaid Hj. Abd Akla. Kuala Lumpur, Malaysia. 3 September 2016.
7 Personal interview with ISMA activist, Amar Yasier. London. May 2016.
8 Imtiyaz Yusuf, in his publication, refers to PAS in Malaysia and PKS in Indonesia as the two prominent Islamist parties in Southeast Asia. For more details, see Imtiyaz Yusuf. The Middle East and Muslim Southeast Asia: Implications of the Arab Spring. Available online via www.oxfordislamicstudies.com/Public/focus/essay1009_southeast_asia.html. [24August 2016].
9 In all tests of significance in SPSS, if $p < 0.05$, there is a statistically significant relationship between the two variables. The p-value in Chi-Square outputs for respondent's level of education is 0.00. This means that the relationship between their level of education and knowledge of the Arab Uprisings is significant.
10 The p-value in Chi-Square outputs for respondent's gender is 0.13. This means that the relationship between their level of education and knowledge of the Arab Uprisings is not significant since the P value is more than 0.05 ($P > 0.05$).
11 The p-value in Chi-Square outputs for respondent's type of membership is 0.00.
12 Personal interview with a female AMANAH activist (name withheld at interviewee's request), Kuala Lumpur, September 2016.
13 Respondent's written opinion/comment on the questionnaire.
14 In his statement, the PAS president, Abdul Hadi Awang also agreed that some media agencies published fake news about the Arab Uprisings by saying that 'The media jumbled, and confused the information and understanding (about the 'Arab Spring') in the new borderless media, where they either spread truth or lies to the whole world'. Fake news and the spread of misinformation not only affected the news on the 'Arab Spring' but also worldwide. Examples of 'fake news' about the Arab Uprisings can be accessed from the website 'Snopes', which compiled all existing fake news written on the 'Arab Spring'. See www.snopes.com/?s=arab+spring (05 October 2017).
15 Personal interview with a senior AMANAH activist (name withheld at interviewee's request), Kuala Lumpur, September 2016.
16 See Chamkhi (2014) for more details on neo-Islamism.
17 Personal interview with a PAS activist (name withheld at interviewee's request), Kuala Lumpur, Malaysia. 19 September 2016.
18 Official statement from Abdul Hadi Awang, the sixth president of PAS, regarding the Arab Spring and its lesson for Malaysia. The original statement is available online at https://www.facebook.com/abdulhadiawang/photos/a.146944298724030/1107443426007441/?type=3&theater [12November 2016].
19 Personal interview with Abdullah Zaik bin Abdul Rahman, the current president of ISMA. Bangi, 5 November 2016.
20 Official statement from Abdul Hadi Awang, 12 November 2016.

70 *Knowledge of the Islamist movements*

21 As pointed out by Nepstad (2013: 337–347), the non-violent civil resistance research has portrayed defections as unequivocally positive. Forced defections can also heavily influence the outcome of non-violent uprisings against authoritarian regimes.
22 Personal interview with the ISMA president, November 2016.
23 Official statement from Abdul Hadi Awang, 12 November 2016.
24 Arab Barometer Survey, Wave III (2012–2014). www.arabbarometer.org/content/arab-barometer-iii-0 [12 Jun 2015].
25 Personal interview with The International Relations Bureau for ISMA's UK branch, Amar Yasier. London, United Kingdom. 10 June 2016.
26 Personal interview with the ISMA president, November 2016.
27 Personal interview with ISMA activist, Mohd Syafiq. ISMA Head Office. Bangi, Malaysia. August 2016.
28 Personal interview with ISMA activist, Asyraf Farique. ISMA Head Office. Bangi, Malaysia. August 2016.
29 Personal interviews with ISMA activists, Asyraf Farique and Mohd Syafiq. ISMA Head Office. Bangi, Malaysia. August 2016.
30 Personal interview with the ISMA president. Bangi, Malaysia. 5 November 2016.
31 PAS delegation had visited the Ennahda Headquarters in Tunis in 2012 and 2015 to congratulate Ghannouchi and his party for their first-ever opportunity to govern Tunisia.
32 Personal interview with the AMANAH National Youth Leader, Muhammad Najib. Kuala Lumpur, Malaysia. September 2016.
33 Respondent's written comments on the questionnaire.
34 For more details on parties and party system change in the MENA after the Arab Uprisings, see Storm (2017) in Szmolka, Inmaculada (ed.), *Political Change in the Middle East and North Africa: After the Arab Spring*, pp. 63–88.
35 By referring to the case of Ennahda and the FJP, shortly after the departure of Mubarak in Cairo and Ben Ali in Tunis, the election results in both countries enabled these Islamist parties to form new governments.
36 See Lise Storm for more details on the party system in Tunisia before the Jasmine Revolution. Lise Storm. (2014). *Party Politics and Prospects for Democracy in North Africa*. Boulder, Colorado: Lynne Rienner, pp. 85–106.
37 Defined here as those who renounce violence and commit to the democratic process, as in the case of the Muslim Brotherhood in Egypt.
38 Personal interview with a PAS activist (name withheld at interviewee's request), Kuala Lumpur, Malaysia. 19 September 2016.
39 Personal interview with the Amanah Central Committee (Former PAS Chief Youth), Suhaizan Kayat. AMANAH Headquarters, Kuala Lumpur, Malaysia. 19 October 2016.
40 See Diane Singerman (2004). The Networked World of Islamist Social Movements. In Wiktorowichz, Quintan (ed.), *Islamic Activism: A Social Movement Theory Approach*. Bloomington, Indianapolis: Indiana University Press, pp. 143–161.

4 The influences and impacts of the Arab Uprisings on the Islamist movements in Malaysia

The aim of this chapter is to focus on the attitudes of respondents towards the post-Arab Uprisings issues, which are directly relevant to the landscape of Malaysian politics as well as the development of political Islam in the country. This chapter will also examine the implications of the post-Arab Uprisings phenomenon on PAS, ABIM, ISMA and AMANAH members and activists: specifically how the events have impacted on their attitudes towards street protests, social media activism, political Islam and moderation, and how the events have influenced their interest in Middle Eastern political affairs.

Why these issues? First, as explained in Chapter 2, there have been protests in Malaysia over the past few years which have pressured the previous Malaysian Prime Minister, Najib Razak, and his one-party dominant government (*Barisan Nasional*) to step down.[1] Their aim is to have a regime change by any means and transform the previous practice of 'semi-democracy' in Malaysia into a more open and democratic system. However, these opposition parties would need significant support from their 'coalition' or alliance members to mobilise any protests. For instance, the passion and energetic character of PAS Islamists, especially amongst the youth members, make them a backbone of street protests and social movements in Malaysia – as can be seen from the *Reformasi* Protest (1998), Bersih 1.0 (2007), Bersih 2.0 (2011) and Bersih 3.0 (2012). The potential involvement of a large number of Islamist opposition activists in future political protests raises concern for the Malaysian ruling government. From the regime perspective, the act of street protest could possibly undermine the country's political stability, and any attempt for political change should be funnelled through a proper and legitimate channel – the election. For them, the opposition politicians and the Islamists should never 'import' the elements of Arab Uprisings protest into Malaysia because this may encourage more political activists and Islamists to take to the streets for the sake of regime change (as occurred in previous protests).[2]

Second, in the wake of the apparently 'Islamist Winter' following the Arab Uprisings, there have been efforts to improve the quality of political

Islam amongst the Islamist groups in Malaysia – including PAS.[3] Although in 'Islam and Democracy' (1996), Esposito and Voll argued that Islam and democratic governance had proven to be compatible in several Muslim nations, including Malaysia, it seems that Malaysian Islamist movements (parties and NGOs), for instance PAS and ISMA, still hold rigid views on several issues, such as Sharia and Islamic rule matters, and political and social relations with non-Muslim citizens and non-Islamic-oriented parties – which may explain why these parties have not come to power since 1957. Nevertheless, the success of Ennahda in the Tunisian Constituent Assembly Election (2011), the PJD in the Moroccan Parliamentary Election (2011) and the FJP in the Egyptian Presidential Election (2012) have seemed to revive the confidence of Malaysian Islamists in raising their Islamist agenda on the national political landscape. The moderate and 'Muslim Democrat' approach of the Ennahda founder, Ghannouchi, could also impact the ideology of Malaysia's Islamist movements, given the established bilateral relations between these parties. All the issues mentioned above have recently led to polemics about the impact of the Arab Uprisings on Malaysian Islamist opposition parties, specifically PAS, ABIM, ISMA and AMANAH.

Attitudes towards the post-Arab Uprisings phenomenon

On the post-Arab Uprisings and its political and economic implications

The respondents were first asked whether post-Arab Uprisings developments had had any impact on economic and political aspects in the affected Arab states. According to Hafez Ghanem (currently the Vice President of the World Bank for the Middle East and North Africa (MENA)), one cannot expect the Arab Uprisings to have resulted in much improvement in terms of greater democracy and freedom, except in Tunisia. The four years following the Arab revolutions have also witnessed increasing fiscal imbalances in Egypt, Tunisia, Morocco and Yemen. In Libya, Yemen and Syria, for instance, civil wars brought uncertainty, which affected their performance in developing the economy and maintaining financial stability (Ghanem 2016a: 28–30). Thus, it is logical that 165 respondents agreed, and 55 strongly agreed that the Arab Uprisings actually had a short-term negative impact on the politics and economy of the affected states. One hundred and fourteen respondents, however, argued that the Arab Uprisings events, in general, had some positive impact in terms of political reform – as occurred in Tunisia, Morocco and Egypt from 2012 to 2013. One hundred and ninety-six respondents, mostly from PAS and AMANAH, were not certain of an exact answer; thus they preferred to neither disagree nor agree with the statement. Table 4.1 indicates the attitudes of PAS, ABIM, ISMA and AMANAH Islamists on the impact of the Post-Arab Uprisings in the Middle East.

Table 4.1 Respondents' perceptions that the post-Arab Uprisings have had a destructive impact based on the political and economic context

Type of Islamist Movement	The Post-Arab Uprisings Have Had a Destructive Impact Based on the Political and Economic Context (Frequency and Percentages)					Total
	Strongly Disagree	Disagree	Neutral	Agree	Strongly Agree	
The Pan Malaysian Islamic Party (PAS)	9 −3.10%	44 −15.30%	108 −37.60%	96 −33.40%	30 −10.50%	287 −100%
The National Trust Party (AMANAH)	7 −7.50%	13 −14.00%	43 −46.20%	23 −24.70%	7 −7.50%	93 −100%
The Muslim Youth Movement of Malaysia (ABIM)	11 −13.60%	18 −22.20%	21 −25.90%	21 −25.90%	10 −12.30%	81 −100%
The Malaysian Muslim Solidarity Front (ISMA)	0 0.00%	12 −17.40%	24 −34.80%	25 −36.20%	8 −11.60%	69 −100%
Total	27 −5.10%	87 −16.40%	196 −37.00%	165 −31.10%	55 −10.40%	530 −100%

Source: Field Research 2016.

From Table 4.1, it is obvious that some respondents from the four movements were uncertain whether the outcome of the Arab Uprisings brought any benefit to Arab politics and economics.

When they were asked whether the Post-Arab Uprisings had supported the democratisation process in the countries involved, their responses showed quite a similar pattern, with 'agree' and 'neither disagree nor agree' opinions remaining frequent choices for all four movements. Overall, 189 respondents (35.6 per cent) chose to be neutral. 20.5 per cent of respondents (109) were of the opinion that the process of democratisation had still not happened, while 43.9 per cent (233) believed that the democratisation process has started in Tunisia and that it will later extend to neighbouring Arab states. Table 4.2 gives details of the respondents' perceptions regarding the issue of democratisation in the post-Arab Uprisings.

When democratisation is discussed in its simplest form it can be defined as political changes that move in a democratic direction, which regularly involves a process of developing, consolidating and establishing democracy in a non-democratic state. The Post-Arab Uprisings phenomenon, to some observers, such as Barbara Zollner, gives a new drive to the discussion of democratisation in the MENA after being 'exceptional' for decades.[4] However, the attempts to bring democracy to each state affected by the Arab Uprisings were somewhat unsuccessful, except for in Tunisia, which

Table 4.2 Respondents' perceptions that the post-Arab Uprisings have supported the democratisation process in the countries involved

Type of Islamist Movement	The Post-Arab Uprisings Have Supported the Democratisation Process in the Countries Involved (Frequency and Percentages)					Total
	Strongly Disagree	Disagree	Neutral	Agree	Strongly Agree	
The Pan Malaysian Islamic Party (PAS)	10 −3.50%	48 −16.70%	108 −27.50%	96 −33.30%	26 −9.00%	287 −100%
The National Trust Party (AMANAH)	1 −1.10%	7 −7.50%	33 −35.50%	40 −43.00%	12 −12.90%	93 −100%
The Muslim Youth Movement of Malaysia (ABIM)	8 −9.90%	8 −9.90%	22 −27.20%	26 −32.10%	17 −21.00%	81 −100%
The Malaysian Muslim Solidarity Front (ISMA)	8 −11.60%	19 −27.50%	26 −37.70%	12 −17.40%	4 −5.80%	69 −100%
Total	27 −5.10%	82 −15.40%	189 −35.60%	174 −32.80%	59 −11.10%	530 −100%

Source: Field Research 2016.

managed certain positive progress. In Yemen, Libya and Syria, civil wars, with intervention from foreign states, continue to undermine the countries and any democratic processes. Meanwhile in Egypt, the rule of Al-Sisi is perceived as the prolongation of Mubarak's dictatorship legacy. Thus, one has to admit that the status of democratisation in the Middle East since the Arab Uprisings events is subjective.

On the Post-Arab Uprisings and the emergence of Daesh, and the issue of Syrian refugees

According to Tarek Osman, the vacuums created by the Arab Uprisings have allowed the 'centuries-old phenomenon' of radical Islam or militant Islamist groups, currently known as Daesh, to re-emerge in the Arab Middle East and wreak havoc all over the world (Osman 2017). Before proceeding to a discussion of the findings of the survey, it is useful to include some fundamental facts about Daesh in the Middle East. This information is based on selected academic publications, including an article published by *Al Jazeera*.[5] For Marc Lynch, the rise of Daesh undoubtedly posed a new set of strategic challenges to the MENA regional security in the aftermath of the Arab Uprisings (Lynch 2016: 224). The birth of the Islamic State group, also known as IS/ISIS/ISIL or Daesh (*Ad-Dawla Al-Islamiyya fil Iraq Wa Al-Sham*), has precipitated a deterioration in the situation in the MENA. Daesh reportedly emerged in Northern Syria in early 2014, when there was an internal split within the Al-Qaeda branch in Iraq. Since then, Daesh has expanded its operation throughout northern Syria by fighting against Syrian rebel groups, most notably in the areas of Raqqa, Kobani and Aleppo. By mid-2014, the war in Syria had reached a stalemate, and the armed opposition group was dominated by Daesh militants (Cockburn 2015: 84). Coincidentally, this occurred in the middle of the Syrian refugee crisis, which saw approximately 4.5 million Syrian citizens (based on a UNHCR report from 2017) displaced from their homes. Without a doubt these two crises were not anticipated by most Syrians, including those who directly participated in the protests against Assad in 2011. One can say that the outcome of the Arab Uprisings in Syria, unlike that in Tunisia, has been abject failure and misery, with a series of civil wars and destruction that has impacted approximately two-thirds of the country.[6] Hence, can we say that the emergence of Daesh and the humanitarian crisis in Syria were due to a failure to achieve the fundamental objectives of the Arab Uprisings (replacing an old dictator with a new democratic leader)? Table 4.3 records the respondents' answers.

Table 4.3 Respondents' perceptions that the failure of the post-Arab Uprisings in Syria has led to the emergence of Daesh and the humanitarian crisis

Type of Islamist Movement	The Post-Arab Uprisings in Syria Has Led to the Emergence of Daesh and the Humanitarian Crisis (Frequency)					Total
	Strongly Disagree	Disagree	Neutral	Agree	Strongly Agree	
The Pan Malaysian Islamic Party (PAS)	32 −11.10%	51 −17.80%	101 −35.20%	67 −23.30%	36 −12.50%	287 −100%
The National Trust Party (AMANAH)	24 −26.10%	17 −18.50%	24 −26.10%	14 −15.2%	13 −14.10%	93 −100%
The Muslim Youth Movement of Malaysia (ABIM)	19 −23.5%	6 −7.40%	21 −25.90%	16 −19.80%	19 −23.50%	81 −100%
The Malaysian Muslim Solidarity Front (ISMA)	10 −14.50%	15 −21.70%	28 −40.60%	11 −15.90%	5 −7.20%	69 −100%
Total	85 −16.1%	89 −16.80%	174 −32.90%	108 −20.40%	73 −13.80%	530 −100%

Source: Field Research 2016.

One hundred eighty-one Malaysian Islamist respondents generally agreed (including 73 respondents who strongly agreed) that if the Arab Uprisings had not been spread to Syria, the country would not have faced the issue of Daesh and the related refugee crisis. Eighty-nine disagreed with such an assumption, and 85 strongly disagreed, while 174 chose to be neutral. The responses to this question show that out of the four Islamist movements, ISMA presented the highest frequency of neutral and sceptical opinions, followed by PAS, AMANAH and ABIM. Meanwhile, AMANAH is the only movement which recorded a new trend, whereby the number of 'strongly disagree' and 'disagree' opinions exceeded the other options. The former scenario somehow reflects the critical view of ISMA members (including its President), who claimed that the role of 'invisible hands' by Western powers once again played a role in supporting Daesh based on a personal agenda rather than being solely to blame for the failure of the Syrian Revolution. According to Abdullah Zaik (ISMA President)[7]:

> ISIS, if we were to look at it in terms of the origin and so on, would cast doubts in terms of the motives of the group being set up. I have the opinion that the role of external parties (MOSSAD, CIA, IRAN) does exist behind IS. The one who names this group as 'Islamic State' is also the West. It is seemingly seeking to offer the world community, especially the Islamic world, two models of administration which are ISLAM (a poor model) or Liberal (a good model). Surely people will not choose ISLAM if the IS model serves as the example and propaganda. This is a project that benefits the Western countries. It also impacts on ISMA in its effort to develop political Islam in Malaysia. Western propaganda also tries to refute any political Islam agenda to the point that Islamist movements become easily labelled as radical.

The PAS President seems to agree with Abdullah's views in saying that[8]:

> A lot of countries have been involved in creating violence (in Syria), whether in terms of giving access to weapons, or sending fighters and money to assassinate, at the expense of truth. Some did it openly, some were more discreet. The emergence of Daesh in the post-Arab Uprisings in Syria led the country to become a new battle ground in an arms race amongst major world powers such as Russia and the USA.

As a result, the majority of Syrian citizens had no choice but to flee the region for their own protection.[9] One of the AMANAH interviewees commented that the powerful role of Israel in influencing US foreign policy (for the sake of Israel's long-term security against any potential threat from Arab countries) should be considered as one of the causes of the Arab world's destabilisation following the post-Arab Uprisings in Syria.[10] This may help explain why the majority of AMANAH members disagreed with the question. Abdul Hadi Awang, the PAS President, has blamed the involvement of Israel in the Syrian conflict, commenting that:

> Even worse, there is the possibility from the information cited through photo recording that Israel is directly involved in giving supplies and treatment for a cause named 'jihad'. This is seen from the political angle. The states that attempt to oust Bashar Asad will also not let Islam emerge victorious. They who uphold the actual Islamic state return an Islamic state with sovereignty and fairness and which becomes a threat, especially to Zionist-Israel which dominates the politics of the larger states, especially America and its allies that have long aspired to become a single power. It is also a dream of Israel to become the centre of global power. All the potential leaders, as recently reported in the US, had vied to obtain the support of the Zionist in every General Election. The relationship between a government and its people with Zionist countries has also become the benchmark in terms of determining the fate of the Arab Spring and the degree of extremity. Any countries that acknowledge the forbidden land of Israel and establish all forms of relationship between the government and the people are the safest. The second degree is that the countries with secret affairs with Israel will also be safe. Countries that reject Israel, or in the case where the people reject Israel openly or do not adopt a peace treaty with the forbidden land, will surely expect the inevitable fall.

Tunisia and the 'Success Story' of the Arab Uprisings

It has become evident that the Arab Uprisings failed to produce democracy, except where they began, in Tunisia (Esposito et al. 2016: 3). Following its two successful elections (in 2011 and 2014) Tunisia was praised by the Freedom House (2017) as the only democratic state in the MENA.[11] The former French colonial state has also been widely viewed as a successful product of the Arab Uprisings, which highlights the fruitful negotiations between the previously banned Islamist party, Ennahda, and other political parties. As pointed out by Esposito et al. (2016: 200),

> Despite significant differences and fierce rivalries in Tunisian politics (in the post-Arab Spring phenomenon), Tunisians were able to move along the road to democratisation, avoiding its derailment because of its stronger civil society organisations, the military's professionalism, and the responsiveness and significant concessions made by Ennahda.

Since the period following the Post-Tunisian Jasmine Revolution in 2011, it seems that Tunisia has positively maneuvered its political transition (from one of the region's most oppressive states) to democracy; its democratic process has not unravelled into civil wars as it did Syria, Yemen and Libya (Osman 2017). It has also not undergone a counter-revolution that returned the country to the autocratic rule of its pre-revolution days, as occurred in Egypt (Culbertson 2016; Sadiki and Bouandel 2016).

Although Tunisia is perceived as an Arab Uprisings success story by many scholars,[12] it is not seen as such by PAS and ISMA Islamists since the majority were not certain about these opinions, and some even disagreed. Several of the respondents acknowledged that their lack of knowledge about the Arab Uprisings in general, and Tunisian politics in particular, led them to remain neutral on the statement. Their other reason for disagreeing or being neutral is that, amongst PAS youth members and ISMA activists, Tunisia is less popular than Egypt in terms of Middle Eastern political news. It was only after Ennahda's rule (2011–2014) that Tunisia became a new 'topic' of interest, although not to the same level of excitement as that generated by the Muslim Brotherhood (MB) in Egypt.[13] However, a number of respondents were in line with Sadiki (2015b) in viewing Tunisia as demonstrating a positive outcome of the Arab Uprisings. Table 4.4 shows the respondents' overall reactions.

Table 4.4 Respondents' perceptions on Tunisia as the 'success story' of the Arab Uprisings

Type of Islamist Movement	Tunisia as the 'Success Story' of the Arab Uprisings (Frequency and Percentages)					Total
	Strongly Disagree	Disagree	Neutral	Agree	Strongly Agree	
The Pan Malaysian Islamic Party (PAS)	9 −3.10%	29 −10.10%	133 −46.20%	86 −29.90%	31 −10.80%	287 −100%
The National Trust Party (AMANAH)	1 −1.10%	4 −4.30%	28 −30.10%	37 −39.80%	23 −24.70%	93 −100%
The Muslim Youth Movement of Malaysia (ABIM)	0 0.00%	6 −7.40%	19 −23.50%	29 −35.80%	27 −33.30%	81 −100%
The Malaysian Muslim Solidarity Front (ISMA)	3 −4.30%	13 −18.80%	37 −53.60%	12 −17.40%	4 −5.80%	69 −100%
Total	13 −2.40%	52 −9.80%	217 −40.90%	164 −30.90%	85 −16.00%	530 −100%

Source: Field Research 2016.

The influences of the Arab Uprisings 79

Based on SPSS analysis, the summary of Table 4.4 can be read as follows:

i   For PAS respondents, 40.7 per cent agreed (in general), followed by 46.2 per cent who were neutral and 13.2 per cent who disagreed (in general).
ii For AMANAH respondents, 64.5 per cent agreed (in general), followed by 30.1 per cent who were neutral and 4.4 per cent who disagreed (in general).
iii For ABIM respondents, 69.1 per cent agreed (in general), followed by 23.5 per cent who were neutral and 7.4 per cent who disagreed (in general).
iv For ISMA respondents, 23.2 per cent agreed (in general), followed by 53.6 per cent who were neutral and 23.1 per cent who disagreed (in general).[14]

Overall, these findings show the mixed attitudes of the Malaysian Islamist movements towards the general view of Tunisia as an Arab Uprisings success story. As previously explained by the interviewees themselves, different levels of exposure to and general knowledge about Tunisian politics are likely to serve as the main reasons for the pattern of reactions to the question.

On the Post-Arab Uprisings and the state of Arab world stability

The Arab world seems to be worse off than it was before the Arab Uprisings in terms of violence, civil war and unrest. For instance, Egypt has returned to military rule, with pluralism and opposition parties – including the MB – facing the most repressive atmosphere in half a century. Syria has become one of the most desolate places on earth, with half of its population displaced and most of its cities destroyed. Much of the Syrian countryside has been reduced to a battleground between, on the one hand, the Assad regime and its foreign allies, and, on the other, a band of enemies of the regime from all over Syria and indeed the world (Alaoui 2016). In the words of March Lynch, 'There will be no return to stability. The Arab uprisings of 2011 were only one episode in a generational challenge to failed political order. Protesters won some battles in 2011, and regimes won them in the following years' (Lynch 2016: 254).

Given such evidence, it is interesting to ask (in the case of Malaysian Islamists) whether the MENA has been more or less stable since the Arab Uprisings. Table 4.5 presents the attitudes of respondents towards the question concerning Arab world stability before the Arab Uprisings events.

The remarkable thing about Table 4.5 is that it does show quite a high level of rejection by respondents (from both the 'strongly disagree' and 'disagree' categories), mainly from PAS and AMANAH. This implies that 207 respondents believed that the MENA was already unsteady (in terms of politics, economics and society) before the start of the Arab Uprisings. Amongst the arguments provided there were references to several major wars which occurred in the Middle East before the 2011 Arab Uprisings – for instance the US-led coalition invasion of Iraq (2003) and the series of Palestinian-Israeli

Table 4.5 Respondents' perceptions that the Arab world was more stable before the start of the Arab Uprisings

Type of Islamist Movement	Strongly Disagree	Disagree	Neutral	Agree	Strongly Agree	Total
The Pan Malaysian Islamic Party (PAS)	37 −12.80%	77 −26.70%	104 −36.10%	54 −18.80%	16 −5.60%	287 −100%
The National Trust Party (AMANAH)	14 −15.10%	22 −23.70%	35 −37.60%	13 −14.00%	9 −9.70%	93 −100%
The Muslim Youth Movement of Malaysia (ABIM)	10 −12.30%	22 −27.20%	13 −16.00%	22 −27.20%	14 −17.30%	81 −100%
The Malaysian Muslim Solidarity Front (ISMA)	8 −11.60%	17 −24.60%	27 −39.10%	13 −18.80%	4 −5.80%	69 −100%
Total	69 −13.00%	138 −26.00%	179 −33.70%	102 −19.20%	43 −8.10%	530 −100%

Source: Field Research 2016.

conflicts. Thus, for these respondents, there was not much difference in terms of regional stability between the periods pre- and post-Arab Uprisings. As pointed out by Hicham Alaoui (2016), although the question is legitimate to ask, it is quite difficult and subjective to answer. One hundred and forty-five respondents, however, agreed that the Arab world had been relatively more peaceful and stable before the Arab Uprisings took place, while 179 respondents preferred to remain neutral on the statement. One of the respondents from ISMA agreed that the Arab world had been more stable before the Arab Uprisings but noted that freedom of speech had been restricted, which might have led to political instability in the future.[15] The PAS President seems to agree that the Arab Uprisings have brought drawbacks rather than benefits to many Arab citizens. As pointed out by Abdul Hadi Awang[16]:

> For those Arab countries where the Arab Spring successfully contributed to the fall of their governments, it caused a lot more chaos than the brutality shown by the previous governments. They experienced political turmoil, a more severe state of security and life to the extent that they had to escape only to become much humiliated refugees, leaving behind their home countries that had a wealth of natural resources to

become beggars in foreign lands - to the point that the Arab world does not welcome its own allies of the same faith and religion. For people who stay behind in the country, they are either fighting amongst themselves or waiting for death, starvation and outbreak to befall them.

The Post-Arab Uprisings phenomenon: an 'Eye-Opener' for rulers of the Arab states?

The Arab Uprisings events have undoubtedly unleashed unprecedented passion for revolution and drive for change within Arab nations. They also taught the majority of Arab citizens to take a new look at – and to openly voice their opposition against – corrupt and repressive regimes in a manner that was not seen in the last two decades of their struggle for freedom and dignity. It seems that Arab dictators may have learned a lesson from the Arab Uprisings – the lesson being that the political power of dictators can be short-lived when they face a powerful, popular and collective grass roots movement. In addition, the Arab Uprisings, as well as other revolutions in modern history, show that removing a dictatorship is easier than replacing it with a democratic regime. This means that there is always a potential for political revolution to be launched, but the consequences remain unpredictable. For Malaysian Islamists, more than half of the respondents (54.7 per cent) believed that the Arab Uprisings should have taught Arab rulers not to take for granted their citizens' voices, as expressed through street protest. One of the respondents from ABIM, Mohamad Saifuddin, a graduate from a higher education institution in Morocco, highlighted that:

> From my own observation (throughout the years as a student in Morocco), the Arab Spring events seemed to serve as an eye-opener to most of the Muslim nations around the world, including Malaysia. It proved that most of the (Muslim-majority) states are still practising corruption and power abuse in many ways (economic, political and social) which leads people to voice their disagreement and dissatisfaction towards their respective ruling regimes.

Saifuddin's opinion is supported by another PAS activist, who believed that the voice of citizens (in the Arab world) via street protest against any corrupted regime (post-Arab Uprisings) is really important to ensure that a mechanism of checks and balances is in place. However, the activist suggested that wise strategies are needed to ensure a positive outcome and that no bloodshed occurs during the process of removing a dictator.[17] Only a small number of respondents (12.4 per cent) rejected the idea that the Arab Uprisings were an 'eye-opener' to the leaders of Arab countries, while 33 per cent remained neutral (mostly from ISMA).

As discussed in Chapter 3, most ISMA members rejected the idea of the Arab Uprisings as a bottom-up movement for political change and firmly believed that Western powers played a role in the protests (a role designed to obtain gain for the West at the expense of the Arab states). Thus, it is not surprising to see that many respondents from ISMA were not certain whether the Arab Uprisings had been, or ought to have been, an 'eye-opener' to every Arab state leader.

Uncertainties in the Post-Arab Uprisings environment: will they lead to another wave of uprisings in the future?

Will there be any second wave of Arab Spring-type uprisings in the future? According to an assessment by the United Nations Arab Development Report (November 2016), only five Arab countries were in a state of conflict (due to civil wars, interstate conflict and political violence) in 2002, whereas by 2016, 11 were in a state of conflict.[18] This same report suggests that by 2020, 75% of the Arab world will be vulnerable to conflict. Lewis Tallon, a Geopolitical Intelligence Analyst who specialises in the MENA, has highlighted that[19]:

> With social media having further developed the interconnectivity of the region's youth since 2011, and many governments facing economic exhaustion and a subsequently degraded ability to respond financially to unrest, it is probable that a second-wave of the Arab Spring would spread more quickly, and more effectively than the first.

Tallon's views are supported by Marc Lynch,[20] a Professor of Political Science at George Washington University, who has pointed out that:

> Many of the conflicts (after the Arab Uprisings of 2011), especially in Syria and Yemen, had no winners at all. There will be more rounds of upheaval, more state failures, more sudden regime collapses, more insurgencies, and more proxy wars.

Furthermore, Tarek Osman confidently predicts that many of the Arab countries that currently appear stable will witness new waves of mass protests and revolts against their ruling regimes – as a result of immense anger among the youth regarding the way their 'Arab Spring revolutions' have failed to achieve their goals (Osman 2017: 247). Given the currently vulnerable situation of certain nations (Syria, Libya and Yemen) in the Arab world, it seems that the majority of respondents (66.1 per cent) also predict that another wave of democratic uprisings will take place in the future. As mentioned by one of the ISMA activists[21]:

> I am quite certain that in ten years from now, the world will probably witness another wave of democratic uprisings in the MENA region due to the failure of the first attempt. With positive support from the international community, it seems that Arab citizens will not lose faith in democracy and good governance.

One hundred and forty-one respondents (29.5 per cent) were not entirely sure about such a prediction. The remaining 39 respondents (7.3 per cent) challenged the statement by arguing that Arab citizens should have learned lessons from the Arab Uprisings and therefore will not reignite the protests so as to maintain peace and stability. Thus, they predict that there will be no second wave of Arab Uprisings protests in the future. Overall, the responses received from the four Islamist movements show quite a similar pattern, with 'agree' as the most popular answer to the question.

Influences of the Arab Uprisings on the Islamist movements in Malaysia

The polemics of the influences of the Arab Uprisings have been given considerable attention by the Malaysian regime, as well as local and foreign media, within the context of Malaysian Islamist opposition parties and NGOs. This section will provide a comprehensive and empirical answer to the question – has the Arab Uprisings phenomenon influenced the Islamist movements in Malaysia (in this case PAS, ABIM, ISMA and AMANAH)? Through in-depth examination of each response to each specific question in the survey, the section provides an analysis of the Arab Uprisings' impact on Malaysia's Islamist movements and the factors that have shaped it.[22] The respondents' reactions to each question will be discussed in the following sub-sections.

The Arab Uprisings and the act of civil disobedience: what impact on PAS, ABIM, ISMA and AMANAH political activism?

In general, political activism can be defined as an institutionalised participation within the context of existing order, which encourages a connection with formal politics at the national level (Stein & Volpi 2014). Meanwhile, the current general definition and popular narratives of 'Arab Uprisings studies' often defines the 2011 Uprisings (in its simplest form) as mass street protests and civil disobedience – managing to topple autocratic leaders in several MENA countries. According to John Rawls, in his famous writing 'A Theory of Justice' (1971), the term 'civil disobedience' can be defined as a politically motivated, public, non-violent act and conscious breach of law undertaken with the aim of bringing about a change in laws or government policies. Mohd Zain Zawiyah et al. (2017: 10) further summarised five significant features in civil disobedience acts based on the studies by Rawls (1971). First, there is disobedience of the law. Second, there is disobedience carried out in public because of frustration with government actions or unjust laws or policies. Third, there are non-violent acts. Fourth, the acts must be undertaken with regard for conscience. Finally, people are willing to accept the consequences of their actions. Rawls's definition seems to reflect the nature of the Arab Uprisings protests in 2011; these highlight several important features of civil disobedience, as seen when the first mass rallies broke out in Tunisia and Egypt.[23]

In non-democratic states (and less, partial and quasi-democratic states – for example Malaysia), Arab Uprisings events might serve as a relevant example to show how the sentiments expressed in 'people power' via civil disobedience can overthrow corrupt regimes when ballot boxes are no longer effective due to regular regime manipulation (Saikal and Acharya, 2014). As pointed out by Gainous, Wagner and Abbott (2015), there has been an increase in the number of mass demonstrations and political marches in Malaysia. Most notably, the Coalition for Clean and Fair Elections (Bersih) has organised five mass rallies in the past six years (2007, 2011, 2013, 2015 and 2016), culminating in the largest and most consistent series of demonstrations in Malaysian political history. Do the Islamists from PAS, ABIM, ISMA and AMANAH feel that civil disobedience and street protests during the Arab Uprisings Revolutions inspired them to participate in civil protests and political rallies in Malaysia? Out of 530 respondents who answered the question, 79 (14.9 per cent) strongly believed that they were inspired by protests in the Arab Uprisings, and 186 (35 per cent) shared a similar (but less strong) attitude. One hundred and eighty respondents (33.9 per cent) gave a neutral response, while 66 (12.4 per cent) disagreed with the statement. Only 20 respondents (3.8 per cent) totally rejected the idea of inspiration for civil disobedience arising from the Arab Uprisings. Table 4.6 shows the respondents' reactions to the question.

Table 4.6 Respondents' views on whether civil disobedience during the Arab Uprisings has given inspiration to Malaysia's Islamist movements

Type of Islamist Movement	Whether Civil Disobedience during the Arab Uprisings Has Given Inspiration to Malaysia's Islamist Movements (Frequency and Percentages)					Total
	Strongly Disagree	Disagree	Neutral	Agree	Strongly Agree	
The Pan Malaysian Islamic Party (PAS)	11 −3.80%	38 −13.20%	105 −36.50%	102 −35.40%	32 −11.10%	288 −100%
The National Trust Party (AMANAH)	2 −2.20%	14 −15.10%	31 −33.30%	33 −35.50%	13 −14%	93 −100%
The Muslim Youth Movement of Malaysia (ABIM)	6 −7.40%	2 −2.50%	22 −27.20%	27 −33.30%	24 −29.60%	81 −100%
The Malaysian Muslim Solidarity Front (ISMA)	1 −1.40%	12 −17.40%	22 −31.90%	24 −34.80%	10 −14.50%	69 −100%
Total	20 −3.80%	66 −12.40%	180 −33.90%	186 −35.00%	79 −14.90%	530 −100%

Source: Field Research 2016.

The influences of the Arab Uprisings 85

Based on SPSS cross tabulation results, the summary of Table 4.6 is as follows:

i   For PAS respondents, 11.1 per cent strongly agreed, followed by 35.4 per cent who agreed, 36.5 per cent who were neutral, 13.2 per cent who disagreed and 3.8 who strongly disagreed.
ii For AMANAH respondents, 14 per cent strongly agreed, followed by 35.5 per cent who agreed, 33.3 per cent who were neutral, 15.1 per cent who disagreed and 2.2 per cent who strongly disagreed.
iii For ABIM respondents, 29.6 per cent strongly agreed, followed by 33.3 per cent who agreed, 27.2 per cent who were neutral, 2.5 per cent who disagreed and 7.4 per cent who strongly disagreed.
iv For ISMA respondents, 15.5 per cent strongly agreed, followed by 34.8 per cent who agreed, 31.9 per cent who were neutral, 17.4 per cent who disagreed and 1.4 per cent who strongly disagreed.

There were no substantial differences in the responses to this question from the four case study groups. The responses from the PAS, ABIM, ISMA and AMANAH Islamist movements demonstrate that the Arab Uprisings protests have influenced their political activism in terms of inspiring members to voice their dissatisfaction (via mass rally) against Malaysia's ruling regime, led by Najib Razak. As stated by Zakiuddin Shariff (PAS member)[24], 'The Arab Uprisings events gave inspiration to Islamist movements in Malaysia (PAS) to continue to struggle against the corrupted ruling regime of UMNO and Barisan Nasional (Party). The Bersih 3.0 protest was one example'.

Another respondent, Abdul Muiz, added that the Arab Uprisings were beneficial in providing an awareness and lesson to the stubborn, greedy and intolerant ruling government in Malaysia – as they showed the potential capability of 'people power' in determining the fate of a corrupted regime.[25] However, there was also a significant number of respondents who were not sure or even denied a connection between motivation from the so-called Arab Uprisings and civil resistance in Malaysia. These scenarios are best understood by one of the PAS youth leaders, who confessed that:

> For us... (the PAS Youth Members) the Bersih 3.0 protest in 2012 was largely inspired by the 'Arab Spring' revolutions, especially when we witnessed that the Ennahda and Muslim Brothers secured executive power in their respective countries. However, since various cases of vandalism and violent incidents reportedly happened (during the Bersih), PAS decided not to join Bersih 4.0 (2015) and Bersih 5.0 (2016) for the sake of promoting our moderation and mature political approaches.[26]

According to PAS President Abdul Hadi Awang, any future Arab Uprisings-style protests in Malaysia (after the Bersih 3.0 event in 2012), for instance the series of upcoming Bersih rallies, should be avoided as they could end in bloodshed, like the Arab Uprisings in 2011.[27] Meanwhile, AMANAH President Mohamad Sabu has lashed out at those comparing the Bersih rallies to the Arab Uprisings. He pointed out that peaceful demonstrations have taken place in the country since before independence, involving various political parties, NGOs and student groups. As stated by Mohamad Sabu[28]:

> Saying that the Bersih rally is like the Arab Spring (protest) is an act of stupidity and pretence. It is an excuse created by those who do not want to join the (coming) Bersih 5.0 (in 2016) rally. Comparing the two would be nonsensical as the first Bersih rally took place in 2007. Only four years later the uprisings and armed rebellions spread across the Middle East, known as the Arab Spring. The Coalition of Clean and Fair Election's first rally in 2007 (Bersih 1.0) proceeded peacefully, followed by Bersih 2.0, Bersih 3.0, and later Bersih 4.0. Demonstrations calling for clean and fair elections have been going on for a long time. It has nothing to do with the Arab Uprisings. It's really stupid for anyone to say Bersih is a copy and continuation of the latter (the Arab Spring).

Del Rosario and Dorsey (2016: 24), political scientists based at, respectively, the National University of Singapore and Nanyang Technological University, raised the same opinion in their publication:

> Well before the 'Arab Spring', a number of Southeast Asian countries experienced their own political upheavals. In all of them, grievances were channelled via organised efforts of civil society. Some have succeeded to get their message across. In all of these countries (who have succeeded) thus far, political strife has not resulted in civil wars. This is perhaps the singular feature that distinguishes protest action in Southeast Asia from the Middle East.

While the AMANAH President strongly rejected attempts to relate the Bersih political protests in Malaysia with the Arab Uprisings in the Middle East, the empirical findings confirm that 49.5 per cent of AMANAH respondents were inspired by the acts of civil disobedience observed during the Arab Uprisings and that this later encouraged them to participate in a series of Bersih protests. Furthermore, the researcher found that respondents' ages and occupational sectors did make a significant difference to their attitudes to the question. Out of 265 respondents who believed they were inspired by the Arab Uprisings, 70.9 per cent came from the age range 16–35 years. In terms of working sector, most of these respondents were also university students or private sector workers.

Thus, it seems that the youth sample, which largely comprised university students and private sector workers, was the group of Malaysian Islamists (across all four movements) who had been most inspired by the civil disobedience element of the Arab Uprisings. As pointed out by John Postill (2014: 95), the Malaysian Bersih 2.0 protests of 2011 undoubtedly shared a common inspiration with the Tahrir Square Protest in its commitment to non-violent civil disobedience (even in the face of police brutality). The research indicates that overall the mass protests witnessed during the Arab Uprisings did impact the political activism of Islamist movements in Malaysia – in particular, through encouragement to participate in local political demonstrations.

The influence of social media factors from the Arab Uprisings

The Arab Uprisings protests involved a factor which helped secure the success of the uprisings – the role of the Internet and social media (see Chapter 4). In Malaysia, the advances in Internet and media technologies have benefitted citizens in many ways, including within the political dimension (Mohd Sani & Zengeni 2010; Melanie 2012; Weiss 2013; Zawiyah et al. 2014). Based on the researcher's observations, many Facebook and Twitter political pages have been created in Malaysia, as well as in other Middle Eastern countries, in recent years. These act as alternative sources of local political news since the majority of mainstream media and TV channels are strictly controlled by the governments, both in Malaysia and in the Middle East.[29]

Regarding the effectiveness of social media during the Arab Uprisings – in terms of its capacity for swift exchange and dissemination of information to millions of people – the study found that it became a major influence on political activism for many Malaysian Islamists. Three hundred and seventy-one respondents (69.9 per cent) believed that the platforms of new social media, such as Facebook, Twitter and YouTube videos (which were used by Arab activists during the Arab Uprisings events), in one way or another impacted political activism by generating enhanced political awareness amongst the Malaysian public as well as initiating political protest against the ruling regime. However, 39 respondents (7.4 per cent) rejected the idea that the Arab Uprisings encouraged the use of social media amongst Malaysian Islamist movements, while 121 (22.8 per cent) preferred to remain neutral. Table 4.7 shows the attitudes of respondents (based on type of Islamist movement) towards the role of social media (as used during the Arab Uprisings) and its impact on PAS, ABIM, ISMA and AMANAH political activism.

In terms of respondents' backgrounds (aside from the type of Islamist movement) the analysis of a Chi-Square test from SPSS indicates that only level of education and type of occupation showed significant differences with regards to respondents' attitudes towards the connection between social media activism during the Arab Uprisings and political activism within Malaysia's Islamist movements.[30] Those respondents with a PhD academic

Table 4.7 Respondents' views that the role of new social media (Facebook, YouTube, Twitter) during the Arab Uprisings influenced the activism of Malaysia's Islamist movements

Type of Islamist Movement	\multicolumn{5}{c}{The Role of New Social Media during the Arab Uprisings Influenced the Activism of Malaysia's Islamist Movements (Frequency and Percentages)}					Total
	Strongly Disagree	Disagree	Neutral	Agree	Strongly Agree	
The Pan Malaysian Islamic Party (PAS)	2 −0.70%	15 −5.20%	73 −25.30%	122 −42.40%	76 −26.40%	288 −100%
The National Trust Party (AMANAH)	2 −2.20%	7 −7.50%	20 −21.50%	37 −39.80%	27 −29.00%	93 −100%
The Muslim Youth Movement of Malaysia (ABIM)	6 −7.40%	2 −2.50%	15 −18.50%	36 −44.40%	22 −27.20%	81 −100%
The Malaysian Muslim Solidarity Front (ISMA)	0 0.00%	5 −7.20%	13 −18.80%	38 −55.10%	13 −18.80%	69 −100%
Total	10 −1.90%	29 −5.50%	121 −22.80%	233 −43.90%	138 −26.00%	530 −100%

Source: Field Research 2016.

qualification expressed a very significant pattern of reaction – all of them (100 per cent) believed that the role of new social media during the Arab Uprisings had influenced the political activism of Islamist movements in Malaysia. 60.8 per cent of respondents with a Master's degree, followed by 70.6 per cent of those with a Bachelor's degree, 66.6 per cent of those with a Diploma and 76.5 per cent of those with a High School qualification all had a positive attitude towards the question.

According to the Malaysian Minister for Higher Education, Idris Jusoh, the latest educational developments in Malaysia suggest that exposure to Internet and media technology amongst students is considered a vital part of the university curriculum (as can be seen in the curricula of numerous Malaysian higher education institutions). Thus, level of education (via exposure to the Internet) might be one of the determining factor of respondents' attitudes on this issue. For type of occupation, the respondents with private sector backgrounds had the highest percentage of positive attitudes (75.9 per cent), followed by those with public sector backgrounds (70.8 per cent) and university students (65.3 per cent). The remaining sectors also recorded more than 60 per cent positive attitudes, except for the retired and pensioner group (42.9 per cent). The explanation for such a finding might well relate to the working environment in each sector, which reflects the increasing use of Internet and media technology. Overall, the advantages of the Internet and social media during the Arab Uprisings in 2011 were important in encouraging a number of Malaysian Islamic activists to utilise these platforms in order to disseminate political awareness and push for political reforms as well as for organising political protests (as witnessed in the series of Bersih events).

The rise of Islamist parties after the Arab Uprisings: does this affect the development of Islamist movements in Malaysia?

The trend of the so-called 'Islamist Winter' saw a number of Islamist parties in the MENA take up power and lead governments in countries including Egypt, Tunisia and Morocco circa 2011–2013. It is important to explore whether or not this phenomena has affected the development of activism amongst Islamist movements in Malaysia. This inquiry began by asking the respondents whether the trend of Islamist parties' 'awakening' in the post-Arab Uprisings was politically inspiring them to achieve power and influencing their political activism in terms of their movements' ideologies and political approaches. The second question asked whether the above scenario had impacted the state of their movements' transnational cooperation with other Arab Islamist parties.

Activism within the Islamist movements in Malaysia and inspiration from the 'Islamist Winter' trend

This section presents the attitudes of respondents towards the scenario of Islamist parties' 'awakening' in the Post-Arab Uprisings – and whether it has inspired Malaysian Islamists from PAS, ABIM, ISMA and AMANAH to continue to struggle for power in the 'Malaysian political game'. As discussed in Chapter 2, given the established relationship between these movements and the Muslim Brothers' parties in the Middle East (for instance the Tunisian Ennahda, Egyptian FJP and Moroccan PJD) the results were close to the researcher's expectations: more than half of the respondents (62.3 per cent – agree and strongly agree) saw the rise of Islamist parties as motivation for them to achieve political power at the national level. 29.2 per cent of the respondents expressed a neutral view towards the question, while 8.5 per cent believed that the performance of Islamist parties in the post-Arab Uprisings elections did not inspire them towards a power struggle in the context of Malaysia's politics. Table 4.8 records the details of respondents' feedback on the question.

Table 4.8 Respondents' views that the rise of Islamist parties in the post-Arab Uprisings has given political inspiration to the Islamist movements in Malaysia

Type of Islamist Movement	Strongly Disagree	Disagree	Neutral	Agree	Strongly Agree	Total
The Pan Malaysian Islamic Party (PAS)	5 −1.70%	16 −5.60%	95 −33.10%	127 −44.30%	44 −15.30%	288 −100%
The National Trust Party (AMANAH)	1 −1.10%	6 −6.50%	25 −29.90%	35 −37.60%	26 −28.00%	93 −100%
The Muslim Youth Movement of Malaysia (ABIM)	2 −2.50%	9 −11.10%	16 −19.80%	24 −29.60%	30 −37.00%	81 −100%
The Malaysian Muslim Solidarity Front (ISMA)	0 0.00%	6 −8.70%	19 −27.50%	36 −52.20%	8 −11.60%	69 −100%
Total	8 −1.50%	37 −7.00%	155 −29.20%	222 −41.90%	108 −20.40%	530 −100%

Source: Field Research 2016.

From Table 4.8, the specific responses from each movement are specified as follows:

i For PAS respondents, 59.6 per cent agreed (in general), followed by 33.1 per cent who were neutral and 7.3 per cent who disagreed (in general).
ii For AMANAH respondents, 65.6 per cent agreed (in general), followed by 29.9 per cent who were neutral and 7.6 per cent who disagreed (in general).
iii For ABIM respondents, 66.6 per cent agreed (in general), followed by 29.9 per cent who were neutral and 13.6 who disagreed (in general).
iv For ISMA respondents, 63.8 per cent agreed (in general), followed by 27.5 per cent who were neutral and 8.7 per cent who disagreed (in general).

It seems that there are no significant differences between the four Islamist movements studied as regards the question about inspiration from the 'Islamist Winter'. As previously stated, most of the respondents acknowledged that they were influenced by the trajectory of the Arab Islamist parties which rose to power in their respective countries following the Arab Uprisings. As acknowledged by Amar Yasier (ISMA activist)[31]:

> The Arab Uprisings more or less had inspired us (ISMA) to participate in the 2013 General Election in Malaysia. As an Islamist NGO, ISMA was motivated by the experience of the Muslim Brotherhood in Egypt (2011–2013) and the trend of Islamist parties awakening in the Middle East. We came to the conclusion that it was the right time for us to participate in the national election by forming our own Islamist Party (Berjasa) since our long term objective has always been to establish an Islamic state in Malaysia. At that time we were confident that our movement had stepped on the right path (to contest in the 2013 Malaysian general election). ISMA has indeed learned something from the Arab Spring especially in the context of involvement in the election.

Abdul Hamid and Che Mohd Razali (2016: 9) agree that ISMA's decision to participate in GE13 as a separate electoral entity could be described as emulating the MB's experience in the Middle East – with encouragement and motivation towards participation in electoral politics given by MB activists.[32] To some extent, an important reason for Malaysian Islamists to be inspired by the success of Arab Islamist parties in the post-Arab Uprisings environment is a very simple one: namely wiser Islamist strategies and leadership. The Islamist parties attracted a high per cent of the public vote after making substantial compromises in terms of political approach and agenda – as can be seen in the case of Ennahda during the post-Ben Ali transition government. Speaking about the Arab Uprisings and its ability to inspire Islamist parties in the MENA, a PAS activist – Syafiq Kamil[33] – points out that the leadership factor should be highlighted as he believes the way new Islamist leaders govern the Arab world will determine the support received from Malaysia's own Islamist movement (PAS). Undoubtedly, understanding the inspiration created in the post-Arab Uprisings environment has generated several new findings relating to Malaysia's Islamist movements. These will be discussed in the following sections.

The post-Arab Uprisings phenomenon and its influence on the political approach of Malaysia's Islamist movements

In order to explore the respondents' opinions regarding the impact of the Arab Uprisings on the political approach of Malaysia's Islamist movements, the researcher conducted a number of short and informal face-to-face interviews with more than 30 Malaysian Islamists, mostly youth members and party supporters. The interviews took place on several different occasions in Malaysia: for instance during the 2016 PAS annual meeting, during the 45th ABIM annual gathering (2016), at AMANAH political speeches and at several ISMA official events. The only question being asked was: does the respondent think that the post-Arab Uprisings developments have influenced their respective Islamist movements' ideology and political approach? Based on the researcher's analysis 'key words' frequently used by the interviewees were identified, specifically: (1) 'moderation' and (2) 'inclusion'. Indeed, the issue of moderation is particularly substantial in the aftermath of the Arab Uprisings as Islamist parties took power in a number of countries (Durac & Cavatorta 2015: 146–147). Half of the interviewees referred to the development of Ennahda in Tunisia and Egypt's coup in 2013 as the real reasons why Malaysia's Islamist movement should be more moderate and inclusive in terms of ideology and political approach – a thought which could transform the long-standing approach of conservative 'Islamism' which has primarily composed the agenda of the Islamic state establishment, support for a number of Islamic privileges as well as the plan to implement sharia amongst the Muslim majority in Malaysia.

The outcome of the interviews might explain why 293 respondents (55.1 per cent) from the questionnaire-survey believed that the post-Arab Uprisings events had somehow influenced the ideological approach of PAS, ABIM, ISMA and AMANAH Islamists in Malaysia. However, there were also 50 respondents (9.4 per cent) who disagreed with the statement and 17 who totally rejected it (3.2 per cent). The remaining 171 respondents (32.2 per cent) could not decide whether the Arab Uprisings had any impact on the party's ideology. Table 4.9 records the summary of respondents' attitudes towards the implications of the post-Arab Uprisings environment,

Table 4.9 Respondents' views that post-Arab Uprisings events have influenced the ideology of Islamist movements in Malaysia

Type of Islamist Movement	Post-Arab Uprisings Events Have Influenced the Ideology of Islamist Movements in Malaysia (Frequency and Percentages)					Total
	Strongly Disagree	Disagree	Neutral	Agree	Strongly Agree	
The Pan Malaysian Islamic Party (PAS)	11 −3.80%	25 −8.70%	107 −37.20%	111 −38.50%	34 −11.80%	288 −100%
The National Trust Party (AMANAH)	1 −1.10%	10 −10.80%	25 −26.90%	44 −47.30%	13 −14.00%	93 −100%
The Muslim Youth Movement of Malaysia (ABIM)	2 −2.50%	6 −11.10%	24 −19.80%	29 −29.60%	20 −37.00%	81 −100%
The Malaysian Muslim Solidarity Front (ISMA)	3 −4.30%	9 −13.00%	15 −21.70%	35 −50.70%	7 −10.10%	69 −100%
Total	17 −3.20%	50 −9.40%	171 −32.20%	219 −41.20%	74 −13.90%	530 −100%

Source: Field Research 2016.

The influences of the Arab Uprisings 93

with specific reference to the experiences of Ennahda and the FJP influencing the ideology of Malaysia's Islamist movements.

In term of percentages, the specific responses for each movement are highlighted below:

i   For PAS respondents, 50.3 per cent agreed (in general), followed by 37.2 per cent who were neutral and 12.5 per cent who disagreed (in general).
ii For AMANAH respondents, 61.3 per cent agreed (in general), followed by 26.9 per cent who were neutral and 11.9 per cent who disagreed (in general).
iii For ABIM respondents, 66.6 per cent agreed (in general), followed by 19.8 per cent who were neutral and 13.6 per cent who disagreed (in general).
iv For ISMA respondents, 60.8 per cent agreed (in general), followed by 21.7 per cent who were neutral and 17.3 per cent who disagreed (in general).

It does seem that the development of Islamist parties in the post-Arab Uprisings setting has affected the way of thinking of the majority of Malaysian Islamists regarding their movement's political approach and ideology. As acknowledged by Muhammad Najib (AMANAH Youth Leader),[34]

> An inspiration from the trend of victory of the Islamic parties in the Middle East is of course, present (within AMANAH). In terms of the political approach, we have been influenced a great deal by AKP. In terms of thinking, we learn a lot from Ennahda, especially the thinking of Sheikh Ghannouchi. This is because he was the one who had a lot of new ideas related to the Islamic politics especially when the concept of al-Faraghat is introduced, which means a vacuum, in the Islamic political thinking. In relation to Ikhwan (Muslim Brotherhood), AMANAH does not really lean towards this movement.

In terms of other relevant background variables, the chi-square test analysis from SPSS found that age and level of education were significant in explaining a pattern within the feedback. The youth members within the movements, aged 16–25 years and 26–35 years, expressed strong feelings regarding the influence of the post-Arab Uprisings environment. The majority of respondents with a PhD academic qualification (66.7 per cent) or a Bachelor's Degree (55.8 per cent) believed that developments in the post-Arab Uprisings period had influenced the political approach of Islamist movements in Malaysia, while respondents with a Diploma (48.6 per cent) showed slightly less agreement.[35] Overall, it is interesting that the respondents' age and type of education are again related to views which conform with the views of their respective movements. The next question will examine in detail the influence of the Arab Uprisings on 'moderation' and 'inclusion', as seen through the eyes of PAS, ABIM, ISMA and AMANAH members.

Influential aspects: moderation and inclusion

Islam proposes a set of fundamental guidelines for promoting peace, maintaining political stability and fostering mutual understanding in multi-faith and multi-cultural contexts (Hassan 2011). Among the values proposed by the Prophet Muhammad is the concept of moderation in all aspects of life, ranging from religious understanding to the relationship of an individual with his or her surrounding community and the political aspects of a nation. Although Sheline (2017: 47) has argued that there is no real agreement on the meaning of moderate Islam, the term 'moderation' itself can generally be defined from the Islamic perspective as being constantly balanced towards the middle way in all matters, including politics. It is between the two extremes of radicalism and disregard, and on a straight path following the Islamic methodology of living. It is the best approach in any political action in order to avoid any extreme or excessive event (Hassan 2011).

The political conflicts in the post-Arab Uprisings have brought daunting challenges for Islamist movements wanting to be seen as relevant and accepted by the world community in general and by their respective citizens in particular. The tragic events comprising Daesh's 'claimed-attacks' in several major world cities (for instance in Paris in 2015) have generated a surge in Islamophobia where many perceive Islamism, Islamists and Islamist movements as volatile, intolerant and extreme. According to Mark Lynch (2016: 250), the failure of the Arab Uprisings in Syria and the emergence of Daesh have revitalised a critique of Islamist movements which had previously fallen into disrepute. Having seen these 'crises', the Ennahda leader, Rachid Ghannouchi, came up with the idea of 'Muslim Democrats' in 2016 as a way to promote the idea of 'neo-Islamism' (see Chapter 3). This term stresses the importance of pluralism and diversity, and rejects party exclusion, division in society and disunity in relation to major national interests within Islamic-oriented political parties. This identity also means the inclusion of the majority of political parties and civil society groups when determining major political choices and decisions.[36] According to Anne Wolf, a Cambridge-based researcher who specialises in the history of Ennahda, 'Ghannouchi insisted that he accepted Western-style multi-party politics as long as it did not marginalize or reject religion, a stance which set him apart from more conservative Islamic movements' (Wolf 2017: 97).

Regarding the current political situation involving Islamist parties in Malaysia, the PAS decision to cut ties with its former secular coalition partner – the Democratic Action Party (DAP) – caused disagreement amongst its members and committees. This led to the internal break within the party in 2015, which gave birth to AMANAH (see Chapter 2). Some members believed that the party should learn a lesson from the Arab Uprisings and the transformation of Ennahda in Tunisia in terms of practising moderation and valuing inclusion.[37] The result of the survey appears to support the claim as 66.8 per cent of respondents agreed that post-Arab

Uprisings events have taught them to embrace a more moderate and inclusive approach when dealing with other non-Islamic-oriented parties and NGOs. The exact responses for each movement in terms of frequency and percentages are as follows:

i   For PAS respondents, 23.3 per cent strongly agreed (67), followed by 37.5 per cent who agreed (108), 16.7 per cent who were neutral (92), 4.5 per cent who disagreed (13) and 8 per cent who strongly disagreed (8).
ii For AMANAH respondents, 48.4 per cent strongly agreed (45), followed by 34.4 per cent who agreed (32), 11.8 per cent who were neutral (11), 3.2 per cent who disagreed (3) and 2.2 per cent who strongly disagreed (2).
iii For ABIM respondents, 37.0 per cent strongly agreed (36), followed by 43.2 per cent who agreed (35), 16.0 per cent who were neutral (13) and 3 per cent who disagreed (3).
iv For ISMA respondents, 15.9 per cent strongly agreed (111), followed by 39.1 per cent who agreed (27), 29.0 per cent who were neutral (20), 13.0 per cent who disagreed (9) and 2.9 per cent who strongly disagreed (2).

The findings indicated that moderation and inclusion are two main issues in the post-Arab Uprisings setting (with specific reference to Ennahda and the FJP) that have affected and could potentially continue to influence the political approach and ideology of Islamist movements in Malaysia. According to PAS activist, Saifuddin[38]:

> The Islamist movements in Malaysia should choose moderation and an inclusive approach as it will create an independent, mature and peaceful political culture in the country. Regarding post-Arab Uprisings developments, there are things that Islamist movements will agree and disagree about as long as it benefits the party and society.

Another PAS activist, Yasin Yunos, stated that[39]:

> Islamist movements all over the world have different approaches and strategies that vary according to local political circumstances, economic performance and social conditions in their respective countries. However, PAS in Malaysia prefers to adopt a moderate approach as well as participating in Malaysia's general election as a method of upholding the political Islam agenda. History and statistical data from past elections have shown that PAS never resorted to any violent methods to topple the ruling regime. A peaceful and stable political sphere in Malaysia has provided a great opportunity for PAS to continue its Islamic propagation objectives and activities as well as promoting political Islam. Despite Arab Spring street protests and violent incidents in the MENA region, it does not change the current moderate approach of PAS in Malaysia.

96 *The influences of the Arab Uprisings*

These opinions from PAS activists seem to align with those of Khalil al-Anani (2017: 4), an Associate Professor at the Doha Institute for Graduate Studies, who has emphasised that:

> Responses of Islamist movements to the fast-changing local, regional, and global environment after the Arab Spring have varied greatly. Some movements adapted and made significant changes in their discourse, organizational structure, and strategy as well as maintained internal coherence and unity to cope with the new environment.

The respondents, especially those from AMANAH and ABIM, have paid great attention, both ideologically and in practice, to both moderation and inclusion. Moreover, these were a significant part of the values which the AMANAH leadership tried to promote amongst its members and to Malaysian citizens in general. Emphasising moderation and inclusion as core values within all four movements, although with different degrees of practice, reflects the readiness of Malaysia's Islamist movements to attract political support from all layers of society. The next section will discuss the relationship between the Islamist movements in Malaysia and the Middle East during post-Arab Uprisings events, based on respondents' attitudes and experiences.

Strengthening cooperation: the Islamist movements in Malaysia and the Middle East and North Africa

Table 4.10 shows respondents' (71.5 per cent) opinions about whether post-Arab Uprisings developments have strengthened cooperation between Islamist movements in Malaysia and the Middle East since the overthrow of former regimes in several Arab states (Tunisia, Egypt and Morocco). Historically, it is recognised that the relationship of PAS, ABIM and ISMA with global Islamist movements and parties has a basis in history (see Chapter 2). PAS and ABIM have established a wider official Islamic connection since the formation of the Islamic Republic of Iran in 1979. Furthermore, with MB movements as a fundamental model of political Islam, PAS and ABIM have maintained the 'Arab-Middle Eastern connection' as part of their vital international agenda. ISMA, via its President, also admitted that MB movements in the Arab world have shaped the movement's political approach since its establishment in the 1990s.[40]

In addition, during the post-Arab Uprisings period, PAS visited Tunisia's Ennahda and the leaders of the Muslim Brothers in the Middle East twice – in 2012 and 2015, respectively. The main objectives were to congratulate them (on the opportunity to govern their respective states) and to learn from their political experience in the new 'era' following the post-transitional governments in Tunisia, Egypt and Morocco.[41] Out of the PAS members who responded to the question, 57.7 per cent believed that post-Arab Uprisings

Table 4.10 Respondents' views that post-Arab Uprisings events have strengthened cooperation between Islamist movements in Malaysia and Islamist movements in the Middle East and North Africa

Type of Islamist Movement	\multicolumn{5}{c}{Post-Arab Uprisings Events Have Strengthened Cooperation between Islamist Movements in Malaysia and Islamist Movements in the Middle East and North Africa (Frequency and Percentages)}	Total
	Strongly Disagree	Disagree	Neutral	Agree	Strongly Agree	
The Pan Malaysian Islamic Party (PAS)	3 −1.00%	25 −8.70%	94 −32.60%	114 −39.60%	52 −18.10%	288 −100%
The National Trust Party (AMANAH)	1 −1.10%	7 −7.50%	30 −32.30%	35 −37.60%	20 −21.50%	93 −100%
The Muslim Youth Movement of Malaysia (ABIM)	4 −4.90%	2 −2.50%	17 −21.00%	39 −48.10%	19 −23.50%	81 −100%
The Malaysian Muslim Solidarity Front (ISMA)	1 −1.40%	12 −17.40%	27 −39.10%	24 −34.80%	5 −7.20%	69 −100%
Total	17 −1.70%	50 −8.70%	171 −32.20%	219 −31.60%	74 −39.90%	530 −100%

Source: Field Research 2016.

events have definitely strengthened the party's cooperation with their Islamist counterparts in the Arab world. One of the respondents explained that it is PAS policy to encourage its members to support any legal Islamist movement in the world, especially when those movements have secured governing power.

Thus, it is not a surprise to see that many Facebook users amongst PAS ABIM, ISMA and AMANAH members changed their Facebook profile pictures to feature the famous 'Four-Finger Salute' image as a symbol of their solidarity with the former Egyptian President, Mohamed Morsi, who was overthrown during the June 2013 military takeover. Many peace rallies were also conducted for the same purpose, including one near the Egyptian Embassy in Kuala Lumpur. Overall, these findings show a pattern of positive attitudes by Malaysian Islamists towards the development of transnational cooperation between Islamist movements in Malaysia and the Middle East during the post-Arab Uprisings period.

Awareness of political issues in the Middle East and North Africa: the 'Arab Uprisings' factor

The purpose of this section is to explore how Malaysian Islamists perceive Arab Uprisings events as raising their awareness of and interest in

98 *The influences of the Arab Uprisings*

political matters in the MENA. Based on the researcher's observations, for much of the past three decades the Iranian Revolution, the Gulf War, the Israel-Palestine conflict, the 2003 US-led coalition invasion of Iraq and the development of AKP in Turkey were among the most popular issues that interested Malaysian Islamists as regards Arab and Middle Eastern political affairs. However, beginning in 2011, the dynamic and changing nature of the political landscape and the progress of the Arab Uprisings phenomenon have caught the attention of the world community in general and the Islamist movements in Malaysia in particular.

Out of the PAS, ABIM, ISMA and AMANAH members, activists and supporters who responded to the question, 69.4 per cent (380) felt that the Arab Uprisings undoubtedly opened new dimensions in Arab world politics and will be the focus of discussion in the years to come because of their lasting implications, not only in the MENA countries but also worldwide. 26.8 per cent of respondents (125) gave a neutral response, while the remaining 3.9 per cent (25) disagreed with the statement. The explanation for such statistical feedback might relate to the relationship between PAS, ABIM and ISMA, and the Islamist movements in the MENA, which is seen as the reason why Arab and Middle East politics always 'come first' for the Malaysian Islamists compared to politics in other regions (Europe, Latin America, East Asia, Oceania, etc.). The research suggests that Arab Uprisings events have encouraged Malaysian Islamists to pay more attention to political issues across the MENA. Amar Yasier (ISMA activist) 'confessed' that[42]:

> Before the 'Arab Spring' I seldom consistently followed any news or updates about Middle East politics (except some issues about the Israel-Palestine conflicts) since I personally thought there was nothing very exciting about the MENA region (in terms of local politics). I instead paid more attention to Malaysian politics as well as developments in the US and UK. But when the Arab Uprisings happened, I perceived these events as highly interesting to follow due to their dynamism and involving lots of actors (both local and foreign) including the Islamists.

Conclusion and summary

The main objectives of this chapter were to examine the attitudes of Malaysian Islamists towards post-Arab Uprisings developments and to establish whether these developments influenced the political activism of the selected Islamist movements in Malaysia. The findings showed that many PAS, ABIM, ISMA and AMANAH Islamists believed the Arab Uprisings had both positive and negative short-term implications, depending on the specific country involved. For instance, some respondents were quite positive about the recent political reform (21.5 per cent) and democratisation processes (43.9 per cent) in Tunisia, Morocco and Egypt (during the FJP rule). However, other respondents (41.5 per cent) did not see much improvement in terms of political and economic stability – referring to the examples of Syria, Yemen and Libya. Paradoxically, the findings also revealed that many respondents were not certain whether Tunisia should be viewed as an example of a 'successful product' of the Arab Uprisings, despite the positive reviews of academics and the international community. The reason for this is probably limited knowledge about the Maghreb region and political development in Tunisia as respondents engage less frequently with its political news than they do with Egypt.

There are a number of respondents (34.2 per cent) who assumed that the impact of the post-Arab Uprisings involved the unleashing of an unexpected event – the birth of Daesh in Northern Syria and the terrorism that followed in several different countries. However, not all agreed with the statement about the connection between the Syrian Uprisings and the emergence of Daesh (32.9 per cent), and some preferred to remain neutral (32.9 per cent). Among the reasons for rejection of the statement were the claims by the ISMA President and an AMANAH activist that there were 'invisible hands' behind the backdrop of Daesh operations, which they believed belonged to Western powers (including Israel) working for personal (Western) gain. The series of terrorist activities carried out by Daesh has undeniably affected the stability of the MENA. Accordingly, for some respondents (39 per cent), the Arab world was seen as more peaceful before the Arab Uprisings (especially before the Syrian uprisings occurred). Indeed, the findings from this part of the study are somewhat complex but still interesting as they indicate a rather balanced view with no dominant response from respondents.

Apart from the adverse side of the post-Arab Uprisings developments discussed above, this study shows that the majority of Malaysian Islamists (54.7 per cent) believe that the phenomenon has been an 'eye-opener' for Arab rulers, who have been forced to listen to the voices of their citizens. Dictatorships within the Arab world have proven that they are not 'immune' to grass root challenges. The vast majority of respondents who agreed with the statement also predicted that another wave of democratic uprisings would take place in the future – given the current political uncertainties in several Arab nations. Regarding the impact of the Arab Uprisings on the Islamist movements in Malaysia, the findings showed that the events have influenced various aspects of PAS, ABIM, ISMA and AMANAH political activism.

First, almost half of respondents (49.9 per cent), largely comprising youths and university students, admitted that the act of street protests during the Arab Uprisings had inspired them to openly express their anger and disappointment with the systematic discrimination of the Malaysian regime of opposition parties as well as the huge corruption scandals involving Prime Minister Najib Razak. Most of these respondents had participated in one of the biggest political protests in Malaysia – the 2013 Bersih 3.0 movement.

Second, it appears that the majority of Malaysian Islamists (69.9 per cent) believe that the Arab Uprisings benefitted from social media via the platforms, such as Facebook, Twitter and YouTube videos – and that social media could serve as a great 'weapon' in future political activism. The respondents agreed that the use of the Internet and social media should be fully utilised by Malaysian Islamist activists in order to generate political awareness as well as to initiate civil disobedience against the ruling regime in the future. The result of the Chi-square test analysis also found that respondents' level of education and working sector were statistically significant in determining their attitudes on this issue.

Third, the positive performance of several Islamist parties in their first 'democratic' elections in the post-Arab Uprisings era appears to have motivated a majority of PAS, ABIM, ISMA and AMANAH Islamists (62.3 per cent) to put more effort into attracting local support in order to reach the ultimate agenda of political Islam in Malaysia. Respondents also learned from Islamist parties in the Middle East that the goal of political Islam can only be achieved by implementing well-considered strategies, which include negotiation in terms of ideology and political approach.

Fourth, without having had direct, in-country experience, the post-Arab Uprisings phenomenon (via the development of Islamist parties) nevertheless influenced the ideology and political approach of Islamist movements in Malaysia. There was emphasis on the practices of moderation and inclusivity in order to attract wider political support. Crucially, these two aspects were seen by respondents as a 'soft approach' when dealing with different layers of society and non-Islamic-oriented parties and NGOs in Malaysia. Amongst the four Islamist movements being studied, AMANAH seemed to most strongly embrace the idea of Ghannouchi's 'Muslim Democrat' or neo-Islamism for the movement's members. 83.1 per cent showed a positive attitude towards the proposition that Malaysia's Islamist movements should adopt a more moderate and inclusive approach, as in the transformation of Ennahda in Tunisia. Related indirectly to this question, the research found that the practice of conservative Islamism (which highlighted the aim of establishing *Daulah Islamiyah* and sharia in Malaysia) was less popular with Islamist parties and NGOs.

Fifth, it seems that post-Arab Uprisings events have somehow strengthened the relationship between Malaysia's Islamist movements and Arab Islamist movements through several 'courtesy calls', such as the one undertaken by PAS with Ennahda representatives. Events that occurred during the post-Arab Uprisings, for instance the victory of the Ennahda Party in the 2011 Tunisian Constituent Assembly Election and the tragedy of the 2013 military coup in Egypt, garnered tremendous support from Islamist politicians and activists in Malaysia.

Finally, this study found that Arab Uprisings events have encouraged approximately 70 per cent of respondents from PAS, ABIM, ISMA and AMANAH to pay more attention to political issues in the Arab world. For them, the lasting impact of the protests makes the 'drama' of Middle East politics worth watching. It is, of course, obvious that the degree of awareness depends on the regularity of engaging with Middle Eastern political news. However, it is worth noting that the strengthening transnational relationship between Malaysia's Islamist movements and Arab Islamist parties after the Arab Uprisings might embolden respondents to 'get closer' to Middle Eastern political affairs.

To sum up, the overall findings of this study demonstrate that Islamist movements in Malaysia have been significantly influenced by political developments that have occurred within the Arab world, especially those during the post-Arab Uprisings era. Undeniably, the impacts of the Arab Uprisings phenomenon were felt by the majority of Malaysian Islamists from PAS, ABIM, ISMA and AMANAH – depending on their knowledge and how they perceived the specific issues within the scope of the research.

Notes

1 Fieldwork at the Coalition for Clean and Fair Election (Bersih) roadshow, Shah Alam, Malaysia. 3 November 2016.
2 'Malaysia's government accuses opposition of fomenting "Arab Spring": Opposition leaders say new law banning street protests is more repressive than those in Burma and Zimbabwe'. Retrieved from www.theguardian.com/world/2011/nov/30/malaysia-goverment-opposition -arab-spring [09 May 2017].
3 Discussion of 'Islamist Winter' can be seen in Chapter 3.
4 Fieldwork at the colloquium entitled '5 Years After the Arab Spring: The Implosion of Social Movements?', Birkbeck, University of London, UK. 10 June 2016. On the other hand, Raymond Hinnebusch argued that the Middle East is not entirely 'exceptional' with respect to parties, although their roles may be more marginal than in developed states. See R.A. Hinnebusch. (2017). Why Political Parties in the Middle East Matter. *British Journal of Middle Eastern Studies*, 44(2): 159–175.
5 To further consider the nature of Daesh, see Michael Martin & Hussein Solomon. (2017). Understanding the Nature of the Beast and Its Funding. *Contemporary Review of the Middle East*, 4(1): 18–49.
6 Shakeeb Asrar. (2017). Syrian Civil War Map: A Map of the Syrian Civil War that Shows Who Controls What after Five Years of Fighting. Available at www.aljazeera.com/indepth/interactive/2015/05/syria-country-divided-150529144229467.html [11 September 2017].
7 Personal interview with the ISMA President Bangi, Malaysia. 5 November 2016.
8 Official statement from PAS President, Abdul Hadi Awang. November 2016.
9 Ibid.
10 Personal interview with an AMANAH activist (name withheld at interviewee's request), Kuala Lumpur, Malaysia. 9 August 2016.
11 See Freedom House Report for Tunisia (2017).
12 Speaking about the success of political transition in Tunisia after the Arab Uprisings, Rafik Abdessalem, former Minister of International Affairs in Tunisia, further explains that Tunisians have survived the democratic process due to the neutrality of military forces and the homogeneity of the Tunisian people (who help to prevent any potential sectarian and religious division within the society). The rationality of political actors, especially the role of the Ennahda Party, has also made a significant contribution towards the effort to consolidate the democratisation process (via the formation of the previous Troika government and current coalition) in the country. Personal interview with Abdessalem in Tunis, Tunisia. December 2017.

13 Personal interviews with (1) The Deputy Chief of Perak PAS Youth, Mohd Hafez Sabri. Ipoh, Malaysia. 28 October 2016. (2) The International Relations Bureau for ISMA's UK branch, Amar Yasier. London, United Kingdom. 10 June 2016.
14 'In general' = Combination of total percentages of agree/strongly agree and disagree/strongly disagree based on each type of Islamist movement in Table 4.4.
15 Personal interview with an ISMA activist, Najmuddin Mohd Faudzir. Bangi, Malaysia. 13 October 2016.
16 Official statement from Abdul Hadi Awang. November 2016.
17 Written opinion/comment left by PAS respondent on the questionnaire form (name withheld at respondent's request).
18 UNDP (2016). Arab Human Development Report. Youth and Prospects for Human Development in a Changing Reality. pp 37–39. Available at www.arabstates.undp.org/content/rbas/en/home/library/huma_development/arab-human-development-report-2016--youth-and-the-prospects-for-/ [15 September 2017].
19 Lewis Tallon. (2017). Second Arab Spring. Available at https://encyclopediageopolitica.com/2016/12/09/2017-second-arab-spring/ [15 September 2017].
20 See Marc Lynch. (2016). *The New Arab Wars: Uprisings and Anarchy in the Middle East*. New York: Public Affairs, pp. 253–254.
21 Personal interview with an ISMA activist, Najmuddin Mohd Faudzir. Bangi, Malaysia. 13 October 2016.
22 Regarding this section, the researcher asked seven major inter-linked questions in the questionnaire, which covered civil disobedience, social media factors, development of Arab-Islamist parties and awareness of Middle Eastern politics in the post-Arab Spring.
23 See also Mohd Zain Zawiyah, et al. (2017). Civil Disobedience and Cyber Democracy. *Mediterranean Journal of Social Sciences*, 8(4): 9–16.
24 Personal interview with PAS activist, Zakiuddin Shariff. Perlis, Malaysia. 13 August 2016.
25 Personal interview with PAS activist, Abdul Muiz. Perak, Malaysia. 16 August 2016.
26 Personal interview with PAS Youth Leader, Mohd Hafez Sabri. Ipoh, Malaysia. 28 October 2016.
27 Official statement from Abdul Hadi Awang. November 2016. See Appendix C for the full statement.
28 Fieldwork at the Coalition for Clean and Fair Election (Bersih) Roadshow, Shah Alam, Malaysia. 3 November 2016. The statements were originally quoted from Mohamad Sabu's speeches at the event. See also Geraldine Tong (2016). Stupid to Compare Bersih to Arab Spring, says Amanah President. [Online] Available: www.malaysiakini.com/news/359055 (15 October 2016).
29 For more discussion on the media restrictions and power of new media in the political context of Malaysia and the Middle East, see M.L. Weiss. (2013). Parsing the Power of New Media in Malaysia. *Journal of Contemporary Asia*, 43(4): 591–412 and K.M. Wagner & Jason Gainous. (2013). Digital Uprising: The Internet Revolution in the Middle East. *Journal of Information Technology & Politics*, 10(3): 261–275.
30 In all tests of significance, if $p < 0.05$, there is a statistically significant relationship between the two variables. The p-value in chi-square outputs for respondent's level of education and type of occupation is 0.002. This means that the relationship between respondents' level of education and type of occupation and attitudes towards the influence of Arab Spring social media activism is significant.
31 Personal interview with the International Relations Bureau for ISMA's UK branch, Amar Yasier. London, United Kingdom. 10 June 2016.

32 In 2011, an ISMA delegation led by its President, Abdullah Zaik Abdul Rahman, paid a courtesy visit to the Vice Mursyidul Am of MB, Mahmud Izzat. ISMA's media representative also interviewed one of the MB activists, Dr Kamal el Helbawy, with regard to the FJP experience in the post-Mubarak era. See also www.ismaeropah.com/isma-lakukan-kunjungan-hormat-ke-atas-naib-mursyidul-am-ikhwan-muslimin/ [04 February 2018].
33 Respondent's written opinion/comment on the questionnaire.
34 Personal interview with the AMANAH National Youth Leader, Muhammad Najib. Kuala Lumpur, Malaysia. September 2016.
35 The P-values for both variables are less than 0.05, which clearly indicate a statistically significant relationship between the variables.
36 Speaking of this new identity, Ghannouchi further clarifies that Ennahda's commitment to consensual democracy, dialogue, negotiation and the search for common ground in the management of Tunisia's affairs and the prioritisation of the national interest over partisan interests and ideological differences will be on the party's main agenda in the coming years. For more details, see 'Concluding Statement of Ennahda's Tenth Party Conference'. Available at www.facebook.com/Nahdha.International/ posts/ 703054 249797836 [12 June 2016].
37 Personal interview with a former PAS Youth Chief – Suhaizan Kayat – who is currently on the AMANAH Central Committee. Batu Caves, Malaysia. 27 August 2016.
38 Written comments/thoughts from a PAS activist, Saifuddin in the questionnaire form.
39 Written comments/thoughts from a PAS activist, Yasin Yunos in the questionnaire form.
40 Personal interview with the ISMA President. Bangi, Malaysia. 5 November 2016.
41 Personal interview with Mohd Hafez Sabri. 28 October 2016.
42 Personal interview with Amar Yasier, London, United Kingdom. 10 June 2016.

5 Revolution or political stability? Malaysia's Islamist movements and lessons from the Arab Uprisings

The purpose of this chapter is to explore the attitudes of the sample respondents (from specific dimensions) to lessons learned from the Arab Uprisings phenomenon within the context of the Malaysian political landscape and the development of Malaysia's Islamist movements. To begin with, every major historical event undoubtedly produces some valuable lessons for humankind, and it seems that the same principle applies in the case of the 2011 Arab Uprisings. Academically speaking, there are plenty of significant studies that highlight the lessons that can be drawn from the Arab Uprisings – for instance by Filiu (2011), As'ad Ghanem (2013), Larbi Sadiki (2015a), Roberts et al. (2016) and Hafez Ghanem (2016a, 2016b). However, none of these authors discuss the above matters from the perspective of countries beyond the Middle East and North Africa (MENA); none adopt the perspective of other majority Muslim nations (e.g. Malaysia). Hence, after years of observation and discussion relating to the Arab Uprisings, this book investigates whether the Malaysian Islamists from PAS, ABIM, ISMA and AMANAH have learned lessons from these momentous events.

The good, the bad and the ugly: what have Malaysian Islamists learned from the Arab Uprisings?

In order to examine this question, the researcher has provided nine statements in the questionnaire that explore the attitudes of respondents towards several issues within the theme of lessons from the Arab Uprisings – for instance the state of political Islam and Islamism, the 'Malaysian Spring' polemics, the acceptance of electoral democracy and the significance of Malaysia's current political stability. The researcher recognises that there are some differences between the actual situation in those Arab states where the Arab Uprisings or Arab Revolutions have demanded immediate 'change of the ruling regime' for various reasons and the Malaysian case of the Bersih protests, where Malaysians, particularly Islamists, still fight against corruption, political injustice and electoral reform (as well as the long-term plan of implementing Sharia). However, it is still possible to draw some lessons relevant for Malaysian Islamists from PAS, ABIM, ISMA and AMANAH. As pointed out by one of the respondents from PAS[1]:

> The political situation in Malaysia is different from the other (Arab) states. The Islamist Movement (PAS) was created earlier along with the journey of Malaysia's independence. In other (Muslim) countries, the Islamist movements are always being threatened, repressed and banned. Apart from that, the approach of Islamist movements in Malaysia is unique as they have their own 'battlefield' which could only be shaped by themselves (the Malaysian Islamists), although there may be some influenced from outside. Thus, I would personally say that the 'Arab Spring' is more or less suitable to serve as a lesson for the development of Malaysian Islamist movements.

Adnan, an ABIM activist, shared the same opinion by stating that[2]:

> Indeed, the 'Arab Spring' was one of the manifestations of Arab civilian voices against autocratic regimes. However, the condition and political scenario in Malaysia is slightly different from the Arab world. Thus, in my view, the 'Arab Spring' should not be followed by us in Malaysia, rather it should be seen as a lesson.

The opinions above are only examples of what Islamists from PAS and ABIM thought about the lessons they learned from the Arab Uprisings. The following sections will specifically highlight all the identified lessons from the Arab Uprisings phenomenon that are relevant to the development of Islamist movements in Malaysia, based on respondents' opinions.

The importance of political strategy and preparation to govern

The Arab Uprisings of 2011 have clearly altered the political context of Islamist opposition and state interactions in the wider Arab world. Like many Islamist political parties in the Middle East, the Islamist movements in Malaysia also originally emerged as movements calling for the application of Sharia and the establishment of an 'Islamic state'. Previously they had evolved as opposition and protest movements; however, in the aftermath of the Arab Uprisings some of the Islamist parties in the MENA tried to develop negotiation and compromise skills. This can be witnessed in the recent development of Ennahda as a way to ensure that the 'ideological rigidity' of Islamism (which was often seen as a source of anxiety for citizens who do not share the vision of 'political Islam') can be effectively minimised.[3]

Throughout the post-Arab Uprisings, the newly progressive Islamists in the Middle East also appeared to legitimately attract support from a large part of society. Major Islamist movements/parties transformed their Islamist approach by discarding exclusive loyalty to the 'Islamic Ummah' and adopting progressive positions: for instance the introduction of the 'Muslim Democrat' idea by Ghannouchi in 2016. According to the Ennahda president[4]:

> Now that the party is separated from religion, what will your party be? (Actually) We are not separated from religion. Islam is our reference. It is a source of inspiration for us, but we do not ask people to elect us because we are more religious than others. We would like to attract people to our freedom regardless of their religion. All Tunisians are welcome to join our party, provided that they accept our party's programme. Our agenda is not based on religion; it is based on real services for people, real solutions to their daily problems, education, good health care and job creation.

These moves undoubtedly caused the citizens in the MENA countries to shift their support from the old secular elites to the Islamist movements, as in the case of Ennahda, the Egyptian FJP and the Moroccan PJD experiences during the first years after the Arab Uprisings. As Naoufel Eljammali demonstrates,[5]

> The most interesting thing now in the Ennahda and this transformation is it will allow the party not to speak only with few persons who are and have a great, direct and strong relationship with the religion (Islam)... but to extend its public to other people. This effort will allow us to be very strong and have a resilient popular base in the country.

However, the unexpected trajectory of the Muslim Brotherhood in Egypt illustrates that some Islamist parties have not completed their evolution from rigid ideological parties – whose sole aim is to remake their societies in their own image – to pragmatic organisations willing to represent and give voice to their followers in a pluralistic political environment.[6] According to El-Fadl (2015), many Egyptians who voted for the Muslim Brotherhood in 2011 and 2012 saw the well-organised Islamist party as an indication of high moral standards and competence that would translate into an effective new Egyptian government. Yet these hopes were dashed when the Brotherhood turned out to be 'high on will and low on skill' as Morsi's focus was more on consolidating presidential control than on dealing with Egypt's dire economic and social problems (El-Fadl 2015: 256–258).

If the Muslim Brotherhood's experience points to the need for political Islam to accommodate a pluralistic society, this seems more relevant in the context of the multi-racial, multi-religious and multi-cultural Malaysian society. Its Islamist parties can either hold on to their rigid ideological base (if any) – trying to shape society to fit within their singular vision – or they can accept their role as an influential force in a democratic pluralistic regime, within which the rule of law must guarantee protection of rights for everyone, regardless of their background. In light of the failure of Egyptian Islamist political elites to provide an alternative model for long-term political change following the January 25 Revolution, the idea of 'Muslim Democrat', championed by the Tunisian Ennahda founder, emerged as an alternative model to the conservative forms of political Islam in many Arab states. As highlighted by Mohamad (an AMANAH activist), 'Tunisia's Islamist movement (Ennahda) shows its support for inclusivity and progressiveness which fall under the framework of Muslim Democrat and democracy. Meanwhile in Egypt, the Islamists failed miserably'.[7]

Likewise, it seems that within the Malaysian political context Islamist political elites, particularly PAS and AMANAH Islamist politicians, will have to reconsider their political approach if they want to formulate political platforms capable of restoring the confidence in peaceful political action of those segments of the population leaning towards Islamism. Islamist political parties and NGOs in Malaysia must fundamentally review the political approaches they have practised over the past several years to find solutions, if they hope to survive and remain prominent local political actors. In particular, they should focus on providing more effective mechanisms to communicate with the Malaysian grass roots (both inside and outside of the Islamist movements), distinguishing between political action and religious activities, and finally formulating a comprehensive political project that reconsiders the relationship between the civil state and Sharia.

According to al-Anani, the failure of the Muslim Brotherhood when it was in power has highlighted the inability of orthodox Islamism to adapt to the political environment that developed from the Arab Uprisings. By orthodox Islamism, what al-Anani meant was the traditional Islamist movements that had emerged over the past century and been burdened by its stagnant structure; its sprawling organisation; and the dominance of a conservative, old-fashioned style of Islamist leadership (Al-Anani 2015: 237). In addition to what is mentioned above by al-Anani, wise strategies comprising inclusion are seen as a crucial factor in altering Islamist ideology and mind-set in order to make it more moderate and progressive, and contribute towards the success of political Islam in Malaysia.

Regarding the results of the survey, it appears that the findings have supported the above statement because as many as 76.8 per cent of the respondents (407) accepted that the development of Islamist parties in the post-Arab Uprisings have taught them and their respective Islamist movements valuable lessons. Only 3.1 per cent of the respondents (16) disagreed with the statement, while 20.2 per cent (107) preferred to remain neutral. Table 5.1 records details of respondents' feedback towards the question on lessons from the Arab Uprisings.

108 Revolution or political stability?

Table 5.1 Respondents' views that the development of Islamist parties after the Arab Uprisings have taught some valuable lessons to Islamist movements in Malaysia

Type of Islamist Movement	The Development of Islamist Parties after the Arab Uprisings Have Taught Some Valuable Lessons to Islamist Movements in Malaysia (Frequency and Percentages)					Total
	Strongly Disagree	Disagree	Neutral	Agree	Strongly Agree	
The Pan Malaysian Islamic Party (PAS)	2 −0.70%	7 −2.40%	63 −22.00%	135 −47.00%	80 −27.90%	288 −100%
The National Trust Party (AMANAH)	1 −1.10%	4 −4.30%	19 −20.40%	41 −44.10%	28 −30.10%	93 −100%
The Muslim Youth Movement of Malaysia (ABIM)	0 0.00%	1 −1.20%	13 −16.00%	30 −37.00%	37 −45.70%	81 −100%
The Malaysian Muslim Solidarity Front (ISMA)	0 0.00%	1 −1.40%	12 −17.40%	28 −40.60%	28 −40.60%	69 −100%
Total	3 −0.60%	13 −2.50%	107 −20.20%	234 −44.20%	173 −32.60%	530 −100%

Source: Field Research 2016.

From Table 5.1, the specific reactions of respondents based on type of Islamist movements can be summarised as follows:

i For PAS respondents, 74.9 per cent agreed (in general), followed by 22.0 per cent who were neutral and 3.1 per cent who disagreed (in general).
ii For AMANAH respondents, 74.2 per cent agreed (in general), followed by 20.4 per cent who were neutral and 5.4 per cent who disagreed (in general).
iii For ABIM respondents, 82.7 per cent agreed (in general), followed by 16.0 per cent who were neutral and 1.2 per cent who disagreed (in general).
iv For ISMA respondents, 81.2 per cent agreed (in general), followed by 17.4 per cent who were neutral and 1.4 per cent who disagreed (in general).

The findings above unquestionably show that the development of Islamist parties after the Arab Uprisings has taught all four case study movements some lessons relevant to Malaysia. According to Abdullah Zaik (ISMA president)[8]:

> The Islamist movements in Malaysia must have their own strengths, views and approaches. We can learn how the Islamist movements operate in other countries. We try to learn from everyone, from what is good from Muslim Brothers, Ennahda and AKP. Not only ISMA, but Islamist movements all over the world must also learn from one another. They have to study the existing administration, before actions to take over power from the regime. In Libya *maqasid syariah* had at least been the main concern of Gaddafi before he was overthrown and assassinated.

The following comments by respondents further clarify the specific lessons which they believe should not be overlooked by Islamist leaders and politicians in Malaysia. As pointed out by an AMANAH youth activist, Nik Abdul Razak, Islamists in Malaysia need to prepare an 'economic model', which may benefit the country's entire population – if the Malaysia Islamists were given an opportunity to rule Malaysia in the future. For Nik Abdul Razak[9]:

> The 'Arab Spring' has taught the Islamist movements to prepare the idea and thought of a political economic framework, which is something they should offer to citizens. The failure of Islamists (for instance the Muslim Brotherhood in Egypt) to tackle the economic issues only means that they just keep using the old capitalist system which probably increases GDP but is not effectively helping the society.

In addition to the economic and Islamic propagation aspects, there were concerns from several AMANAH and ISMA respondents (including the ISMA president) about the need for solid preparation before assuming power from a previous regime. For these respondents, the tragedy of the Muslim Brotherhood in Egypt highlighted the weakness of the movement in preparing for uncertainty, let alone governing the whole country. The following comments further explain the respondents' opinions regarding lessons that could be learned from the Arab Uprisings in general and the case of the Muslim Brotherhood in Egypt in particular:

> Most Islamist movements in the Middle East are seen to have failed in predicting the changes that can happen in the Arab world. They did not equip themselves regarding the changes that they wished to achieve. At the moment, Islamist movements are beginning to understand that with the collapse of a president or a leader, the existing government may fall, but the proxy of the old regime actually stays on. Thus, the stance of Islamist movements today is quite careful, where they are aware of their

own current capabilities. Any changes that take place must be considered in terms of shortcomings, objectives and *siyasah syariah* (political Islam). The objective must be clear.

(Abdullah Zaik, ISMA president)

In my opinion, the Arab Spring or the failure of the Arab Spring as is happening in Egypt is because of lack of preparation on the part of the Islamic movements. We see Ikhwan in Egypt which is not ready to rule due to lack of experience and other factors of army sabotage, the anti-Morsi movement and so on. Ennahda may be seen to have some preparation. Ikhwan is not seen as equipping itself for rule, especially after gaining access to power where its capability to generate the economy, preserve political stability and other issues are open to debate.

(Muhammad Najib, ISMA Youth Leader)

The 'Arab Spring' was good and relevant. However, we (Islamists) failed when the Muslim Brothers, specifically the ones in Egypt took power and assumed office. Rapid changes were made. However, it seemed the weak progress of improving the political system 'killed' the Islamist movement's reputation. The Muslim Brothers also seemed too rush to propose the Sharia Law bill, while a large part of the society was still lacking understanding of fundamental Islamic thought.

(AMANAH activist)

The 'Arab Spring' was good but the political practice of rushing (to get power) had caused the new Islamist government in Egypt to be ousted which led another worst regime to govern (the Al-Sisi regime).

(Raduan Mat Taib, ABIM senior member)

We have to have proper planning before any change is implemented, which is in the context of changing the leaders and taking over power. Today, we see that countries involved in the Arab Spring do not have the capability to develop that well. There are even some countries like Libya that still do not have qualified leaders. This implies that the effort to oust the leaders is not by means of revolution or by mass rally. With the aim to oust the government in this condition there is no proper planning from revolutionary fighters. By taking as an example the experiences of Ikhwanul Muslimin in Egypt, the decision to place Morsi on the presidential seat has caused him to become unable to defend the FJP administration in Egypt. This stems from the absence of properly arranged plans. Here, clearly ISMA has been able to see the mistakes of Ikhwanul Muslimin.

(Mohd Syafiq, ISMA activist)

Interestingly, during an interview with Asyraf Farique (an independent researcher within ISMA), the interviewee voiced two crucial points regarding lessons that could be learned by Islamist movements in Malaysia and by ISMA in particular. The first is the need for Islamist movements to follow fundamental phases (within the context of *Harakah Islamiyyah* or political Islam) as well as adopt readiness before acquiring political power. The second is that Islamist movements or parties must think critically and stay alert regarding any potential external threats, especially those from Western powers like America or Israel. The following paragraphs present these original points from Asyraf:

> Firstly, as an Islamist movement, we cannot simply jump from one phase to another. The phase implied starts from the individual, family, society, country (*khilafah*) and international level. The Islamist movement needs to take into account the situation, strength and level of maturity in politics before making changes or having power. When transcending from one phase to another, the impact is so tremendous that it can stunt an organization as happened to Ikhwanul Muslimin in Egypt. This should be prevented from happening in Malaysia. In the Middle East the Islamist movements should not skip a phase or *marhalah* from one to another without considering the strength possessed.
>
> Secondly, the 'Arab Spring' events teach ISMA to view the political scenarios that happen and not just look at local politics, as in Egypt where Ikhwanul Muslimin only looks at the dictatorship and plays in the space that supports the elimination of a dictator, but does not look at the potential of foreign intervention that lingers, as shown by countries like America and Israel. This has to be clear because if we are that naïve we will suffer the consequences.
>
> (Asyraf Farique, ISMA activist & independent researcher)

The first point seems relevant as it overlaps with the other respondents' opinions regarding the significance for Islamists of political strategy and preparation for ruling before political power is assumed. However, the second point is quite debatable as the argument more or less lies on 'anti-Western' and anti-Israel sentiments. As explained in Chapter 2, ISMA is quite consistent in showing a 'radical' view when it comes to the matter of relations between Islam and the Western world. Thus, it is no surprise to hear such an opinion from an ISMA member, even with regard to the topic of lessons learned from the Arab Uprisings. Nevertheless, the research findings highlight the fact that the Arab Uprisings have provided lessons for Malaysian Islamists – these include the importance of political strategy and preparation for governing.

The necessity of cooperation between Islamists and non-Islamists

In the context of the Malaysian political landscape, the formation of political alliances or coalitions among the diverse political parties (be it from the ruling government or opposition bloc) is not new. However, the relationship typically fluctuates, especially when it comes to issues involving the interests of Islamists and Secularists. Hence, when speaking about political strategy, should the Islamist movements in Malaysia cooperate with any non-Islamic-oriented political parties or organisation? Since Malaysia's formation in 1957, there had been a number of tensions and disagreements between Islamists or Muslim conservatives and liberalists or secular intellectuals.[10]

However, it appears that Islamists have on the whole gained the dominant voice among Malaysian Muslims, especially since the Islamic resurgence in the 1970s. In terms of political Islam, a number of these Islamist politicians and activists saw Sharia as divinely inspired and unchangeable as well as valid for the on-going agenda of their movements. Sometimes, Malaysian Islamists, especially those from PAS, view the bold measures taken to bolster the party's appeal to non-Muslims (particularly the softening of its stance on the Islamic state agenda) as having caused the Islamist movements to compromise too much. Some PAS members even asked their leadership why the Islamic state agenda had to be put on the 'back burner' when it was the fundamental purpose behind their party. There were also cases whereby Islamists in Malaysia 'attacked' the few liberal voices seeking to reinterpret the Muslim sources to align with a modern context and human rights.[11]

Nevertheless, it seems that the experiences of Ennahda and the FJP in the period after the Arab Uprisings have indirectly taught the general Islamist movements in Malaysia that the act of rigidness might reduce support for them in the multi-cultural society of Malaysia. The Ennahda founder, Ghannouchi, during his speech in a forum held in Washington in 2013, highlighted the importance of establishing a positive political relationship between the Islamists and Secularists for the sake of liberating Tunisia from a dictatorship. The relevant excerpt from Ghannouchi's speech appears below[12]:

> The conflict between Secularists and Islamists, which has continued for decades, has wasted many energies and helped dictatorships to control the fate of our countries, and on that basis, the secular and Islamic alliance is vital to a free society capable of managing its differences on the basis of dialogue.

The experiences of Ennahda and the Muslim Brotherhood in the Middle East undoubtedly taught Malaysian Islamists the significance of cooperation between Islamist and non-Islamist politicians. As pointed out by an AMANAH (female) activist[13]:

Revolution or political stability? 113

The 'Arab Spring' has taught us that Islamist movements (in Malaysia) need to learn, adapt and make changes that suit Malaysia's current circumstances. They certainly cannot be rigid, simple-minded, short-sighted and practise the act of holier than-thou.

Another AMANAH activist supported these comments by stating that[14]:

> The Muslim Brotherhood was successful in gaining support from a large part of their citizens; however the new governments formed in the aftermath of the Egyptian revolution seemed unprepared to govern and lacked cooperation with others and the practice of inclusivity. This situation led to the collapse (indefensible) of their rule in Egypt during the post-Mubarak regime. The 'Arab Spring' teaches a valuable lesson for Malaysian Islamists. We have to create our own way (in politics).

Meanwhile, Razali Salleh, who is an ABIM activist, feels that the Arab Uprisings have taught the Islamist movements in Malaysia that better engagement with non-Muslims and non-Islamists will be a starting point in implementing the agenda of political Islam.[15]

> The struggle to uphold Islam must be made through soft *dakwah* (Islamic preaching) not through enforcement, labelling (infidels, *kafirs*, liberals etc) and badmouthing, which will not reflect the beauty of the Islamic culture. We (Malaysian Muslims) have to approach as many Muslims and non-Muslims as we can, rather than creating a gap between groups that are not in-line with our ideology.

In addition to the above opinions, the study found that some Malaysian Islamists from PAS, ABIM, ISMA and AMANAH learned from the development of Islamist parties after the Arab Uprisings that cooperation between Islamist movements and non-Islamic-oriented political parties and organisations (for instance the Nationalists, Secularists, Leftists and human rights groups) might eventually contribute to political stability. Out of 530 respondents who answered the question, 89 respondents (16.8 per cent) strongly believed that there must be a respectable cooperation between Islamist parties and non-Islamist parties for the sake of maintaining political stability in the country. One hundred and sixty respondents (30.1 per cent) shared a similar (but less strong) attitude. One hundred and fifty-six respondents (29.4 per cent) gave a neutral response, while 85 respondents (16.0 per cent) disagreed with the statement. Only 41 respondents (7.7 per cent) totally rejected the importance of political cooperation between Islamist and non-Islamist parties or groups in Malaysia. Table 5.2 summarises the responses.

Table 5.2 Respondents' attitudes towards the importance of political cooperation between Islamist and non-Islamist parties or groups in Malaysia

Type of Islamist Movement	\multicolumn{5}{l	}{Respondents' Attitudes towards the Importance of Political Cooperation between Islamist and Non-Islamist Parties or Groups in Malaysia (Frequency and Percentages)}	Total
	Strongly Disagree	Disagree	Neutral	Agree	Strongly Agree	
The Pan Malaysian Islamic Party (PAS)	25 −8.70%	46 −16.00%	102 −35.40%	81 −28.10%	34 −11.80%	288 −100%
The National Trust Party (AMANAH)	4 −4.30%	5 −5.40%	17 −18.30%	37 −39.80%	30 −32.30%	93 −100%
The Muslim Youth Movement of Malaysia (ABIM)	1 −1.20%	7 −8.60%	19 −23.50%	33 −40.70%	21 −25.90%	81 −100%
The Malaysian Muslim Solidarity Front (ISMA)	11 −15.90%	27 −39.10%	18 −26.10%	9 −13.00%	4 −5.80%	69 −100%
Total	41 −7.70%	85 −16.00%	156 −29.40%	160 −30.10%	89 −16.80%	530 −100%

Source: Field Research 2016.

The two positive and negative categories of feedback were combined to produce a more generalised view for each movement, which is summarised as follows:

i   For PAS respondents, 39.9 per cent agreed (in general), followed by 35.4 per cent who were neutral and 24.7 per cent who disagreed (in general).
ii For AMANAH respondents, 72.1 per cent agreed (in general), followed by 23.5 per cent who were neutral and 9.7 per cent who disagreed (in general).
iii For ABIM respondents, 66.6 per cent agreed (in general), followed by 29.9 per cent who were neutral and 9.8 per cent who disagreed (in general).
iv For ISMA respondents, 18.8 per cent agreed (in general), followed by 26.1 per cent who were neutral and 55 per cent who disagreed (in general).

Examining the types of Islamist movements might help highlight some differences amongst the responses. As can be seen from Table 5.2 and its summary, ISMA presents an interesting pattern of reaction as more than half of its members rejected the statement, even though its president generally 'realised' that there should not be any more conflict between Islamists and Nationalists in Malaysia in the future.[16] Meanwhile, AMANAH shows the highest percentage of positive feedback when compared to ABIM and PAS. These findings undoubtedly reflect the variety of current political approaches and the ideologies of each movement as well as the degree of Islamism that has been adopted.[17] Goodwin (2009), in his theory of 'the Adjustment to Change' (ACT), proposed that the personal characteristics of individuals and the nature of events are the predictors of individuals' evaluations of social change. However, based on the findings in this study, the researcher proposes a new criterion, which might also determine the degree of acceptance or evaluation of individuals towards any social change events – this is the group's characteristics: for instance its ideology and political approach. In other words, different movements' ideologies and political approaches might produce different attitudes in respondents. Thus, it is not a surprise to learn that many AMANAH members who embrace the idea of progressive and moderate political Islam support the idea of cooperation between Islamists and non-Islamic-oriented groups. On the other hand, ISMA, a movement which is perceived as quite 'radical' in terms of its relations with secular parties, showed a more negative attitude towards the statement.

Political stability or regime change? The magnitude of stability in Malaysia's current political scenario

The third lesson that can be learned from the Arab Uprisings from the perspective of the sample of Malaysian Islamists is that the importance of maintaining political stability should always be prioritised, even when the country is facing economic crisis and political turmoil. Broadly speaking, the current political situation in Malaysia is relatively stable, although it was previously categorised as a semi-democratic state. To some Malaysians the act of mass street protest is believed to temporarily affect the country's peace and stability, and the normal daily lives of its citizens, such as in the series of Bersih events, when all major roads, public places and buildings were forced to close for several days. If one looks at the post-Arab Uprisings in Libya, Syria and Yemen, the consequences are very serious, with on-going conflicts and wars. These countries were in a relatively better condition before the launch of public protest that later turned into the popular Arab Uprisings phenomenon.

As a response to the question about whether political stability is valued above regime change via street protest, more than half of the respondents (55.4 per cent) preferred to avoid any attempt at political change via street demonstrations for the sake of maintaining the current political stability in

116 Revolution or political stability?

Table 5.3 Respondents' views that political stability is valued above a regime change through street protest

Type of Islamist Movement	Political Stability Is Valued above a Regime Change through Street Protest (Frequency and Percentages)					Total
	Strongly Disagree	Disagree	Neutral	Agree	Strongly Agree	
The Pan Malaysian Islamic Party (PAS)	8 −2.80%	25 −8.70%	87 −30.20%	106 −36.80%	62 −21.50%	288 −100%
The National Trust Party (AMANAH)	12 −12.90%	19 −20.40%	26 −28.00%	24 −25.80%	12 −12.90%	93 −100%
The Muslim Youth Movement of Malaysia (ABIM)	11 −13.60%	8 −9.90%	21 −25.90%	23 −28.40%	18 −22.20%	81 −100%
The Malaysian Muslim Solidarity Front (ISMA)	1 −1.40%	1 −1.40%	18 −26.10%	27 −39.10%	22 −31.90%	69 −100%
Total	32 −6.00%	53 −10.00%	152 −28.60%	180 −33.90%	114 −21.50%	530 −100%

Source: Field Research 2016.

Malaysia. 28.6 per cent of respondents gave a balanced reaction against 16 per cent of 'hardcore' activists who were firmly against the statement. Overall, Table 5.3 indicates that nearly half of the respondents from PAS, ABIM and ISMA favour maintaining political stability, which may indirectly make them less interested in participating in any future street protest that could harm the country's peace. In other words, the post-Arab Uprisings have taught some respondents that political stability is to be prioritised over a regime change through an Arab Uprisings style of street protest.

From Table 5.3, the feedback from respondents based on type of Islamist movements can be summarised as follows:

i   For PAS respondents, 58.3 per cent agreed (in general), followed by 30.2 per cent who were neutral and 11.5 per cent who disagreed (in general).
ii For AMANAH respondents, 38.7 per cent agreed (in general), followed by 28 per cent who were neutral and 33.3 per cent who disagreed (in general).
iii For ABIM respondents, 50.6 per cent agreed (in general), followed by 25.9 per cent who were neutral and 23.5 per cent who disagreed (in general).
iv For ISMA respondents, 71 per cent agreed (in general), followed by 26.1 per cent who were neutral and 2.8 per cent who disagreed (in general).

It is evident from the above data that both ISMA and AMANAH have shown a clear contradictory opinion regarding the issue of street protest (for the purpose of regime change) and the importance of political stability. ISMA seems highly supportive of avoiding political demonstrations for the sake of maintaining political stability in Malaysia, followed by PAS and ABIM. Less than half of AMANAH respondents agreed with the statement. Based on this finding, the researcher assumes that (within the context of lessons learned from the Arab Uprisings) there is a relationship between the stand of Malaysian Islamist movements concerning the act of street protest and how they view the protests' possible effects on political stability. For instance, after the Bersih 3.0 event in 2013, AMANAH was the only Islamist party in Malaysia that continuously participated in a similar style of public protest (Bersih 4.0 and Bersih 5.0) against the ruling regime. Meanwhile, ISMA and PAS (via the voices of their presidents) strongly rejected any street protest action against the government, based on their evaluation of the lessons learned following the Arab Uprisings. As pointed out by Abdullah Zaik (ISMA president):

> I am always against the idea of Islamist movements taking part in BERSIH because they will not get the outcome they wish for. We should think about local politics in Malaysia in the right frame of mind. The current political stability is far better maintained than allowing the potential for chaos to happen. Due to the pluralistic society that we have in Malaysia, I have this concern that a bigger turmoil will take place if the practice of street demonstrations becomes a habit. At another level, without the strong support of Islamist movements in Malaysia, BERSIH (objectives) will not succeed.

Written comments were also left on the questionnaire by respondents from PAS, AMANAH and ISMA to justify why they believed that the Arab Uprisings had taught them to value political stability more so than to promote 'revolution'. All the comments are detailed below:

> The current political situation in Malaysia definitely needs a holistic change. However, the change that is to be made should be done in a proper and organised way to ensure that no one will be affected or harmed as well as to prolong the current political stability.
> (PAS activist)

> Peace and serenity are something that should be maintained. If there would have been a political crisis or chaos in Malaysia, many irresponsible groups or parties would have taken advantage. The level of political maturity amongst Malaysians is also low. Hence their political considerations are always mixed up with emotions without any guidance from religion (Islamic teachings).
> (Shaiful Maszri, AMANAH activist)

The 'Arab Spring' should be wholly exposed to all Malaysian citizens, especially those who are not involved in Islamist movements. This is because any misunderstanding of the 'Arab Spring' could lead to a negative perception towards the existing Islamist movements in Malaysia. It is crucial for Malaysians to realise the value of maintaining political stability in the country.

(Muhammad Azlin, PAS activist)

If the outcome of regime change (via revolution) leads to an uncertainty which will later allow 'foreign' agendas to penetrate the state's sovereignty, then the action for political change must be avoided. Malaysia is a country whereby Islam and the Malays make up its identity. This identity must be retained and respected by every layer of citizen, based on the previous social contract agreement. Malaysia will be able to maintain its stability if these matters are being seriously taken into consideration.

(ISMA youth activist)

Again, from all the comments and the pattern of responses received, the researcher found that group characteristics or approaches might help determine individual perception on certain issues that derived from dramatic social change (i.e. the Arab Uprisings).

Does Malaysia actually need any Arab Uprisings-style revolution?

Despite Malaysia's currently shaky political ground and economic situation, as well as the inspiration (from the Arab Uprisings) that affected the political activism of its Islamist movements (see Chapter 4), it seems that 277 Malaysian Islamists (52.3 per cent) learned from the Arab Uprisings that the country does not need to emulate the Arab Uprisings style of mass protest in order to maintain peace and political stability. For these respondents, the politics and economic conditions in Malaysia are somehow different (and probably better) when compared to those of other countries in the Arab world. Thus, in their eyes, to organise similar protests is pointless. Furthermore, one of the respondents highlighted the fact that Malaysia is currently recognised as a moderate Muslim nation amongst the Organisation of Islamic Cooperation (OIC) members and regarded as such by the Western world. Therefore, any action which could damage this reputation should be avoided. Indeed, many of the angry Arab youths who have taken to the streets to peacefully demand an immediate transformation and regime change may not find many options through which to pursue their aim – except for public protest or revolution.

Developments following the Arab Uprisings in Syria, Libya, Egypt and Yemen have led these respondents to believe that dramatic regime change should include a proper plan in order to avoid any 'anarchism' and political and economic disruption in the future. In contrast, 123 respondents

Table 5.4 Respondents' views that Malaysia does not need any Arab Uprisings-style revolution in the future (based on lessons learned after the Arab Uprisings in the MENA)

Type of Islamist Movement	\multicolumn{5}{c}{Malaysia Does Not Need Any Arab Uprisings-Style Revolution in the Future (Frequency and Percentages)}	Total
	Strongly Disagree	Disagree	Neutral	Agree	Strongly Agree	
The Pan Malaysian Islamic Party (PAS)	17 −5.90%	28 −9.80%	78 −27.20%	88 −30.70%	76 −26.50%	288 −100%
The National Trust Party (AMANAH)	20 −21.50%	28 −30.10%	22 −23.70%	11 −11.80%	12 −12.90%	93 −100%
The Muslim Youth Movement of Malaysia (ABIM)	9 −11.10%	11 −13.60%	19 −23.50%	22 −27.20%	20 −24.70%	81 −100%
The Malaysian Muslim Solidarity Front (ISMA)	1 −1.40%	9 −13.00%	11 −15.90%	21 −30.40%	27 −39.10%	69 −100%
Total	47 −8.90%	76 −14.30%	130 −24.50%	142 −26.80%	135 −25.50%	530 −100%

Source: Field Research 2016.

(23.2 per cent) supported the act of street demonstrations (although not with the same momentum as in the Arab Uprisings) as long as the existing government of Najib Razak remained in power. For them, the act of civil disobedience functions as a checks and balances mechanism to the ruling government in order to improve the quality of democracy. The remaining 130 respondents (24.5 per cent) were neutral towards the statement. Table 5.4 summarises their reactions to the issue of Malaysia and an Arab Uprisings-style revolution.

From Table 5.4, the respondents' reactions regarding the polemics of the 'Malaysian Spring' (based on type of Islamist movements) can be summarised as follows:

i   For PAS respondents, 57.2 per cent agreed (in general) that Malaysia does not need any Arab Uprisings-style revolution in the future, followed by 27.2 per cent who were neutral and 15.7 per cent who disagreed (in general).
ii For AMANAH respondents, 24.7 per cent agreed (in general) that Malaysia does not need any Arab Uprisings-style revolution in the future, followed by 23.7 per cent who were neutral and 51.6 per cent who disagreed (in general).

iii For ABIM respondents, 51.9 per cent agreed (in general) that Malaysia does not need any Arab Uprisings-style revolution in the future, followed by 23.5 per cent who were neutral and 24.7 who disagreed (in general).

iv For ISMA respondents, 69.5 per cent agreed (in general) that Malaysia does not need any Arab Uprisings-style revolution in the future, followed by 15.9 per cent who were neutral and 14.4 per cent who disagreed (in general).

It seems that there are some differences between the four Islamist movements studied as regards the necessity of having an Arab Uprisings-style revolution in the form of public protest or street demonstration in Malaysia. ISMA and AMANAH once again showed noticeably opposite trends in their responses as the former recorded higher percentages of rejection towards the question, while the latter remained firm on supporting the act of civil resistance. As pointed out by Amar Yasier, an ISMA activist[18]:

> Street demonstrations are not seen as a proper way to oust a leader. Malaysians should obey the law of the country. ISMA itself does not encourage any element of ousting rulers through street protests. This may explain why ISMA has never participated in any series of BERSIH.

For PAS and ABIM, more than half of the respondents agreed that the post-Arab Uprisings events have taught them that there is no real urgency for Malaysians, or Islamists, to imitate the protest actions of Arab revolutionaries in 2011 and 2012.

Respondents were also asked whether an attempt at power transfer through acts of civil disobedience and street protest could potentially produce a positive political change. The purpose of this question was to investigate whether the uncertainty factor (from street protests) might serve as the reason why some respondents were sceptical about the polemics of the 'Malaysian Spring'. The respondents' responses can be seen in Table 5.5.

From Table 5.5, the respondents' reactions regarding whether acts of civil disobedience and street protest in Malaysia suggest a positive political transition can be summarised as follows:

i For PAS respondents, 8.3 per cent agreed (in general), followed by 29.5 per cent who were neutral and 62.2 per cent who disagreed (in general).

ii For AMANAH respondents, 15.1 per cent agreed (in general), followed by 43.0 per cent who were neutral and 41.9 per cent who disagreed (in general).

iii For ABIM respondents, 14.8 per cent agreed (in general), followed by 22.2 per cent who were neutral and 62.9 per cent who disagreed (in general).

iv For ISMA respondents, 0.0 per cent agreed (in general), followed by 17.4 per cent who were neutral and 82.6 per cent who disagreed (in general).

Table 5.5 Respondents' views on whether acts of civil disobedience and street protest suggest a positive political transition (based on the lessons learned after the Arab Uprisings in the MENA)

Type of Islamist Movement	Whether Acts of Civil Disobedience and Street Protest Suggest a Positive Political Transition (Frequency and Percentages)					Total
	Strongly Disagree	Disagree	Neutral	Agree	Strongly Agree	
The Pan Malaysian Islamic Party (PAS)	88 −30.60%	91 −31.60%	85 −29.50%	19 −6.60%	5 −1.70%	288 −100%
The National Trust Party (AMANAH)	16 −17.20%	23 −24.70%	40 −43.0%	10 −10.80%	4 −4.30%	93 −100%
The Muslim Youth Movement of Malaysia (ABIM)	24 29.60%	27 −33.30%	18 −22.20%	10 −12.30%	2 −2.50%	81 −100%
The Malaysian Muslim Solidarity Front (ISMA)	29 42.00%	28 −40.60%	12 −17.40%	0 −0.00%	0 −0.00%	69 −100%
Total	157 −29.60%	169 −31.80%	155 −29.20%	39 −7.30%	11 −2.10%	530 −100%

Interestingly, these findings show that the majority of ISMA, ABIM and PAS members are convinced that acts of Arab Uprisings-style street protest do not necessarily produce a positive outcome. For AMANAH, only approximately 42 per cent of members agreed with this popular opinion, while nearly half chose to be neutral. Hence, it seems that some respondents learned from the developments following the Arab Uprisings that power transfer through civil disobedience and street protest does not guarantee a positive political transition. According to ISMA activist Mohd Syafiq[19]:

> In Malaysia, we have a democratic system that chooses leaders through the election. Bringing down leaders through demonstration without proper planning will only invite foreign intervention – if the leaders step down. What worries me is that, if this happens, possibly Malaysia will have to repeat the unfortunate tragedy of the Middle East. Politically speaking, what we see (ISMA) in Malaysia is that the way to change our leaders is not by way of demonstration seeking to oust the leaders, but it is to be done through mature politics. An election is a relevant alternative for now where political parties can influence the people to support the ideas and approaches adopted.

Abdul Hadi Awang, the PAS president, even issued a statement to clarify why PAS rejected any effort to create a Malaysian version of the Arab Uprisings and warned Malaysians about the risk of applying what had been done in the MENA. As analogically stated by Abdul Hadi:

> The fruit yielded from the 'Arab Spring' was more nauseous to the mind and intoxicating to one's sanity, and further destroyed the self-integrity of an Ummah. In Malaysia there is no season named 'spring', there are only rainy and drought seasons. So, don't create this non-existent season here. Wait and istiqamah with Islam, you will be safe and secure; without Islam, one is nothing but condemned.

The findings also indicate that there is a relationship between group characteristics: in this case the political approach of different Islamist movements and the respondents' attitudes towards the issue of a 'Malaysian Spring'. As explained in Chapter 2, over the past few years, the majority of AMANAH members (including a few from ABIM) have still actively participated in a series of mass protests against the ruling regime, encouraged by their movement's leaders. PAS also engaged aggressively in street demonstration activities in Malaysia. However, since the internal split within the party that gave birth to AMANAH in 2015, it changed its approach to mass demonstration activity and refused to join the series of Bersih mass protests in 2015, 2016 and 2017. This decision by the top leadership of PAS has indirectly influenced the way of thinking of the majority of PAS members regarding the polemics of a Malaysian Spring (as can be seen from previous findings).

ISMA, on the other hand, remains firm on its policy of rejecting the act of street protest against the ruling government. To counter the arguments from ISMA, the AMANAH president, Mohamad Sabu, emphasised that such acts should be seen as a relevant platform for Malaysians to voice their 'anger' about corruption amongst civil servants, power abuses by politicians and price hikes in foods and commodities. He also plans to organise another mass demonstration prior to the 14th general election, the date of which has not yet been announced.[20]

The importance of improving the quality of democracy in Malaysia

As stated in Chapter 2, since independence in 1957, Malaysian political leadership has been largely dominated by a coalition government (*Barisan Nasional* or BN), led by representatives of the country's majority Malay Muslim population – the United Malays National Organisation (UMNO). None of the opposition parties, including the Islamists, have ever won in the series of 'first-past-the-post' elections in Malaysia, despite tremendous efforts to break up UMNO and BN domination in the parliament. Some observers, such as Case (1993, 2007), Means (1996) and Abbott (2009, 2011), claim that the Malaysian regime has in some ways systematically manipulated the elections, also instituting other political restrictions in order to remain in power. The current circumstances of political competition are regarded as 'electoral authoritarianism' or semi-democracy.[21] The regime is habitually seen to be giving a false impression that democratic elections are somehow taking place in Malaysia, and the country's politics is moving towards democratic consolidation (Tapsell 2013: 614).

In reality Malaysia is still practising the old style of 'electoral one party dominant' system, which has been criticised by Malaysian academics – Wong et al. (2010: 920) referred to it as an 'act of democracy that never produces democracy'. In other words, these academics stressed that although an election is regarded as an important mechanism for selecting leaders within the prism of democracy, this has never been true in Malaysia. Its democratic status is always plagued by two major issues, which are that: (1) the elections have never been free and fair, and (2) it has not experienced party alternation since 1957 (Wong et al. 2010: 920).

Despite these political circumstances, Liow (2011: 375) argues that the past two decades have witnessed the proliferation of Islamist political parties in Malaysia, which have committed themselves to engagement in the political process, including elections. It seems that most (if not all) Malaysian Islamists still value the purpose of an election for power politics and political change. Within the context of lessons learned from the Arab Uprisings, the respondents were asked whether an election is considered as a relevant medium to determine the direction of Malaysian political leadership, given that street demonstrations inspired by the Arab Uprisings have recently gained momentum as an alternative process (to end the long dominance of UMNO and the BN regime).

Out of 530 Malaysian Islamist politicians, activists and supporters from PAS, ABIM, ISMA and AMANAH who responded to the question, 146 (27.5 per cent) strongly supported the proposition that a democratic political system and associated elections are the best medium through which to determine the future of political change in Malaysia. Two hundred and seventeen respondents (40.9 per cent) shared a similar (but less strong) opinion. One hundred and twenty-four respondents (23.4 per cent) had a neutral feeling, while 38 respondents (7.2 per cent) disagreed with the statement. Only six respondents (1.1 per cent) completely rejected democracy and the electoral system as a vehicle for political transition in Malaysia. Table 5.6 presents the specific pattern of reactions to the question from different Islamist movements.

From Table 5.6, it is clear that each Islamist movements recorded more than half of its sample (ABIM = 82.7 per cent; AMANAH = 75.1 per cent; PAS = 63.9 per cent; ISMA = 60.8 per cent) as supporting a democratic political system and elections as a relevant option to 'topple' the current regime of Najib Razak in Malaysia. As explained by a few random respondents (via written comments on the questionnaire), there are several reasons why democracy and elections are still preferred, especially when

Table 5.6 Respondents' views on whether democracy and elections are the best medium for political change in Malaysia (based on lessons learned following the Arab Uprisings in the MENA)

Type of Islamist Movement	Whether Democracy and Elections Are the Best Medium for Political Change in Malaysia (Frequency and Percentages)					Total
	Strongly Disagree	Disagree	Neutral	Agree	Strongly Agree	
The Pan Malaysian Islamic Party (PAS)	5 −1.70%	17 −5.90%	82 −28.50%	108 −37.50%	76 −26.40%	288 −100%
The National Trust Party (AMANAH)	1 −1.10%	6 −6.50%	16 −17.20%	37 −39.80%	33 −35.30%	93 −100%
The Muslim Youth Movement of Malaysia (ABIM)	0 0.00%	2 −2.50%	12 −14.80%	41 −50.60%	26 −32.10%	81 −100%
The Malaysian Muslim Solidarity Front (ISMA)	0 0.00%	13 −18.80%	14 −20.30%	31 −44.90%	11 −15.90%	69 −100%
Total	6 −1.10%	38 −7.20%	124 −23.40%	217 −40.90%	146 −27.50%	530 −100%

Source: Field Research 2016.

the developments following the Arab Uprisings in the MENA are taken into consideration. Among the reasons mentioned were:

> The changes that suit Malaysia's *waqi'* (political context) are through elections. The operation of Islamist movements should consider the *waqi'* of the specific country.
>
> (PAS activist)

> The best way to 'topple' the BN & UMNO regime is through elections, not street rallies or demonstrations
>
> (Wan Mohd Nurmisuari, PAS activist)

> The 'Arab Spring' events were one manifestation of the failure of democratic principles (in involved states). Malaysia has to ensure its democratic principles are being respected and productive despite not going through the same type of mass movements as during the Arab Spring.
>
> (Ramdani, ABIM activist)

> The Islamist movements in Malaysia should be more serious in facing the question of democracy as part of change in wider Malaysian politics. Democracy needs to be seen as a tool (to obtain power) rather than a goal.
>
> (Nik Abdul Razak, AMANAH Youth activist)

In addition, speaking about elections, the ISMA president, Abdullah Zaik, seems to support a voting mechanism, provided that it is within the framework of political Islam. He is optimistic that there will be a political change in Malaysia in the future; he predicts the fall of the UMNO party (which currently leads the government) but not through mass uprisings. According to him[22]:

> In Malaysia, will UMNO decline? My answer will be that UMNO will come to its end one day. But will it take the way of the Arab Spring revolution? My answer will be, not at all. An election is a good alternative and is accepted in Islam because it gives opportunity and space to make changes harmoniously. But it must move within the political Islam framework. Whatever changes are done must be within a strategic framework where, in effect, it will not lead to collapse as we have seen happening in (some of) the Arab countries.

Overall, given the context in the Middle East following the Arab Uprisings, support for electoral democracy is the most likely scenario for the future of political activism for Malaysia's Islamist movements. The survey found that Malaysian Islamist activists and politicians opted for democracy and elections as their preferred means, rather than mass uprisings or street protests.

Making sense of the 'Malaysian Spring' polemics: reality or fallacy?

Are the series of protest events organised by the Coalition for Clean and Fair Election movement (Bersih) seen as an indirect effort to create a 'Malaysian Spring' in Malaysia?[23] At the beginning of the book, the researcher highlighted some polemics about the potential for a 'Malaysian Spring' to occur in the future due to the series of civil resistance actions launched by the Bersih between 2011 and November 2016. In 2013, prior to the 13th general election, there was also a campaign called the 'Malaysian Spring' initiated by local Malaysian activists as a symbol to spread the message of hope and get people to participate in the process of political change. According to Barnes (2013), after the 2013 election, in response to alleged government election fraud, a coalition of opposition parties in Malaysia has continued the Malaysian Spring campaign to pressure the ruling government. As a result a number of pro-government politicians and some local and foreign journalists accused these demonstrations and the campaign of being a type of indirect effort to topple the existing regime (which could also be considered a 'Malaysian Spring' as per the 'Arab Spring' uprisings).[24]

Aidila Razak, a Malaysian journalist who is currently based at the *Malaysiakini* online news portal, stated that the term 'Malaysian Spring' was used as a symbol of Malaysia's 'Awakening' – a campaign that had 'a life' during the 13th general election.[25] Such comments led Barnes (2013) to assume that the Malaysian regime feared that use of 'Spring' amongst protesters could

Table 5.7 Respondents' views on whether the series of protest events organised by the Bersih were an indirect effort to create a 'Malaysian Spring'

Type of Islamist Movement	Whether the Series of Protest Events Organised by the Bersih Were an Indirect Effort to Create a 'Malaysian Spring' (Frequency and Percentages)					Total
	Strongly Disagree	Disagree	Neutral	Agree	Strongly Agree	
The Pan Malaysian Islamic Party (PAS)	28 −9.70%	52 −18.10%	103 −35.80%	81 −28.10%	24 −8.30%	288 −100%
The National Trust Party (AMANAH)	19 −20.40%	25 −26.90%	17 −18.30%	23 −24.70%	9 −9.70%	93 −100%
The Muslim Youth Movement of Malaysia (ABIM)	12 −14.80%	15 −18.50%	12 −14.80%	23 −28.40%	19 −23.50%	81 −100%
The Malaysian Muslim Solidarity Front (ISMA)	4 −5.80%	11 −15.90%	22 −31.90%	20 −29.00%	12 −17.40%	69 −100%
Total	63 −11.90%	103 −19.40%	154 −29.00%	147 −27.70%	64 −12.10%	530 −100%

Source: Field Research 2016.

potentially be linked to a conspiracy by opposition parties to overthrow the government through violent street demonstrations – although the Prime Minister, Najib Razak, declared that the government was not afraid of any kind of 'Malaysian Spring'.[26]

The findings from this research indicate that 154 respondents (some of whom admitted that they had participated in past Bersih demonstrations) were not certain whether the efforts by the movement should be viewed as an attempt to create a 'Malaysian Spring'. However, 211 respondents felt that it somehow tried to launch an Arab Uprisings-style protest in Malaysia, although there is no solid evidence to support this view – hence its rejection by 166 respondents. Table 5.7 records responses regarding the polemics of the 'Malaysian Spring'.

From Table 5.7, the respondents' reactions regarding the polemics of the 'Malaysian Spring' (based on type of Islamist movements) can be summarised as follows:

i For PAS respondents, 36.4 per cent agreed (in general), followed by 35.8 per cent who were neutral and 27.8 per cent who disagreed (in general).
ii For AMANAH respondents, 34.4 per cent agreed (in general), followed by 18.3 per cent who were neutral and 47.3 per cent who disagreed (in general).

iii For ABIM respondents, 51.9 per cent agreed (in general), followed by 14.8 per cent who were neutral and 33.3 per cent who disagreed (in general).
iv For ISMA respondents, 46.4 per cent agreed (in general), followed by 31.9 per cent who were neutral and 21.7 per cent who disagreed (in general).

As can be seen in Table 5.7, the number of respondents who supported the idea that the Bersih movements were a continuation of an 'Arab Uprisings-style protest version' in Malaysia was quite low. Only ABIM recorded more than 50 per cent of respondents as having a positive attitude to the question. When respondents were asked whether an 'Arab-Uprisings' style of street protest or revolution would take place in Malaysia in the future (based on the current political and economic situation), most of them (184) were not certain, followed by the same number of respondents who disagreed. Those remaining (163) were positive that 'Malaysian Spring' uprisings would take place in the country in the future, depending on political and economic conditions. The respondents mentioned many reasons for supporting their opinion on 'Malaysian Spring' polemics.[27] As pointed out by Amran Shamsuddin (AMANAH activist):

> The possibility of having an 'Arab Spring' style revolution in Malaysia is too small. This is due to the changing nature of current Malaysian generations - a number of youths and young people appear to be politically apathetic'.

PAS activist, Shafiq, referred to one verse in the Quran to support his opinion that the polemics of the 'Malaysian Spring' are very unlikely to take place in Malaysia in the future:

> ... 'And if they incline to peace, then incline to it [also] and rely upon Allah. Indeed, it is He who is the Hearing, the Knowing.' (Surah Al-Anfal 61). This is the verse from the Quran to support my argument that there will be no kind of 'Arab Spring' revolution in Malaysia. Malaysia still upholds a peaceful democratic system.

Moreover, one of the respondents from ABIM suggested that any action or attempt for political change via revolution should consider all the potential negative consequences, and Islamists should first seek guidance or advice from Muslim clerics (Ulama) before undertaking such actions:

> The 'Arab Spring' was a losing movement because many people died while attempting to overthrow the regime. Ulama (Muslim scholars) thought to protect our souls instead of involving us in war. These events

(the 'Arab Spring' revolutions) brought more backfire than benefits. The ABIM movement moves forward by promoting a culture of learning and finding knowledge. Malaysian Muslims and Islamists should always refer to Muslim scholars (fatwa) before undertaking any political action that involves the fate of Ummah.

Meanwhile, another ABIM activist, Abd Rahman, believed that the condition of any mass uprising is influenced by surrounding (internal) factors relevant to specific places or states. Thus, he felt that it would be difficult to create the exact situation of the Arab Uprisings in Malaysia, even if for the same purpose (of toppling a corrupted regime). His views were supported by an Islamist counterpart from AMANAH, who points out that:

> The situation in Malaysia is different with that of the Arab Middle East world. It can be seen from a variety of angles - economics, culture, demography, thought and international and geopolitical influence. Having said that, current movements (Islamist) are not necessarily bound to follow what happened in the Arab states in Malaysia.

During an interview with the former PAS activist, Muhammad Najib, who left the party to join AMANAH in 2015, he emphasised that revolution or a 'Malaysian Spring' will never take place in Malaysia due to local values of peace and moderation, which are embedded within the attitudes of the majority of Malaysians. He also confirmed that only during Bersih 3.0 in 2013 was there a moment when protesters were perhaps close to toppling the regime. However, the outcome was not produced what most participants had expected – to have a holistic political change in Malaysia. As stated by Najib[28]:

> Actually, when talking about street demonstrations in Malaysia, I have the view that revolution will not happen. If there is a revolution, it should have happened in 1998 during the *reformasi* protests because that was the best moment to bring down BN and for revolution to take place, but in the end it did not happen. This may be because of the eastern values to which Malaysian society has been so accustomed - the tendency towards peace and stability. Thus, it is quite impossible for the (political) revolution to happen. In addition is the fact that most demonstrators will normally come home after a hard day on the street and continue to live their normal lives the next day.

Moreover, Najib also touched upon other factors that might 'prevent' 'Arab Spring'-style protests' being launched in Malaysia:

> For the Arab Uprisings style of street protest, I think that this would be hard to do in Malaysia. The Prime Minister Najib Razak will not be defeated from the streets. However, if I was asked if these mass protests

(Bersih events) can get to the level of the 'Arab Spring', I feel that Bersih 3.0 is the last mass protest that almost affected the BN government. I also took part in Bersih 3.0. I admit that the Malaysian government is still at the level of semi-democracy. Nevertheless, no matter how bad the (Malaysian) government currently is, I personally feel that street protests in Malaysia will not be like the 'Arab Spring'. Additionally, after the Peaceful Gathering Act was introduced, there are no more obstacles for people to demonstrate against. Finally, people's mood to fight against the government has taken a dive. The political turmoil among the opposition parties also makes the people tired. The role of social media has given birth to a lot of keyboard warriors voicing their rights clearly, where they change the platform from street protests to the virtual world. The factors stated above may support the view that the 'Arab Spring' will not be happening in Malaysia.

These points about cultural aspects were also echoed by Amar Yasier, an ISMA activist, who stated that[29]:

It may happen (the Malaysian Spring) but it will not work out. The culture of rebellion is not the culture of the general public in Malaysia. It is difficult to ask the majority of people to take part in the same protest. Organisers or demonstrators may be able to gather a lot of people, but I am of the opinion that they may find it hard or may not be successful in defeating the regime in this way.

What is perhaps most vital about the polemics of the 'Malaysian Spring', as critically voiced by the ISMA president, is the different level of 'suffering' between Malaysians and Arab nations; this might explain why no Arab Uprisings style of revolution will take place in Malaysia. Interestingly, Abdullah Zaik based his argument on Machiavelli's theory on revolution as he felt that the situation in the Arab states appeared to match with the theory's assumption. In the words of Abdullah Zaik (ISMA president)[30]:

Earlier on, ISMA saw the 'Arab Spring' or that particular term 'Spring' as inaccurate because it did not reflect a hopeful, promising season which is generally associated with a good ending. This does not happen in the post-'Arab Spring'. The Arab Uprisings have taken place in Arab countries due to the fact that dictatorship rule reached a level where every individual in the community was threatened and suffering. This does not happen in Malaysia. In Malaysia even though we have cases of fraud and corruption and cruelty by the ruling power we have not reached the point where the authority breaks into individual homes, disturbing wives and children and killing them (as happened in Egypt and Syria). According to Machiavelli's revolutionary theory, a revolution will take place if the situation becomes this severe. For example, in Indonesia, Iran and Egypt, the secret police at one time were very active and rampant. In Egypt, the relationship between the government and the people seems non-existent to the point that the police would kill a civilian without feeling guilty, as was reported to have happened to Khaled Said. When the police act to this extreme, it has become the pretext for a revolution.

The ISMA president also used his experience of visiting Egypt to support his argument that Malaysia does not need to 'import' the elements of Arab Revolutions for the sake of political change. He said:

> When I was in Egypt in 2006, I managed to ask the public about the current situation (social and political) in Cairo. The feedback I received was that the people there had expected that in five years there would be uproar among the people and an uprising would be impending. This is really happening. In Malaysia, from the perspective of Fiqh or political Islam, the (political) change that is to be done must be in a framework that is easy to control. This means that we are able to control anything bad that might happen. For instance, with the fall of the dictator or leader, what is the advantage that can be achieved? We should consider the graver consequences should a leader be overthrown (as compared to if he stays). Thus, ISMA does not see that importing the Arab Revolutions is something positive. In making any change, we have to refer to our own capabilities when it comes to deciding on any political action.

From the comments voiced by respondents, it is clear that many Islamist movement members, activists, politicians and supporters in Malaysia are quite sceptical or neutral about the polemics of the 'Malaysian Spring'. Most of them simply disagreed (or neither disagreed nor agreed) that the series of Bersih demonstrations were an indirect effort to topple the ruling government (in a similar way to the Arab Uprisings), as had been suggested by several pro-government media outlets, politicians and authorities in Malaysia. Moreover, the arguments put forward by some respondents – that a revolution similar to the Arab Uprisings would be very unlikely in Malaysia – seem sensible, particularly if one refers to a number of notions or assumptions in the Theory of Revolution, specifically as regards revolutionary movements and their prospects for success. In 1989, Jeff Goodwin and Theda Skocpol insisted that the nature of quasi-democracy in Malaysia has not facilitated the growth of revolutionary coalitions in the country. They further explained why some 'inclusionary' authoritarian regimes, such as Malaysia, are immune to revolutionary movements, which can be seen in the following quote:

> Although these regimes lack of civil rights, they either sponsor mass political mobilization or regulate the official representation of, and

bargaining among, various social groups, including working class and other lower strata groups. They impose controlled forms of political participation on key social groups, co-opting leaders and handing out certain benefits in the process; this tends to undercut possibilities for political action independent of the existing regime.

(Goodwin & Skocpol 1989: 495–496)

At present, Malaysia does not seem to be the type of regime that is vulnerable to the emergence of revolutionary movements and revolutionary coalitions, let alone ready to be overthrown by revolutionaries. Furthermore, its Islamist movements appear to lack the characteristics of successful revolutionary movements, such as those that emerged in Iran, Nicaragua and the Philippines in the 1970s through the 1990s. Those characteristics for success, as suggested by Foran (1992: 255) and Lane (2009: 113), involved a united and organised opposition with an alternative ideology and political policy – which the Bersih movement in Malaysia is currently lacking.

Ennahda's perspectives on the findings

During the winter of 2018, the researcher managed to conduct face-to-face interviews with four key figures of the Ennahda movement in Tunisia regarding several outcomes of the study, particularly concerning the impact of the Arab Uprisings on political activism and the approaches of Islamist movements in Malaysia, the issues of 'Malaysian Spring' polemics and the Arab Spring's lessons (see findings in Chapters 3 and 4). The responses received from those interviewees stressed that the Tunisian revolutionaries and the government formed after the uprisings never once intended to 'export' the so-called 'Jasmine Revolution' or 'Arab Spring' to other countries (which contrasts with the 1979 Iranian Revolution). Regarding the question about the impact of the Arab Uprisings, particularly as concerns Ennahda's recent experiences with other Islamist movements and political parties,[31] Ghannouchi responded as follows:

> Our (Jasmine Revolution) experience was a local experience. We do not have any ambition to export our experiences (to any other countries). Every Muslim country has a full right and even a duty to make and discover the local solution between Islam and realities, between Islam and the milieu and the problems currently in place. Despite the fact that Muslims generally believe in the same Islam, the religion has been (mistakenly) interpreted in many ways which has led to the current realities where Islam and Islamism appear (to the Muslim rulers) to have many sorts of ideologies and policies. Since the problems and situations are different between Malaysia, Egypt and Tunisia for instance… all Muslims (particularly Muslim politicians) in their countries need to rethink and understand their own situation. They need to read the

Quran and think deeply about their realities and try to make a sort of 'marriage' (solution) between Islam and the local realities for the benefit of the people.

From Ghannouchi's perspective, it is clear that there is emphasis on local circumstances and the correct interpretation of Islam that first must be properly addressed by Muslims (including those in Malaysia) before it can be influenced and infused by the so-called 'Arab Spring' phenomenon. His opinion is in line with several respondents from PAS and ABIM, who noted the different political and economic situations in Malaysia and the Middle East (e.g. Tunisia), which led the Malaysian Islamists to view the phenomenon of the 2011 Arab Uprisings in the local context as lessons rather than a 'direction'.

Naoufel Eljammali[32] further clarifies the reason why Tunisia (and Ennahda in particular) is reluctant to export its post-'Arab Spring' experiences to other countries, such as Malaysia (with its Islamist movements). As explained by Eljammali:

> Because we are a very small state… we are not very enthusiastic to export any political experience (of the post-Jasmine Revolution) outside the country as it will cause us harm and lots of problem. But we are telling the world that we are here and standing for democracy, good governance and economic reform. Of course, we are willing to share some ideas, some principles and thoughts with Malaysian Islamists, but without any intention to export anything from Tunisia. You cannot dissociate the idea of the Jasmine Revolution from the Ennahda party. We were one of the main political parties which was standing before the revolution and standing for democracy. And (for) other countries maybe they cannot understand and dissociate our experience from the idea of revolution itself. That is why we are very careful with this kind of tendency which can push us to give the (false) impression that we are showing lessons to the world and exporting a kind of revolutionary idea. We must confess that what we are doing within the Ennahda party (as a Muslim political party) is 'revolutionary'. And as I mentioned earlier it will be very good to share with other political parties (which are near to us in terms of identity, ideas, thoughts and principles) the best way to deal with political reform and so on.

Although Eljammali personally argues that Tunisia should not and will not externally export its 'revolutionary' experience, it is clear that the Jasmine Revolution has already indirectly caused a great snowballing effect amongst neighbouring countries, such that the region erupted into the so-called 'Arab Spring'. Despite Ennahda's willingness to share ideas and thoughts that might benefit other political parties and groups outside Tunisia, it seems that PAS, ABIM, ISMA and AMANAH (as prominent

Islamist movements in Malaysia) have already observed and learned several significant lessons from the Arab Uprisings phenomenon and the political 'journey' of Ennahda itself. Regarding those lessons, Rafek Abdessalem[33] (former Tunisian Minister of Foreign Affairs) has emphasised that Malaysian Islamist parties must cooperate with other non-Islamic-oriented political parties (e.g. Secularist, Nationalist) and not 'work in silo' for the benefit of the heterogeneous population in Malaysia. According to him:

> One of the main lessons from our experience is the need to work with other political forces. Because a major threat for political stability and democratic process is ideological or ethnic or religious polarisation. When you have a diversified society or population like in Malaysia, there is a need for Muslims and non-Muslims to work together... there is a need for moderates, Islamists and secularists to work together. This is very essential for any modern society, because there are no political forces that have the ability to manage any political situation by themselves. Take for example in Tunisia, we have a long legacy of political failure, economic crisis and external intervention in our political affairs. So, there is a strong need for different ideological political forces to have a united front in favour of economic and political reform – as can be seen in our current coalition government.

Osama al-Saghir, an Ennahda member of parliament, further commented on the significance of political strategy and preparation to govern – which was perceived as one of the lessons learned by Malaysian Islamists. He seems antipathetic to those conservative Islamists who were using and manipulating religion for personal political mileage. Instead, he insists that Islamists, whether they are from moderate, conservative or Nationalist parties and organisations, should put tremendous effort and determination into offering real political and socio-economic reform that will eventually benefit citizens. According to al-Saghir[34]:

> Us, as Islamist or Muslim politicians, sometimes we are too theoretical, playing with the image of Islam and less its practise...sometimes the Islamists go to the streets and make mistakes in the name of Islam. For instance, someone who says: 'you have to vote for me, because I am trying to implement the words of Allah (via sharia law)'. This is wrong. People should not vote for an Islamist because he chooses Islam. Instead, they should view the capacity of the Islamist in delivering a noble agenda for the benefit of the people. And this may seem the hard way. Sometimes an Islamist chooses to go the easy way by saying 'vote for me because I am a Muslim and representing the Islamic agenda'. The truth is, you are not going to represent the Islamic agenda by words... it has to be by facts, real projects and real efforts.

Concerning the lessons derived from the 2013 Egyptian coup and the FJP's experiences, Eljammali agrees that Malaysian Islamists should avoid any attempt to concentrate power in their party's own hands and implement aggressive change or reform in politics, economics and society (if ever given the opportunity to govern a state).

Another issue discussed during the researcher's fieldwork in Tunisia was how the post-Arab Uprisings developments have strengthened the cooperation between Malaysian Islamist movements and Arab Islamist parties (e.g. Ennahda). 71.5 per cent of respondents (see Chapter 4) agreed that the relationship between Islamist movements in Malaysia and those in the Middle East had been enhanced since the 2011 political transition. Abdessalem[35] acknowledged this finding by saying:

> Since we are now a legal political entity in Tunisia, and part of the Tunisian coalition government, we are very keen to consolidate the already established relationship with our 'friends' and 'brothers' in Malaysia based on a national political agenda. We have recently sent our delegation (including myself and Ghannouchi) to Malaysia to meet with Abdul Hadi Awang, the PAS President for the purpose of exchanging ideas and experiences. We are also in favour of having constructive cooperation with other political forces such as with the ruling party (UMNO) and opposition parties in Malaysia. We have to be open to other political forces (apart from Islamists), either in the Middle East or Asia.

Although aware of the polemics of the 'Malaysian Spring' (along with the fact that 49.9 per cent of respondents were inspired by the act of mass street protest during the Arab Uprisings), Abdessalem disagrees with the idea of Malaysian political activists and opposition politicians emulating the 2011 revolution (as previously expressed through Bersih demonstrations). Whilst he admits that Malaysia is not an ideal example of democracy since the country is ruled by a 'dictatorship' (or at least a competitive autocratic regime), he points out that there is no real urgency for Malaysians to launch a revolution against the current ruling regime since political parties and civil society in Malaysia are still given a reasonable space to operate and participate in politics and elections – which is better than in Arab states before the 2011 revolution.

With respect to the issues concerning Daesh, Abdessalem (as a representative of Ennahda) explicitly highlights the fact that the party refuses to acknowledge any conspiracy theories (concerning the role of the United States, Israel or Iran and Daesh), as were previously claimed by the PAS and ISMA presidents, by some respondents. Instead, Ennahda sees the emergence of Daesh as by-product of the political mess, political crisis and sectarian division in the Arab region, especially following the civil war in Iraq.

In short, despite being somehow influenced by the Arab Uprisings as well as inspired by the wave of Islamism and the success of Ennahda since Ben

Ali's departure in 2011, the Malaysian Islamist movements appear to hold some views different from those of the Tunisian Islamist party. In this sense, it shows that Islamist movements and parties, from one country to another, are diverse in practice – primarily due to differences in local context. Nevertheless, Ennahda has accepted what the PAS, ABIM, ISMA and AMANAH Islamists learned from their experiences and the Arab Uprisings phenomenon in a positive way, which indirectly consolidated the relationship between Islamist politics in Malaysia and those in Tunisia (and possibly elsewhere in the Arab world).

Conclusion and summary

The main goal of this chapter was to investigate the lessons learned by respondents from the four main Islamist movements in Malaysia about developments following the Arab Uprisings in the MENA. Through his fieldwork the researcher established five main lessons from the Arab Uprisings within the context of the development of Malaysia's Islamist movements. The lessons from the Arab Uprisings (derived mainly from the experiences of Islamist parties in the Arab world) were analysed based on respondents' feedback to several diverse questions as well as a number of in-depth interviews with movement leaders and activists. Indeed, the survey found that more than 70 per cent of respondents from each of the Malaysian Islamist movements being studied had a positive attitude towards the development of Arab Islamist parties and recent political circumstances in the Middle East (after the Arab Uprisings), believing that these had taught them valuable lessons. A summary of the five main lessons is highlighted in the following paragraphs.

The first lesson is that Islamist parties in Malaysia need to improve their political strategy in order to survive in the Malaysian political game. As mentioned by the ISMA president, in terms of political operations, the Islamist movements in Malaysia (and in other parts of the world) need to learn from each other's experiences before attempting to hold political power. Among the specific strategies suggested by respondents are: (1) The Islamist parties and movements in Malaysia should develop a 'manifesto' that proposes a comprehensive economic model that seeks to benefit all citizens. Respondents suggest that failure to do so will reflect upon the competency of Islamists to govern the state in the long run; (2) The Islamist parties and movements in Malaysia need to have undertaken solid preparation and have proper plans in place before (and after) assuming power from the incumbent government. Any agenda for political change must be fully considered in terms of short- and long-term consequences. Most importantly, Islamists must develop their own strengths and approaches when facing pressures from citizens as well as foreign parties. This lesson, as explained by respondents, derived primarily from the tragic case of the Egyptian Muslim Brotherhood during the June 2013 military takeover.

The second lesson is that in order to attract strong support from the different layers of society, the Islamist movements in Malaysia must not 'work alone'. Instead, they should have thoughtful cooperation with other non-Islamic-oriented groups and parties that exist in their country. The study found that 46.9 per cent of Malaysian Islamist respondents from PAS, ABIM, ISMA and AMANAH learned from the development of Islamist parties after the Arab Uprisings (especially the Egyptian Muslim Brotherhood and the Tunisian Ennahda) that collaboration between Islamist movements/parties and non-Islamic-oriented political parties and organisations (for instance the Nationalists and Secularists) might contribute to stability in the current political situation in Malaysia. In terms of responses from specific movements, 72.1 per cent of respondents from AMANAH showed tremendous support for the proposition of establishing a positive relationship with non-Islamists in Malaysia, compared to 66.6 per cent of ABIM and 39.9 per cent of PAS respondents. Meanwhile, only 18.8 per cent of ISMA members considered cooperation with non-Islamists as something positive. For the researcher this variation in feedback undoubtedly reflects the role of group characteristics, with a movement's political approach and ideology influencing individual perceptions about certain political issues. In other words, Islamist movements, such as AMANAH and ABIM, that express a progressive and moderate political approach are more likely to cooperate with non-Islamic-oriented parties in Malaysia, than ISMA and PAS, which strongly uphold the agenda of political Islam.

The third lesson from the Arab Uprisings phenomenon is that political stability should always be prioritised and maintained above any unplanned actions for regime change through revolution or street protest. The study found that 55.4 per cent of respondents, mainly from ISMA and PAS, preferred to avoid any attempt to overthrow the regime through revolution – for the sake of maintaining the current political stability. Almost half of ABIM respondents also agreed with the above statement, while fewer than 40 per cent of AMANAH respondents responded in a similar way. Some respondents stated that the 'failures' following the Arab Uprisings in Syria, Libya, Egypt and Yemen had taught them to value political stability more than to promote revolution. Interestingly, it does seem that the stance of Malaysia's Islamist movements on the act of street demonstration has been indirectly inculcated into respondents' attitudes, although there were some who did not conform with the party position.

The fourth lesson is that in order to promote a peaceful and effective political transition Malaysians in general and Islamists in particular do not necessarily need to apply the Arab Uprisings style of revolution as a method for 'toppling' the current ruling regime. More than half of respondents from ISMA, PAS and ABIM supported the statement that acts of civil disobedience and street protests do not suggest a positive political change, whilst approximately the same percentage of AMANAH respondents rejected the proposition. The reason for this difference (as previously explained) lies in the movement's stand on participation in street demonstrations. ISMA and PAS clearly rejected the act of street protest as a method for overthrowing a ruling regime, as based on statements from their leaders. AMANAH, on the other hand, remains consistent in encouraging its members to take to the streets for the sake of ending the long 'semi-democratic' rule of the UMNO and BN in Malaysia.

The fifth lesson from the Arab Uprisings is that improving the quality of democracy in Malaysia should be highly valued, given the fact that the old-fashioned political system – commonly known amongst academics as 'semi-democracy' or 'electoral authoritarianism' – is still in place. Although the act of street protest has recently gained impetus in pressuring the ruling regime, it is evident that the majority (68.4 per cent) of respondents prefer an election as the practical medium for political change in Malaysia. There were a number of reasons given by respondents to support this argument. One was that an election is seen as a constructive alternative for political change that is suitable to Malaysia's political environment and in line with the principle of Islamic teaching that emphasises the element of citizens' freedom to elect their leader. No significant conflict emerged between the four Islamist movements in the research since the majority (more than 60 per cent) showed tremendous support for democracy and elections.

Finally, there are the issues of the 'Malaysian Spring' campaign and its connection with the series of mass demonstrations popularly known as Bersih, which journalists and government authorities suggested were an attempt to topple the regime through 'Arab Spring'-style uprisings. These polemics seem to unfold when significant numbers of Malaysian Islamist activists and politicians (who also participated in such mass protests) remained neutral or disagreed with such claims. Only 39.8 per cent of respondents believed that the act of civil disobedience organised through the Bersih was a reflection of indirect efforts to create a 'Malaysian Spring'. Some respondents also predicted that there would be no Arab Uprisings-style revolution taking place in Malaysia in the future. They suggested that this was due to the different political, economic and social circumstances in Malaysia as compared to those in the MENA countries. Moreover, an analysis from the perspective of the Theory of Revolution suggested to the researcher that Malaysia's Islamist movements lacked the attributes of a successful revolutionary movement (such as that which existed in Iran during the 1979 Iranian Revolution). Hence, the polemics of a 'Malaysian Spring' are determined to be fallacy rather than reality.

Notes

1 Personal interview with a PAS activist (name withheld at interviewee's request), Kuala Lumpur, Malaysia. 19 September 2016.
2 Personal interview with an ABIM activist, Adnan. Shah Alam, Malaysia. 29 October 2016.
3 During an interview with Osama al-Saghir (Ennahda member and Tunisian MP), he explains that for many years before the revolution, most Tunisians

138 Revolution or political stability?

and secular politicians could not differentiate between radical Islamist groups who adopted violence (e.g. Taliban, Al-Qaeda) and moderate Muslim parties who supported democracy. Thus, after the revolution, with more freedom of speech and expression, Ennahda decided to clarify its identity as a moderate, conservative and democratic Muslim party in Tunisia.

4 Ghannouchi's statement (published via his official Facebook account) on the idea of 'Muslim Democrat' as a new identity of Ennahda during the party's 10th Congress in Tunis, May 2016. www.facebook.com/rached.ghannoushi/?ref=br_rs [19 October 2017].

5 Personal interview with member of Ennahda Political Bureau, Naoufel Eljammali. Tunis, Tunisia. January 2018.

6 After Morsi won the presidential election, despite reminders by the moderates to tread carefully, many of the leading members of the Muslim Brotherhood invoked a 'historical imperative' to start an 'Islamic Enlightenment' project. The seeds for the coup on 3 July 2013 against Mohamed Morsi and the subsequent ban on the Muslim Brotherhood were sown by their attempt to implement the Islamisation policy without dealing effectively with socio-economic problems. This allowed the intelligence and military under the old Mubarak regime to take advantage of the ensuing anti-Morsi and anti-Muslim Brotherhood sentiments to regain power in one fell swoop under the pretext of saving the revolution from the Islamists. For more details see Khaled Abou El Fadl. (2015). Failure of a Revolution: The Military, Secular Intelligentsia and Religion in Egypt's Pseudo-Secular State. In Sadiki, Larbi (ed.), *Routledge Handbook of the Arab Spring*. London: Routledge, pp. 253–269.

7 An AMANAH activist, Mohamad's written opinion/comment on the questionnaire.

8 Personal interview with the ISMA president. Bangi, Malaysia. 5 November 2016.

9 An AMANAH activist, Nik Abdul Razak's written opinion/comment on the questionnaire.

10 The disagreement on political Islam (Sharia Law or Hudud) was considered as one of the reasons that caused a series of tensions between Malaysian Islamists (PAS and ISMA) and secularists (UMNO and DAP), which led PAS to break off ties at the national level with UMNO in 1977 and the Democratic Action Party (DAP) in 2015.

11 See, for example, the list of media statements on scores of issues by Malaysia's 'Liberal Islamic Group', the Sisters in Islam, against Malaysian Islamist parties and authority bodies. www.sistersinislam.org.my/news.php?cat.27.

12 See Ghannouchi's official Facebook timeline. www.facebook.com/rached.ghannoushi/photos/a.176765715693374.28928.175565099146769/1657945594242038/?type=3&theater.

13 Written opinion/comment on the questionnaire by an AMANAH women activist.

14 Written opinion/comment on the questionnaire by an AMANAH activist.

15 Written opinion/comment on the questionnaire by Razali Saleh, an ABIM activist.

16 Personal interview with the ISMA president. Bangi, November 2016.

17 See Chapter 2 for details of PAS, ABIM, ISMA and AMANAH Islamist ideologies and political approaches.

18 Personal interview with The International Relations Bureau for ISMA's UK branch, Amar Yasier. London, United Kingdom. 10 June 2016.

19 Personal interview with ISMA activist, Mohd Syafiq. ISMA Head Office. Bangi, Malaysia. August 2016.

20 Predeep Nambiar (2017). Mat Sabu: Mari Lepas Geram di Himpunan Rakyat Marah (Mat Sabu: Let's Release Our Anger at the People's Anger Rally) Free Malaysia Today. www.freemalaysiatoday.com/category/bahasa/2017/01/10/mat-sabu-mari-lepas-geram-di-himpunan-rakyat-marah/ [25 October 2017].

21 See William Case (2018) for discussion on electoral authoritarianism and semi-democracy in Malaysia.
22 Personal interview with the ISMA president. Bangi, Malaysia. 5 November 2016.
23 Background on the series of selected Bersih movements in Malaysia is given in Chapter 2.
24 Amongst the selected foreign and local news reports that covered stories about the 'Malaysian Spring' are the following:

  i Fabio Scarpello. (2011). Though Not a 'Malaysian Spring', Bersih Shakes Up Local Politics. *World Politics Review*. www.worldpoliticsreview.com/articles/9671/though-not-a-malaysian-spring-bersih-shakes-up-local-politics. [17 October 2017].
  ii Peter Boyle. (2012). Malaysian Spring: Bersih 3.0 Democracy Movement Plans Mass Sit-In. *International Journal of Socialist Renewal*. http://links.org.au/node/2831 [17 October 2017].
  iii Jonah Fisher. (2012). Could Street Protests Herald a Malaysian Spring? *BBC News*. www.bbc.co.uk/news/world-asia-pacific-18058036 [17 October 2017].
  iv James Crabtree. (2012). Anwar in Bid to Lead 'Malaysian Spring'. *Financial Times*. www.ft.com/content/5df58246-3d3c-11e1-8129-00144feabdc0?mhq5j=e7 [17 October 2017].
  v M.M Chu. (2013). Malaysian Spring: Cops Say Malaysian Spring Is Arab Spring, Stop It. Says.com. http://says.com/my/news/malaysian-spring-plants-flowers-to-inspire-hope-for-a-better-change-in-malaysia-pru13 [17 October 2017].
  vi C.H. Wong. (2013). Fears Grow for a Malaysian Spring. *Asia Times*. www.atimes.com/atimes/Southeast_Asia/SEA-01-290513.html [17 October 2017].

25 Aidila Razak. (2013). Malaysian Spring Frozen Out of M'sia Day Art Show. *Malaysiakini*. www.malaysiakini.com/news/238969#EfIfVSe7V6qkFtr [17 October 2017].
26 See also,

  i Daniel Barnes. (2013). The Prospects of a Malaysian Spring. www.futuredirections.org.au/publication/the-prospects-of-a-malaysian-spring/ [17 October 2017].
  ii G. Vinod. (2013). We Are Not Afraid of Malaysian Spring. *Free Malaysia Today*. www.freemalaysiatoday.com/category/nation/2013/06/26/we-are-not-afraid-of-malaysian-spring/ [17 October 2017].

27 All comments were collected from respondents' written opinions in the questionnaire.
28 Personal interview with the AMANAH National Youth Leader, Muhammad Najib. Kuala Lumpur, Malaysia. September 2016.
29 Personal interview with Amar Yasier of The International Relations Bureau for ISMA's UK branch. London, United Kingdom. 10 June 2016.
30 Personal interview with the ISMA president. Bangi, Malaysia. 5 November 2016.
31 Personal interview with Rached Ghannouchi. Tunis, Tunisia. January 2018.
32 Personal interview with Naoufel Eljammali in the Tunisian parliament, Tunis, Tunisia. January 2018. He is a former Tunisian Minister of Employment and Vocational Training and a current member of the Ennahda Political Bureau.
33 Personal interview with the current advisor to the Ennahda Party President on International Relations, Rafek Abdessalem. Tunis, Tunisia. December 2017.
34 Personal interview. Tunis, Tunisia. January 2018.
35 Ibid.

6 Concluding remarks and perspectives

The purpose of this study has been to investigate the relationship between the phenomenon of the 2011 Arab Uprisings in the MENA and the Islamist movements in Malaysia. For this reason, the researcher chose a questionnaire-based survey, as well as in-depth interviews, to examine the knowledge, perceptions and influences of the Arab Uprisings on the experiences of four selected Malaysian Islamist movements. Intensive fieldwork was carried out in the autumn and winter of 2016 amongst 530 Malaysian Islamist members from the four movements – PAS, ABIM, ISMA and AMANAH – across West Malaysia, particularly in Kuala Lumpur, Selangor, Perak, Kelantan, Kedah and Perlis. The researcher managed to identify five lessons learned by members of the Malaysian Islamist movements from the experiences following the Arab Uprisings.

In many recent studies the impact of the 2011 Arab Uprisings, within and beyond the regions of the MENA, has been discussed in case studies of countries that have either been drivers of, or been affected by, the phenomenon. However, little attention has been paid to its implications for Malaysian political development, particularly from the perspective of political activism amongst Malaysia's Islamist movements. Although there are a few studies discussing the connection between the Arab Uprisings and Malaysia – such as Osman Bakar (2012), Mohd Safar Hashim (2015), Syed Abdul Razak Al-Sagoff (2015) and Nidzam Sulaiman and Kartini Aboo Talib @ Khalid (2017) – none of these works considered the attitude and reaction of Malaysian Islamists towards the phenomenon. This book reflects on how the development of Arab Uprisings in the last six years – for example, the nature of revolutionary movements, the act of civil disobedience, the role of Islamists and the wave of political Islam – is affecting the activism and ways of thinking of the most influential Islamist groups in Malaysia. It also looks at how the journey of Arab Islamist parties coming to power after the 2011 Uprisings has impacted the political approach of selected Malaysian Islamist parties.

The decision to study the relationship between the Islamist movements in Malaysia and the recent 'Arab Revolutions' was driven by two main factors. First, the tendency of Malaysian Islamists to be inspired, influenced and affected by developments in the Middle East and the Islamic world is self-evident – as shown in the case of the 1979 Iranian Revolution. Most of the Malaysian Islamist movements were also originally established based on resources and 'guidelines' provided by the legacy of the Egyptian Muslim Brotherhood. The respectable relationship between the Malaysian Islamist movements and prominent Arab Islamist leaders such as Ghannouchi (Ennahda) and Muhammad Badie Abdul Majid (Egyptian Muslim Brotherhood) seems to support the proposition that the period following the Arab Uprisings might have impacted the attitude and insight of Malaysian Islamists (either directly or indirectly) – in terms of Islamic political activism and approach. The fact that the period following the Arab Uprisings appeared to increase the popularity of the Islamists in several MENA states (although this did not last long) seemed sufficient to re-energise the momentum of Malaysian Islamists regarding their aim of establishing an 'Islamic state', along with an Islamisation agenda, in the country.

Second, due to Malaysian Islamists' long history of frustration and struggle against the ruling regime – most notably through open expression and participation in a series of mass protests widely known as Bersih in Malaysia – it is the researcher's argument that their political activism could also have been inspired by the Arab Uprisings phenomenon. In addition, there was the 'Malaysian Spring' (see Chapter 5), when a number of pro-government politicians (including Prime Minister Najib Razak) and some local and foreign journalists claimed that the Bersih events were some kind of indirect effort to overthrow the current Malaysian ruling regime through street protests (in a similar way to the 'Arab Spring' revolutions). These polemics suggest that the study of Arab Uprisings within the context of Malaysian contemporary politics, specifically from the viewpoint of Islamists, is highly interesting, valuable and worthy of research as it will eventually contribute to the body of knowledge on Malaysian Islamist movements as well as the global reactions towards the development of post-Arab Uprisings. The research findings have been discussed in-depth in Chapters 3–5, based on specific themes and questions in the survey. The findings successfully answered all the main research questions and objectives, as discussed and summarised below.

The first objective was to identify the knowledge, perceptions and views of Islamist movements in Malaysia (PAS, ABIM, ISMA and AMANAH) towards the Arab Uprisings phenomenon in the MENA (Chapter 3). The investigation began with the question – to what extent did Malaysian Islamists really know about and understand the Arab Uprisings? The study found that 82.7 per cent of respondents from PAS, ABIM, ISMA and AMANAH were well-informed about the protests. The finding seems consistent with the general claims by Abdul Malek (2011), Osman Bakar (2012) and Abdul Hadi Awang (2016) that some of the Malaysian public had excitedly paid attention to the developments associated with the 2011 Arab Uprisings. Only 17.3 per cent of respondents did not know about them (see Chapter 3 for their reasons). Overall, it was clear that the interaction between Malaysia and the Arab Muslim world was (in one way or another) generated by the positive awareness and attention of Malaysian citizens (particularly the Islamists) who were concerned about contemporary issues in the MENA.

The next question was – what are the perceptions of PAS, ABIM, ISMA and AMANAH Islamists of the Arab Uprisings? More than 70 per cent of respondents viewed the protests as a symbol of political revolution and non-violent resistance against former Arab dictators due to the long-term practice of political repression as well as the deteriorating state of economic performance. A similar percentage believed that Islamism and the role of Arab Islamist movements played a tremendous part in mobilising protesters during the 2011 Arab Uprisings. The former perception is in line with other studies concerning general issues relating to the Arab Uprisings. The latter, however, appears misleading since many Islamists were 'absent' during the protests in order to avoid any misinformation that the Arab Uprisings were some kind of 'Islamic Revolution'. Moreover, Arab Islamist groups, such as the Muslim Brotherhood in Egypt, never publicly declared that they participated in the revolutions in the name of 'Islam' or as part of the struggle for political Islam – although they supported efforts to overthrow the incumbent Arab regimes, which had long been tyrannically suppressing the Islamists (e.g. in Tunisia, Egypt, Libya and Syria).

The second objective was to examine the extent of the influence of the 2011 Arab Uprisings phenomenon and the impact of post-Arab Uprisings developments (in several states) on the political approach and activism of different Islamist movements in Malaysia (Chapter 4). This was achieved by asking the question – to what extent have the 2011 Arab Uprisings phenomenon and post-Arab Uprisings developments influenced and shaped the ideology, political activism and approach of PAS, ABIM, ISMA and AMANAH in Malaysia? It became clear that, during the first several years of the Arab Uprisings, almost half of the respondents (49.9 per cent) were somehow influenced or inspired by the success of civil disobedience and street protest acts in toppling several former Arab regimes. This trend was evidenced in a series of Bersih protests (2013 and 2015), whereby the respondents admitted that they were motivated to 'occupy' the streets of Kuala Lumpur and Independence Square to press for the immediate resignation of Najib Razak from Putrajaya – due to alleged corruption, monetary scandals; several incidents of political injustice towards opposition leaders (e.g. the detention of former opposition leader Anwar Ibrahim in 2015); price hikes in food, gas and commodities; and the claim of previous electoral manipulation by the regime (see Chapter 2). Almost 70 per cent of respondents also acknowledged the role played by social media in their political activism (e.g. initiating civil disobedience acts, mobilising protesters and generating political awareness) after they witnessed the effectiveness of technology (online social media) in the Arab revolts in 2011.

Relating to the development of Islamist parties after the Arab Uprisings, 62.3 per cent of Malaysian Islamists were motivated by the so-called 'Islamist Winter' trend (the unexpected and dramatic wins by the Ennahda

Party in Tunisia, the PJD in Morocco and the FJP in Egypt in the first elections following the political transition after the Arab Uprisings) to put more effort into realising their parties'/movements' objectives regarding the future establishment of an 'Islamic country' in Malaysia through election and political power. The respondents also agreed that this objective can only be achieved using proper strategies – for instance by embracing values of moderation as well as being politically inclusive in order to gain strong political support from multiple layers of society. This particular finding seems coherent with a study by Maszlee Malik (2017), concluding that the transformation of Ennahda's identity in 2016 (from an Islamic fundamentalist party to an Islamic democratic party) managed to put 'pressure' on certain Islamist movements in Malaysia (the author used ABIM, AMANAH and IKRAM for his case studies) to adopt a neo-Islamism approach instead of supporting the long conservative approach of Islamism which concentrated on the establishment of an Islamic state and Sharia.

The third and final objective of this study was to identify the lessons learned by the Malaysian Islamists from the events following the Arab Uprisings and to explain the dynamic views and approaches of selected Islamist movements with regard to issues of civil disobedience, Arab world affairs and political Islam (Chapter 5). The findings (lessons from the Arab Uprisings) have focussed predominantly on the importance of: (1) improving political strategy (in order to survive in the political game and 'uncertain' environment), (2) maintaining political stability (by avoiding the potential for political disorder and regime change via violent revolution), (3) being inclusive (by cooperating with any non-Islamic-oriented political parties and movements), (4) promoting peaceful political transition in the country (by supporting free and fair elections as the alternative and practical medium for political change) and (5) 'upgrading' the current practice of democracy used by the regime and future government in Malaysia (by implementing reasonably competitive elections as well as guaranteeing basic civil rights). The findings also focus on the role of group characteristics (e.g. the political approaches and ideologies of different parties/movements) and their standpoints on the political Islam agenda and participation in political protests – which constituted the reasons for different responses on certain issues being tackled in the survey.

Implications of the findings on the discourse on political Islam

In the words of Samer Shehata (2012), political Islam has been one of the most dynamic and contentious political forces in the Middle East for over three decades, and this has led to broad consensus about its significance. However, he argues, less agreement has been achieved regarding the character and category of Islamist politics. Indeed, the wave of political Islam coming from the Middle East will always be a key peripheral element in the development of Islamist movements in Malaysia. The understanding, approach and practice of political Islam in the context of Malaysian Islamist parties and movements, as presented by the research findings, have implications for how one should consider the different paradigms of Islamist politics.

Undeniably, the Islamist parties and movements in Malaysia are ideologically and practically diverse. PAS, ABIM and ISMA are inspired by the legacy of the Egyptian Muslim Brotherhood, while AMANAH is largely motivated by the AKP's success and committed to Ennahda's new Islamic Democratic principles. PAS is committed to election as a practical means for political change, while AMANAH and ABIM champion mass street protests (along with electoral participation). PAS is consistent with promoting the 'Islamic state' agenda, while AMANAH concentrates on the 'welfare state' and good governance projects. ABIM prefers soft *dakwah* and tolerance while implementing the agenda of Islamisation. ISMA, in contrast, often voices 'extreme words' for the same purpose. AMANAH and ABIM are open to political cooperation with non-Islamists, while PAS and ISMA seem to share the opposite approach. Some Malaysian Islamists are sceptical of American and Western involvement in the Middle Eastern conflicts, whilst others are open to assistance from external democracies. Despite these differences, political Islam in Malaysia shows a positive trend – as this research found that moderation, along with the practice of inclusivity, has been widely accepted as the relevant approach for Islamist movements in Malaysia.

Tentative perspectives: what is likely to happen in Malaysia with the Islamist movements?

The post-1979 Iranian Revolution and the 2011 Arab Uprisings have indirectly posed a challenge for Malaysia's Islamist movements in remaining relevant and significant in the eyes of the general population. This is especially a concern for the non-Muslim community since global political Islam and Islamist movements have usually been perceived negatively due to their tendency to resort to extremism and violence (Durac and Cavatorta 2015: 140).

Despite these formidable challenges, this research established that the Islamist parties and civil society groups in Malaysia remain determined and committed to their political struggle through electoral or voting channels – albeit with different political approaches. Indirectly, it also seems that the practice of semi-democracy will be continued by the current regime – unless there is a 'historic' political change in the upcoming general election. The fact that more than 60 per cent of respondents support democracy and elections as the best medium for political change reflects the fact that the majority of Malaysian Islamists are refusing to adopt violent and extreme methods to legitimise future goals. The researcher believes that this finding is crucial to foreseeing (in some way) the future direction of PAS, AMANAH, ABIM and ISMA as popular Islamist parties and movements in Malaysia within the context of democratic promotion and improvement. With the next (15th) general election predicted to be held sometime in 2023 there is already huge excitement building regarding the 'ideological' battle between PAS and AMANAH, which will compete for certain parliamentary seats.

With the establishment of several Islamist parties and civil society movements, coupled with other factors – for instance the advancement of social media, the post-Arab Uprisings, the development of moderate Arab Islamist parties – the researcher believes that it is very likely that the trend of increased Islamist involvement in political life will continue for the next few years. Without any doubt, PAS and AMANAH will remain prominent Islamist political parties in the country – either in opposition or within the government block. The researcher is also certain that the trend for political protest via street demonstration will reoccur in the future. However, based on the findings, it seems that one can expect less participants or protesters from the Islamist groups, particularly PAS, due to 'lessons' learned from after the Arab Uprisings.

Bibliography

Abbott, Jason. P. (2009). Malaysia's Transitional Moment? Democratic Transition Theory and the Problem of Malaysian Exceptionalism. *Southeast Asia Research*, 17(2): 175–200.

Abbott, Jason. P. (2011). Electoral Authoritarianism and the Print Media in Malaysia: Measuring Political Bias and Analyzing Its Cause. *Asian Affairs: An American Review*, 38(1): 1–38.

Abdo, Ragheb. (2012). Islamist Moderation in Practice: Democratic Practices and their Shifting Meanings. Master Thesis, McGill University.

Abdul Hamid, A.F. & Che Mohd Razali, C.H. (2016). Middle Eastern Influences on Islamist Organizations in Malaysia: The Cases of ISMA, IRF and HTM. *Trends in Southeast Asia*. ISEAS – Yusof Ishak Institute.

Abdul Malek, Zulkifly. (2011). From Cairo to Kuala Lumpur: The Influence of the Egyptian Muslim Brotherhood on the Muslim Youth Movement of Malaysia (ABIM). Master Thesis, Georgetown University.

Abdul Rahman, Ahmad Azam. (2003). Dakwah dan Pembentukan Khayra Ummah: Pengalaman ABIM (Da'wah and the Establishment of a Good Nation: ABIM's Experience) In Idris, Muhamad Razak (ed.), *Model Dakwah ABIM*. Kuala Lumpur: Biro Dakwah dan Tarbiah ABIM, pp. 1–8.

Achy, Lahcen. (2011). *The Carnegie Papers: Tunisia's Economic Challenge*. Washington: Carnegie Middle East Center.

Ahmad, Talmiz. (2013). The Arab Spring and Its Implications for India. *Strategic Analysis*, 37(1): 119–127.

Agathangelou, A.M. & Soguk, Nevzat (eds.). (2013). *Arab Revolutions and World Transformations*. Abingdon: Routledge.

Akbarzadeh, Shahram. (2014). The Arab Revolution Is Bad News for Iran. In Saikal, Amin & Acharya, Amitav (eds.), *Democracy and Reform in the Middle East and Asia: Social Protest and Authoritarian Rule after the Arab Spring*. London: I.B. Touris, pp. 105–120.

Al-Anani, Khalil. (2012). Islamist Parties Post-Arab Spring, *Mediterranean Politics*, 17(3): 466–472.

Al-Anani, Khalil. (2015). The 'Anguish' of the Muslim Brotherhood in Egypt. In Sadiki, Larbi (ed.), *Routledge Handbook of the Arab Spring: Rethinking Democratisation*. Abingdon: Routledge, pp. 227–239.

Al-Anani, Khalil. (2017). Understanding Repression-Adaptation Nexus in Islamist Movements. In Project on Middle East Political Science, *Islam in a Changing Middle East: Rethinking Islamist Politics*. POMEPS Studies 26, pp. 4–7.

Bibliography

Al-Arian, Abdullah. (2014). A State without a State. Islam in a Changing Middle East: Islamist Social Services. Project on Middle East Studies. POMEPS Studies 9.

Al-Battat, Ahmad Rasmi S., et al. (2013). The Effect of the Arab Spring Revolution on the Malaysian Hospitality Industry. *International Business Research*, 6(5): 92–99.

Al-Sagoff, Syed Abdul Razak. (2015). Reaksi Masyarakat, Kerajaan Malaysia dan Dunia Terhadap Fenomena 'Arab Spring' (The Reactions of Malaysian Government, Society and the World to the Arab Spring Phenomenon). In Mujani, Wan Kamal & Musa, Siti Nurulizah (eds.), *'Arab Spring': Faktor Dan Impak*. Bangi: Penerbit Fakulti Pengajian Islam UKM, pp. 115–129.

Alam, Anwar. (2014). The Arab Spring: A View from India. In Sadiki, Larbi (ed.), *Routledge Handbook of the Arab Spring*. Abingdon: Routledge.

Alaoui, Hicham. (2016). *Is the Arab World Better Off, Five Years after the Arab Spring?* Yale Macmillan Center Council on Middle East Studies. Available at: https://cmes.macmillan.yale.edu/news/arab-world-better-five-years-after-arab-spring.

Aljazeera. (2011a). Khamenei Hails "Islamic" Uprisings. Available at: www.aljazeera.com/news/middleeast/2011/02/201124101233510493.html [22 November 2015].

Aljazeera. (2011b). Timeline: Egypt's Revolution. Available at: www.aljazeera.com/news/middleeast/2011/01/201112515334871490.html [20 September 2015].

Amuzegar, Jahangir. (1991). *The Dynamics of the Iranian Revolution*. New York: The State University of New York Press.

Anderson, Lisa. (2011). Demystifying the Arab Spring: Parsing the Differences between Tunisia, Egypt, and Libya. Available at: www.foreignaffairs.com/articles/libya/2011-04-03/demystifying-arabspring.

Antang, Suzalie Mohamad. (2007). Islamist Movements in the Field of Political Participation in Malaysia. *TAFHIM*, 2(2): 57–92.

Arab Barometer Survey. (2014). Wave III (2012–2014). Available at: www.arabbarometer.org/content/arab-barometer-iii-0.

Aras, Bülent & Ekim, Sinan. (2015). Malaysia and the Arab Spring. Project on the Middle East and the Arab. Spring, 7 July.

Arieff, Alexis. (2012a). *Political Transition in Tunisia*. Washington: Congressional Research Service.

Arieff, Alexis. (2012b). Political Transition in Tunisia. In De Leon, J.C. & Jones, C.R. (eds.), *Tunisia and Egypt: Unrest and Revolution*. New York: Nova Science, pp. 1–43.

Ashour, Omar. (2010). *The De-Radicalization of Jihadists: Transforming Armed Islamist Movements*. Abingdon: Routledge.

Ashour, Omar. (2015). Between ISIS and a Failed State: The Saga of Libyan Islamists. *Working Paper, Project on U.S. Relations with the Islamic World*.

Asrar, Shakeeb. (2017). Syrian Civil War Map: A Map of the Syrian Civil War that Shows Who Controls What after Five Years of Fighting. Available at: www.aljazeera.com/indepth/interactive/2015/05/syria-country-divided-150529144229467.html [11 September 2017].

Asseburg, Muriel. (2013). The Arab Spring and the European Response. *The International Spectator: Italian Journal of International Affairs*, 48(2): 47–62.

Astro, Awani. (2015). Bersih 4: Four Things You Need to Know. Available at: http://english.astroawani.com/malaysia-news/bersih-4-four-things-you-need-know-71003 [20 October 2015].

Astro, Awani. (2013). Musa Hassan: 'Arab Spring' boleh berlaku di negara ini (Musa Hassan: 'Arab Spring' Could Happen in this Country). Available at: www.

astroawani.com/berita-malaysia/musa-hassan-arab-spring-boleh-berlaku-di-negara-ini-6913 [2 June 2015].
Awang, Abdul Hadi. (2016). Iktibar Arab Spring: Politik Matang dan Sejahtera. Available at: www.facebook.com/abdulhadiawang/photos/a.146944298724030/1107443426007441/?type=3&theater [12 November 2016].
Axworthy, Michael. (2014). *Revolutionary Iran: A History of the Islamic Republic.* London: Penguin Group.
Ayeb, Habib. (2011). Social and Political Geography of the Tunisian Revolution: The Alfa Grass Revolution. *Review of African Political Economy,* 38(129): 467–479.
Babbie, Earl. (2016). *The Practice of Social Research* (14th ed.). Boston: Cengage Learning.
Bahari, Mohd Azhar & Saat, Ishak. (2014). *Angkatan Belia Islam Malaysia (ABIM) 1971–2004.* Johor: Penerbit UTHM.
Baharuddin, Shamsul Amri. (2009) *Managing a 'Stable Tension': Ethnic Relations in Malaysia Re-Examined.* A Khazanah Merdeka Series.
Bakar, Osman. (2005). Malaysia's Path to Modernization and Democratization. In Hunter, Shireen T. & Malik, Huma (eds.), *Modernization, Democracy, and Islam.* Westport: Praeger Publisher, pp. 235–252.
Bakar, Osman. (2012). The Arab Spring: Malaysian Responses. *IAIS Malaysia,* 743–746.
Bakr, Noha. (2012). The Egyptian Revolution. Available at: www.um.edu.mt/data/assets/pdffile/0004/150394/Chapter4Noha_Bakr.pdf [17 June 2013].
Barnes, Daniel. (2013). The Prospects of a Malaysian Spring. www.futuredirections.org.au/publication/the-prospects-of-a-malaysian-spring/ [17 October 2017].
Batstone, Jade. (2014). The Use of Strategic Nonviolent Action in the Arab Spring. *Peace Review,* 26(1): 28–37.
Bayat, Asef. (1987). *Workers and Revolution in Iran.* New York: Zed Books.
Bayat, Asef. (1996). The Coming of a post-Islamic Society. *Critique: Critical Middle East Studies,* 9: 43–52.
Bayat, Asef. (2005a). Islamism and Social Movement Theory. *Third World Quarterly,* 26(6): 891–908.
Bayat, Asef. (2005b). What Is post-Islamism? *Isim Review,* 16: 5.
Bayat, Asef. (2007). *Making Islam Democratic: Social Movements and the Post-Islamist Turn.* Stanford: Stanford University Press.
Bayat, Asef. (2011). The Post-Islamist Revolution: What the Revolts in the Arab World Mean. Foreign Affairs. Available at: www.foreignaffairs.com/articles/north-africa/2011-04-26/post-islamist-revolutions [12 June 2015].
Bayat, Asef. (ed.). (2013). *Post-Islamism: The Changing Faces of Political Islam.* Oxford: Oxford University Press.
BBC. (2011) Profile: Egypt's Wael Ghonim. Available at: www.bbc.co.uk/news/world-middle-east-12400529 [21 September 2015].
Beetham, David & Boyle, Kevin. (1995). *Introducing Democracy: 80 Questions and Answers.* Cambridge: Polity Press.
Benakcha, Narrimane. (2012). The Algerian Regime: An Arab Spring Survivor. *Journal of International Affairs.* Available at: https://jia.sipa.columbia.edu/online-articles/algerian-regime-arab-spring-survivor [17 September 2015].
Benchemsi, Ahmed. (2012). Morocco: Outfoxing the Opposition. *Journal of Democracy,* 23(1): 57–69.
Bernama News. (2013). No Basis for 'Arab Spring' Protest in Malaysia – Najib. Available at: www.bernama.com/bernama/v8/newsindex.php?id=960539 [25 May 2015].

Bibliography

Bernhagen, Patrick. (2009). Measuring Democracy and Democratization. In Haerpfer, C.W., et al., *Democratization*. Oxford: Oxford University Press, pp. 24–39.

Bishara, Azmi. (2011). *The Great Popular Tunisian Revolution*. Doha: Arab Center for Research & Policy Studies.

Bishara, Marwan. (2013). 'Year Four: The Seasons Turn on the Arab Spring'. Available at: www.aljazeera.com/indepth/opinion/2013/12/year-four-seasons-turn-arab-spring-2013121762345793639.html [06 October 2017].

Boubakri, Amor. (2015). Interpreting the Tunisian Revolution: Beyond Bou'zizi. In Sadiki, Larbi (ed.), *Routledge Handbook of the Arab Spring: Rethinking Democratisation*. Abingdon: Routledge, pp. 65–76.

Boyle, Peter. (2012). Malaysian Spring: Bersih 3.0 Democracy Movement Plans Mass Sit-In. *International Journal of Socialist Renewal*. Available at: http://links.org.au/node/2831 [17 October 2017].

Bradley, John. R. (2012). *After the Arab Spring: How Islamists Hijacked the Middle East Revolts*. New York: Palgrave Macmillan.

Bramsen, Andrew William. (2012). Islamic Party Formation: The Role of Ideology, Institutions and Historical Memory. PhD Thesis, University of Notre Dame.

Brinton, Crane. (1965). *The Anatomy of Revolution*. New York: Vintage.

Brooke, Steven. (2015). The Muslim Brotherhood's Social Outreach after the Egyptian Coup. *Working Paper: Project on U.S. Relations with the Islamic World*.

Bryman, Alan. (1988). *Quantity and Quality in Social Research*. London: Unwin Hyman.

Brynen, Rex, et al. (2012). *Beyond the Arab Spring: Authoritarianism & Democratization in the Arab World*. London: Lynne Rienner.

Buera, Anas Abubakr. (2015). Libya's Arab Spring-Revolution against a 42-Year Dictatorship: Prospects of Governance and Democracy. In Sadiki, Larbi (ed.), *Routledge Handbook of the Arab Spring: Rethinking Democratisation*. Abingdon: Routledge, pp. 105–118.

Carter Center. (2011). National Constituent Assembly Elections in Tunisia: Final Report. Available at: www.cartercenter.org/resources/pdfs/news/peace_publications/election_reports/tunisia-final-Oct2011.pdf [5 June 2015].

Carter Center. (2015). Legislative and Presidential Elections in Tunisia: Final Report. Available at: www.cartercenter.org/resources/pdfs/news/peace_publications/election_reports/tunisia-final-rpt-2014-elections.pdf [5 June 2015].

Case, William. (1993). Semi-Democracy in Malaysia: Withstanding the Pressures for Regime Change. *Pacific Affairs*, 66(2): 183–205.

Case, William. (2001). Malaysia's Resilient Pseudodemocracy. *Journal of Democracy*, 12(1), 43–57.

Case, William. (2007). Malaysia: The Semi-Democratic Paradigm. *Asian Studies Review*, 17(1): 75–82.

Case, William. (2017). Stress Testing Leadership in Malaysia: The 1MDB Scandal and Najib Tun Razak. *The Pacific Review*, 30(5): 633–654.

Cavatorta, Francesco. (2015). No Democratic Change…and Yet No Authoritarian Continuity: The Inter Paradigm Debate and North Africa after the Uprisings. *British Journal of Middle Eastern Studies*, 42(1): 135–145.

Cavatorta, Francesco & Merone, Fabio. (2015). Post-Islamism, Ideological Evolution and 'la tunisianité' of the Tunisian Islamist Party al-Nahda. *Journal of Political Ideologies*, 20(1): 27–42.

Chamkhi, Tarek. (2014). Neo-Islamism in the post-Arab Spring. *Contemporary Politics*, 20(4): 453–468.

Bibliography 151

Champion, Marc. (2011). Morocco Joins in, Defying Predictions. *The Wall Street Journal*. Available at: www.wsj.com/articles/SB10001424052748703498804576156180408970252 [29 September 2015].

Chew, Amy. (2013) The Rising Force in Malaysia's Opposition: The Pan-Malaysian Islamic Party Is Gaining the Upper Hand within the Coalition Headed by Anwar Ibrahim. *Aljazeera*. Available at: www.aljazeera.com/indepth/features/2013/02/201321092433869462.html [16 October 2015].

Chinnasamy, Sara. (2018). *New Media Political Engagement and Participation in Malaysia*. Oxon: Routledge.

Chong, Alan. (2014). Arab Uprising's Contagion: Electronic Vicariousness and Democratic Empathy in Malaysia and Singapore. In Saikal, Amin & Acharya, Amitav (eds.), *Democracy and Reform in the Middle East and Asia: Social Protest and Authoritarian Rule after the Arab Spring*. London: I.B. Touris, pp. 203–232.

Christopher, Alexander. (2011). Tunisia's Protest Wave: Where it Comes from and What it Means. *Foreign Policy*. Available at: http://foreignpolicy.com/2011/01/03/tunisias-protest-wave-where-it-comes-from-and-what-it-means/ [20 January 2015].

Chu, Mei Mei. (2013). Malaysian Spring: Cops Say Malaysian Spring Is Arab Spring, Stop It. Says.com. http://says.com/my/news/malaysian-spring-plants-flowers-to-inspire-hope-for-a-better-change-in-malaysia-pru13 [17 October 2017].

Clark, Janine A. (2012). Islamist Movements and Democratic Politics. In Brynen, Rex, et al. (eds.), *Beyond the Arab Spring: Authoritarianism & Democratization in the Arab World*. London: Lynne Rienner, pp. 119–146.

Cockburn, Patrick. (2015). *The Rise of Islamic State: ISIS and the New Sunni Revolution*. London: Verso.

Crabtree, James. (2012). Anwar in Bid to Lead 'Malaysian Spring'. *Financial Times*. Available at: www.ft.com/content/5df58246-3d3c-11e1-8129-00144feabdc0?mhq5j=e7 [17 October 2017].

Creswell, John W. (2014). *Research Design: Qualitative, Quantitative & Mixed Methods Approaches* (4th ed.). Los Angeles: Sage.

Culbertson, Shelly. (2016). Tunisia Is an Arab Spring Success Story. Available at: http://observer.com/2016/04/tunisia-is-an-arab-spring-success-story/.

Currie, Kellie. (2012). Asia and the Arab Spring. Available at: www.iemed.org/observatori-en/arees-danalisi/arxius-adjunts/anuari/med.2012/currie_en.pdf [13 April 2015].

Dagi, Ihsan. (2013). Post-Islamism à la Turca. In Bayat, Asef (ed.), *Post-Islamism: The Changing Faces of Political Islam*. Oxford: Oxford University Press, pp. 35–70.

Dahl, Robert A. (2000). *On Democracy*. New Haven: Yale University Press.

Dannreuther, Roland. (2014) The Arab Spring and the European Response. *Journal of European Integration*, 37(1): 77–94.

Davies, James C. (1962). Toward a Theory of Revolution. *American Sociological Review*, 27: 5–19. doi:10.2307/2089714.

De La Sablonnière, Roxane., et al. (2013). Dramatic Social Change: A Social Psychological Perspective. *Journal of Social and Political Psychology*, 1(1): 253–272.

Del Rosario, Teresita Cruz & Dorsey, James M. (2016). *Comparative Political Transitions between Southeast Asia and the Middle East and North Africa: Lost in Transition*. New York: Palgrave Macmillan.

Diamond, Larry. (1990). Democracy in Developing Countries. *International Affairs*, 66(3): 636.

Diamond, Larry. (2012). The Coming Wave: China and East Asian Democracy. *Journal of Democracy*, 23(1): 5–13.

Driss, Ahmed. (2011). *Thoughts on the Tunisian Revolution.* Madrid: Elcano Royal Institute.
Durac, Vincent. (2012). Yemen's Arab Spring: Democratic Opening or Regime Maintenance?, *Mediterranean Politics,* 17(2): 161–178.
Durac, Vincent. (2013). Protest Movements and Political Change: An Analysis of the 'Arab Uprisings' of 2011. *Journal of Contemporary African Studies,* 31(2): 175–193.
Durac, Vincent & Cavatorta, Francesco. (2015). *Politics and Governance in the Middle East.* London: Palgrave.
Edward, Salmi & Mujani, Wan Kamal. (2015). 'Arab Spring': Faktor, Kesan dan Pengaruhnya Terhadap Masyarakat di Malaysia (The Arab Spring: Factor, Effect and Influence among the Society in Malaysia). In Mujani, Wan Kamal & Musa, Siti Nurulizah (eds.), *'Arab Spring': Faktor Dan Impak.* Bangi: Penerbit Fakulti Pengajian Islam UKM, pp. 94–106.
Eickelman, Dale F. & Piscatori, James. (2004). *Muslim Politics.* Princeton: Princeton University Press.
El Fadl, Khaled Abou. (2015). Failure of a Revolution: The Military, Secular Intelligentsia and Religion in Egypt's Pseudo-Secular State. In Sadiki, Larbi (ed.), *Routledge Handbook of the Arab Spring: Rethinking Democratisation.* Abingdon: Routledge, pp. 253–269.
El-Katiri, Mohammed. (2014). *Revival of Political Islam in the Aftermath of Arab Uprisings: Implications for the Region and Beyond.* Carlisle: U.S War Army College.
Emadi, Hafizullah. (1995). Exporting Iran's Revolution: The Radicalization of the Shiite Movement in Afghanistan. *Middle Eastern Studies,* 31(1): 1–12.
Esposito, John L. (1986). *Islam in Asia: Religion, Politics & Society.* Oxford: Oxford University Press.
Esposito, John L. (1998). *Islam and Politics* (4th ed.). New York: Syracuse University Press.
Esposito, John L. & Piscatori, James. (1990). Introduction. In Esposito, J.L. (ed.), *The Iranian Revolution: Its Global Impact.* Florida: University Presses of Florida, pp. 1–17.
Esposito, John L., Sonn, Tamara & Voll, J.O. (2016). *Islam and Democracy after the Arab Spring.* Oxford: Oxford University Press.
Esposito, John L. & Voll, John O. (1996). *Islam and Democracy.* Oxford: Oxford University Press.
Fawcett, Lousie. (2016) *International Relations of the Middle East* (4th ed.). Oxford: Oxford University Press.
Fealy, Greg. (2014). 'Look Over Here!': Indonesian Responses to the Arab Spring. In Saikal, Amin & Acharya, Amitav (eds.), *Democracy and Reform in the Middle East and Asia: Social Protest and Authoritarian Rule after the Arab Spring.* London: I.B. Touris, pp. 233–249.
Filiu, Jean-Pierre. (2011). *The Arab Revolutions: Ten Lessons from the Democratic Uprisings.* London: Hurst & Company.
Filstead, William J. (1970). *Qualitative Methodology: Firsthand Involvement with the Social World.* Chicago: Markham Publishing Company.
Fisher, Jonah. (2012). Could Street Protests Herald a Malaysian Spring? Available at: www.bbc.co.uk/news/world-asia-pacific-18058036.
Foran, John. (1992). A Theory of Third World Social Revolutions: Iran, Nicaragua, and El Salvador Compared. *Critical Sociology,* 19(2): 3–27. doi:10.1177/08969 2059201900201.

Bibliography 153

Foran, John. (1993). Theories of Revolution Revisited: Toward a Fourth Generation. *Sociological Theory*, 11: 1–20. doi:10.2307/201977.

Fradkin, Hillel. (2013). Arab Democracy or Islamist Revolution? *Journal of Democracy*, 24(1): 5–13.

Freedom House. (2015). Freedom in the World-Malaysia. Available at: https://freedomhouse.org/report-types/freedom-world# [22 June 2015].

Freedom House. (2017). Malaysia. Available at: https://freedomhouse.org/country/malaysia [28 September 2017].

Funston, John N. (1985). The Politics of Islamic Reassertion in Malaysia. In Ibrahim, Ahmad, et al. (eds.), *Reading on Islam in Southeast Asia*. Singapore: Institute of Southeast Asian Studies, pp. 171–179.

Gainous, Jason, Wagner, Kevin M. & Abbott, Jason P. (2015). Civic Disobedience: Does Internet Use Stimulate Political Unrest in East Asia?. *Journal of Information Technology & Politics*, 12(2): 219–236.

Gelvin, James L. (2012). *The Arab Uprisings: What Everyone Needs to Know*. Oxford: Oxford University Press.

Ghanem, As'ad. (2013). The Palestinians – Lessons from the Arab Spring. *Contemporary Arab Affairs*, 6(3): 422–437.

Ghanem, Hafez. (2016a). *The Arab Spring Five Years Later: Toward Greater Inclusiveness*. Washington: Brookings Institution Press.

Ghanem, Hafez (ed.). (2016b). *The Arab Spring Five Years Later: Case Studies*. Washington: Brookings Institution Press.

Ghabra, Syafeeq. (2015). The Egyptian Revolution: Causes and Dynamics. In Sadiki, Larbi (ed.), *Routledge Handbook of the Arab Spring: Rethinking Democratisation*. Abingdon: Routledge.

Ghannouchi, Rached. (2016). Opening speech at the 10th National Party Conference of Ennahda. Available at: www.facebook.com/Nahdha.International/?fref=nf [25 May 2016].

Ghazali, Mohd Rumaizuddin. (2003). Model Dakwah ABIM: Meniti Sejarah, Membangun Ummah (ABIM's Model of Da'wah: Through History, Developing Nation). In Idris, Muhamad Razak (ed.), *Model Dakwah ABIM*. Kuala Lumpur: Biro Dakwah dan Tarbiah ABIM, pp. 9–22.

Goodwin, Jeff & Skocpol, Theda. (1989). Explaining Revolutions in the Contemporary Third World. *Politics & Society*, 17(4): 489–509.

Goodwin, Robin. (2006). Age and Social Support Perception in Eastern Europe: Social Change and Support in Four Rapidly Changing Countries. *British Journal of Social Psychology*, 45(4): 4799–4815. doi:10.1348/014466605X72144.

Goodwin, Robin. (2009). *Changing Relations: Achieving Intimacy in a Time of Social Transition*. Cambridge: Cambridge University Press.

Goodwin, Robin. (n.d.). Introducing Adjustment to Change Theory (ACT). Available at: www.actproject.co.uk/.

Goodwin, Robin & Gaines Jr., Stanley. (2009). Terrorism Perception and Its Consequences Following the 7 July 2005 London Bombings. *Behavioral Sciences of Terrorism and Political Aggression*, 1(1): 50–65.

Goodwin, Robin, Nizharadze, George, Luu, Lan Anh Nguyen, Kosa, Eva & Emelyanova, Tatiana (2001). Social Support in a Changing Europe: An Analysis of Three Post-Communist Nations. *European Journal of Social Psychology*, 31(4): 4379–4393. doi:10.1002/ejsp.49.

Goodwin, Robin, & Tang, Catherine S. (1998). The Transition to Uncertainty? The Impacts of Hong Kong 1997 on Personal Relationships. *Personal Relationships*, 5(2): 2183–2190. doi:10.1111/j.1475-6811.1998.tb00166.x.

Bibliography

Goodwin, Robin, et al. (2005). Terror Threat Perception and Its Consequences in Contemporary Britain. *British Journal of Psychology*, 96: 389–406.

Goldstone, Jack A. (1980). Theories of Revolutions: The Third Generation. *World Politics*, 32: 425–453. doi:10.2307/2010111.

Goldstone, Jack A. (1982). The Comparative and Historical Study of Revolutions. *Annual Review of Sociology*, 8: 187–207.

Goldstone, Jack A. (2001). Towards a Fourth Generation of Revolutionary Theory. *Annual Review of Political Science*, 4: 139–187. doi:10.1146/annurev.polisci. 4.1.139.

Göle, Nilüfer. (2002). Islam in Public: New Visibilities and New Imaginaries. *Public Culture*, 14(1): 173–190.

Grugel, Jean. (2002). *Democratization: A Critical Introduction*. Hampshire: Palgrave Macmillan.

Guazzone, Laura. (2013). Ennahda Islamists and the Test of Government in Tunisia. *The International Spectator*, 48(4): 30–50.

Gürbüz, Vedat M. (2003). The Iranian Revolution. *Ankara Üniversitesi SBF Dergisi*, 58(4): 107–122.

Haddad, Yvonne Y., et al. (1991). *The Contemporary Islamic Revival: A Critical Survey and Bibliography*. London: Greenwood Press.

Halliday, Fred. (1999). *Revolution and World Politics: The Rise and Fall of the Sixth Great Power*. London: Macmillan Press Ltd.

Hanafi, Sari. (2012). The Arab Revolutions: The Emergence of a New Political Subjectivity. *Contemporary Arab Affairs*, 5(2): 198–213.

Hardy, Roger. (2013). Democracy or Disorder? The Four Lessons of the Arab Spring. Available at: www.bbc.co.uk/news/world-middle-east-23266790 [22 June 2016].

Hasan, Noorhaidi. (2013). Post-Islamic Politics in Indonesia. In Bayat, Asef (ed.), *Post-Islamism: The Changing Faces of Political Islam*. Oxford: Oxford University Press, pp. 157–186.

Hashim, Mohd Safar. (2015). 'Arab Spring' atau Arab Nightmares: Antara Hakikat dan Persepsi Kebangkitan Arab (*The Arab Spring: Between Truth and Perception of the Arab Uprising*). In Wan Kamal Mujani & Siti Nurulizah Musa, *'Arab Spring': Faktor Dan Impak*. Bangi: Penerbit Fakulti Pengajian Islam UKM. pp. 107–114.

Hassan, Mohd Kamal. (2011). *Voice of Islamic Moderation from the Malay World*. Perak: Emerging Markets Innovative Research (M) Sdn Bhd.

Hassan, Saliha. (2003). Islamic Non-Governmental Organisations. In Weiss, Meredith & Hassan, Saliha (eds.), *Social Movements in Malaysia: From Moral Communities to NGOs*. Canada: RoutledgeCurzon.

Haynes, Jeffrey. (2013). The 'Arab Uprising', Islamists and Democratization. *Mediterranean Politics*, 18(2): 170–188.

He, Baogang. (2014). China's Responses to the Arab Uprisings. In *Democracy and Reform in the Middle East and Asia: Social Protest and Authoritarian Rule after the Arab Spring*. London: I.B. Touris, pp. 161–186.

Held, David (ed.). (1993). *Prospects for Democracy*. Cambridge: Polity Press.

Heydemann, Steven. (2013). 'Tracking the Arab Uprising': Syria and the Future of Authoritarianism. *Journal of Democracy*, 4(4): 59–73.

Heywood, Andrew. (2013). *Politics*. (4th ed.). Hampshire: Palgrave Macmillan.

Hill, Jonathan N.C. (2016). *Democratisation in the Maghreb*. Edinburgh: Edinburgh University Press.

Hinnebusch, R.A. (2015). Change and Continuity after the Arab Uprising: The Consequences of State Formation in Arab North African States. *British Journal of Middle Eastern Studies*, 42(1): 12–30.

Hinnebusch, R.A. (2017). Why Political Parties in the Middle East Matter. *British Journal of Middle Eastern Studies*, 44(2): 159–175.
Holík, Jiří. (2011). Malaysia: Between Democracy and Authoritarianism. Research Paper 5/2011, Association for International Affairs.
Honwana, Alcinda. (2013). *Youth and Revolution in Tunisia*. London: Zed Books.
Hooi, Ying Khooi. (2014). Electoral Reform Movement in Malaysia: Emergence, Protest and Reform. *SUVANNABHUMI*, 6(2): 85–106.
Hooi, Ying Khooi. (2016). Malaysia's 13th General Elections and the Rise of Electoral Reform Movement. *Asian Politics & Policy*, 8(3): 418–435.
Hookway, James & Fernandez, Celine. (2015) Critics of Malaysian Government Cite Censorship Pressure: Prime Minister Najib Razak Is Struggling to Contain Fallout from Investigations into 1MDB. Available at: www.wsj.com/articles/critics-of-malaysian-government-cite-censorship-pressure-1447976847.
Howard, Philip N. & Hussain, Muzammil M. (2013). *Democracy's Fourth Wave? Digital Media and the Arab Spring*. Oxford: Oxford University Press.
Hudson, Michael. (2015). Arab Politics after the Uprisings: Still Searching for Legitimacy. In Sadiki, Larbi (ed.), *Routledge Handbook of the Arab Spring: Rethinking Democratisation*. Abingdon: Routledge.
Huntington, Samuel Phillips. (1991). *The Third Wave: Democratization in the Late Twentieth Century*. Norman: University of Oklahoma Press.
Isakhan, Benjamin, Fethi, Mansouri & Akbarzadeh, Sharam (eds.) (2012). *The Arab Revolutions in Context: Civil Society and Democracy in a Changing Middle East*. Melbourne: Melbourne University Press.
Ismael, Jacqueline S. & Ismael, Shereen T. (2013). The Arab Spring and the Uncivil State. *Arab Studies Quarterly*, 35(3): 229–240. doi:10.13169/arabstudquar.35.3.0229.
Jackson, Ashley. (2006). *The British Empire and the Second World War*. New York: Hambledon Continuum.
Jeppie, Shamil. (2014). Revolutions in North Africa: A View from the South of the Continent. In Sadiki, Larbi (ed.), *Routledge Handbook of the Arab Spring: Rethinking Democratisation*. Abingdon: Routledge.
Jomo, Kwame S. & Cheek, Ahmad S. (1992). Malaysia's Islamic Movements. In *Fragmented Vision: Culture and Politics Contemporary Malaysia*. Sydney: Allen and Unwin.
Kaisan, Abdul Rahman. (2013). Political Observes Reject the Possibility of Arab Spring. *The Borneo Post*. Available at: www.theborneopost.com/2013/01/13/political-observers-reject-possibility-of-arab-spring/ [22 June 2015].
Kamrava, Mehran (ed.). (2014). *Beyond the Arab Spring: The Evolving Ruling Bargain in the Middle East*. London: Hurst & Company.
Karakoç, Jülide. (2015). *Authoritarianism in the Middle East: Before and After the Arab Uprisings*. London: Palgrave Macmillan.
Kemal Eldin, Osman Salih (2013). The Roots and Causes of the 2011 Arab Uprisings. *Arab Studies Quarterly*, 35(2): 184–206.
Kerckhove, F.D. (2012). *Policy Update Paper: Egypt's Muslim Brotherhood and the Arab Spring*. Canadian Defence and Foreign Affairs Institute.
Kimmel, Michael S. (1990). *Revolution – A Sociological Interpretation: Revolutions in Sociological Perspectives*. Cambridge: Polity Press.
Kingsbury, Damien. (2017). *Politics in Contemporary Southeast Asia: Authority: Democracy and Political Change*. Oxon: Routledge.
Kobayashi, Masaki. (1996). The Islamist Movement in Sudan: The Impact of Dr Hassan al-Turabi's Personality on the Movement. PhD Thesis, University of Durham.

Bibliography

Koplow, Michael. (2011). Why Tunisia's Revolution Is Islamist-Free: And How their Absence Explains the Quick Fall of Ben Ali's Regime. *Foreign Policy.* Available at: http://foreignpolicy.com/2011/01/14/why-tunisias-revolution-is-islamist-free-2/ [03 January 2015].

Korotayev, Andrey V. & Zinkina, Julia V. (2011). Egyptian Revolution: A Demographic Structural Analysis. *Entelequia Revista Interdisciplinar,* 13, 139–169.

Krejcie, Robert V. & Morgan, Daryle W. (1970). Determining Sample Size for Research Activities. *Educational and Psychological Measurement,* 30: 607–610.

Krznaric, Roman. (2007). *How Change Happens: Interdisciplinary Perspectives for Human Development.* Oxford: Oxfam.

Kuhn, Randall. (2012). On the Role of Human Development in the Arab Spring. *Population and Development Review,* 38(4): 649–683.

Kurzman, Charles & Türkoğlu, Didem. (2015). Do Muslims Vote Islamic Now? *Journal of Democracy,* 26(4): 100–109.

Lane, David. (2009). 'Coloured Revolution' as a Political Phenomenon. *Journal of Communist Studies and Transition Politics,* 25(2–3): 113–135.

Lawson, George. (2015). Revolution, Nonviolence, and the Arab Uprisings. *Mobilization: An International Quarterly,* 20(4): 453–470.

Lemière, Sophie (ed.). (2014). *Misplaced Democracy: Malaysian Politics and People.* Petaling Jaya: SIRD.

Levitsky, Steven & Way, L.A. (2002). The Rise of Competitive Authoritarianism. *Journal of Democracy,* 13(2): 51–65.

Liow, Joseph C. (2009). *Piety and Politics: Islamism in Contemporary Malaysia.* Oxford: Oxford University Press.

Liow, Joseph C. (2011). Islamist Ambitions, Political Change, and the Price of Power: Recent Success and Challenges for the Pan-Malaysian Islamic Party, PAS. *Journal of Islamic Studies,* 22(3): 374–403.

Liow, Joseph C. (2013). Angkatan Belia Islam Malaysia (ABIM). Oxford Bibliographies. Available at: www.oxfordbibliographies.com/view/document/obo-9780195390155/obo-9780195390155-0197.xml?rskey=lraZpO&result=1&q=ABIM#firstMatch [15 September 2015].

Liow, Joseph C. (2015). The Arab Spring and Islamist Activism in Southeast Asia: Much Ado about Nothing? *Working Paper, Project on U.S. Relations with the Islamic World.*

Lust, Ellen. (2011). Opposition Cooperation and Uprisings in the Arab World. *British Journal of Middle Eastern Studies,* 38(3): 425–434.

Lynch, Marc. (2014). Islam in a Changing Middle East: Rethinking Islamist Politics. Project on Middle East Political Science Paper 6.

Lynch, Marc. (2016). *The New Arab Wars: Uprisings and Anarchy in the Middle East.* New York: Public Affairs.

Malay Mail. (2014). ISMA Claims Vilified Simply for Defending Islam. *Malay Mail Online.* Available at: www.themalaymailonline.com/malaysia/article/isma-claims-vilified-simply-for-defending-islam [21 September 2015].

Malaysian National News Agency. (2013). Political Observes Reject the Possibility of Arab Spring. *The Borneo Post.* Available at: www.theborneopost.com/2013/01/13/political-observers-reject-possibility-of-arab-spring/ [22 June 2015].

Malik, Maszlee. (2017). From Political Islam to Democrat Muslim: A Case Study of Rashid Ghannouchi's Influence on ABIM, IKRAM, AMANAH and DAP. *Intellectual Discourse,* 25(1): 21–53.

Malloch-Brown, Lord Mark. (2011). The Economics of the Arab Spring. *The World Today*, 67(10): 8–10.
Malloch-Brown, Mark. (2011). *The Unfinished Global Revolution: The Road to International Cooperation*. New York: Penguin Books.
Mandaville, Peter. (2014). *Islam and Politics* (2nd ed.). New York: Routledge.
Martin, Michael & Solomon, Hussein. (2017). Understanding the Nature of the Beast and Its Funding. *Contemporary Review of the Middle East*, 4(1): 18–49.
Masoud, Tarek. (2011). The Upheavals in Egypt and Tunisia: The Road To (And From) Liberation Square. *Journal of Democracy*, 22(3): 20–34.
Mat Isa, Nasharudin. (2001). *The Islamic Party of Malaysia (PAS): Ideology, Policy, Struggle and Vision Towards the New Millennium*. Kuala Lumpur: PAS.
Matesan, Iona E. (2012). The Impact of the Arab Spring on Islamist Strategies. *Journal of Strategic Security*, 5(2): 27–46.
Matveev, A.V. (2002). The Advantages of Employing Quantitative and Qualitative Methods in Intercultural Research: Practical Implications from the Study of the Perceptions of Intercultural Communication Competence by American and Russian Managers. *Russian Journal of Communication*. Available at: www.russcomm.ru/eng/rca_biblio/m/matveev01_eng.shtml [31 January 2015].
Mcauliffe, Anneliese. (2015). 'Malaysia's Democracy Is in Worse Shape than We Thought: Malaysia's Pro-Democracy Rally Shows a Country Deeply Divided along Ethnic Lines.' *AlJazeera*. Available at: www.aljazeera.com/indepth/opinion/2015/08/malaysia-democracy-worse-shape-thought-1508310659017.html [20 October 2015].
Means, G.P. (1996). Soft Authoritarianism in Malaysia and Singapore. *Journal of Democracy*, 7(4): 103–117.
Melanie, Radue. (2012). The Internet's Role in the Bersih Movement in Malaysia – A Case Study. *International Review of Information Ethics*, 18 (December): 60–70.
Menashri, David (ed.). (1990). *The Iranian Revolution and the Muslim World*. Oxford: West View Press.
Merone, Fabio & Volpi, Frédéric. (2014). Trajectories of Tunisian Islamism. In Stein, Ewan, et al. (eds.), *A CASAW-AHRC People Power and State Power Network Report: Islamism and the Arab Uprisings*. CASAW.
Miller, Erica. (2006). Democratic Islamists? A Case Study on the Pan-Malaysian Islamic Party (PAS). Master Thesis, Tufts University.
Milne, R.S. & Mauzy, Diane K. (1999). *Malaysian Politics under Mahathir*. London: Routledge.
Milton-Edwards, Beverly. (2012). Revolt and Revolution: The Place of Islamism. *Critical Studies on Terrorism*, 5(2): 219–236.
Mir-Hosseini, Ziba & Tapper, Richard. (2006). *Islam and Democracy in Iran: Eshkevari and the Quest for Reform*. London: I.B. Tauris.
Moaddel, Mansor & Gelfand, M.J. (2017). *Values, Political Action, and Change in the Middle East and the Arab Spring*. Oxford: Oxford University Press.
Mohamed, Alias. (1990). *Malaysia's Islamic Opposition: Past Present and Future*. Kuala Lumpur: Gateway Publishing House.
Mohamed Osman, Mohamed Nawab. (2014). Muslim Student Activism in Malaysia: A Case Study of GAMIS. In Lemière, Sophie (ed.), *Misplaced Democracy: Malaysian Politics and People*. Petaling Jaya: SIRD.
Mohamed Osman, Mohamed Nawab. & Saleem, Salina. (2016). *The Impact of Islamic Civil Society Organisations on Malaysian Islam and Politics*. Malaysia Update: S. Rajaratnam School of International Studies.

Bibliography

Mohd Zain, Mohd Izani. (2014). From Islamist to Muslim Democrat: The Present Phenomenon of Muslim Politics in Malaysia. *International Journal of Islamic Thought*, 6 (December): 37–45.

Mohd Redhuan Tee, Abdullah. (2013). Political Observes Reject the Possibility of Arab Spring. *The Borneo Post*. Available at: www.theborneopost.com/2013/01/13/political-observers-reject-possibility-of-arab-spring/ [22 June 2015].

Mohd Sani, Mohd Azizuddin & Zengeni, Knocks Tapiwa. (2010). Democratisation in Malaysia: The Impact of Social Media in the 2008 General Election. In Asian Studies Association of Australia (ASAA) 18th Biennial Conference 2010, 5–8 July 2010, The University of Adelaide, Australia.

Monutty, Muhammad Nor. (1990). Perception of Social Change in Contemporary Malaysia: A Critical Analysis of ABIM's Role and Its Impact among Muslim Youth. PhD Thesis, Temple University.

Müller, Dominik M. (2014). *Islam, Politics and Youth in Malaysia: The Pop-Islamist Reinvention of PAS*. Oxon: Routledge.

Mullin, Corinna. (2015). Tunisia's Revolution and the Domestic-International Nexus. In Sadiki, Larbi (ed.), *Routledge Handbook of the Arab Spring: Rethinking Democratisation*. Abingdon: Routledge, pp. 89–104.

Murad, Dina. (2014). Abdullah Zaik: The Man behind ISMA. The Stars. Available at: www.thestar.com.my/news/nation/2014/05/22/abdullah-zaik-man-behind-isma/ [13 June 2015].

Musa, Hassan. (2013). "Arab Spring" Can Happen if Losing Party Dissatisfied. *Astro Awani*, 10 February 2013. Available at: http://english.astroawani.com/malaysia-news/musa-hassan-arab-spring-can-happen-if-losing-party-dissatisfied-6910?cp [13 June 2015].

Mutalib, Hussin. (2008). *Islam in Southeast Asia*. Singapore: ISEAS.

Nair, Sheila. (2007). The Limits of Protest and Prospects for Political Reform in Malaysia. *Critical Asian Studies*, 39(3): 339–368.

Najib Razak. (2013). No Basis for 'Arab Spring' Protest in Malaysia. *Malaysian National News Agency*. Available at: www.pmo.gov.my/home.php?menu=newslist&news_id=11664&news_cat=13&cl=1&page=1731&sort_year=2013&sort_month [22 June 2015].

Nambiar, Predeep. (2017). Mat Sabu: Mari Lepas Geram di Himpunan Rakyat Marah. (Mat Sabu: Let's Release Our Anger at the People's Anger Rally) Free Malaysia Today. Available at: www.freemalaysiatoday.com/category/bahasa/2017/01/10/mat-sabu-mari-lepas-geram-di-himpunan-rakyat-marah/ [25 October 2017].

Nelson, Joan M. (2014). Will Malaysia Follow the Path of Taiwan and Mexico? *Journal of Democracy*, 25(3): 105–119.

Nepstad, Sharon Erickson. (2011). Nonviolent Resistance in the Arab Spring: The Critical Role of Military-Opposition Alliances. *Swiss Political Science Review*, 17(4): 485–491.

Nepstad, Sharon Erickson. (2013). Nonviolent Civil Resistance and Social Movements. *Sociology Compass*, 7(7): 590–598.

Ng, Cynthia. (2014). What Is Sedition Act 1948? Available at: http://english.astroawani.com/malaysia-news/what-sedition-act-1948-43073 [30 January 2018].

Noor, Farish Ahmad. (2003). Blood, Sweat and Jihad: The Radicalization of the Political Discourse of the Pan-Malaysian Islamic Party from 1982 Onwards. *Contemporary Southeast Asia*, 25(2): 200–232.

Noor, Farish Ahmad. (2004). *Islam Embedded: The Historical Development of the Pan-Malaysian Islamic Party PAS (1951–2003)*, vol. 1. Kuala Lumpur: MSRI.

Noor, Farish Ahmad. (2014). *The Malaysian Islamic Party PAS 1951–2013*. Amsterdam: Amsterdam University Press.

Noueihed, Lin & Warren, Alex. (2012). *The Battle for the Arab Spring: Revolution, Counter-Revolution and the Making of a New Era*. New Haven: Yale University Press.

Nourzhanov, Kirill. (2014). Central Asia and the Arab Spring: Discourses of Relevance and Threat in the Region. In Saikal, Amin & Acharya, Amitav (eds.), *Democracy and Reform in the Middle East and Asia: Social Protest and Authoritarian Rule after the Arab Spring*. London: I.B. Touris, pp. 121–142.

Othman, Mohammad Redzuan & Haris, Abu Hanifah. (2015). The Role of Egyptian Influences on the Religious Dynamics and the Idea of Progress of Malaya's Kaum Muda (Young Faction) before the Second World War. *British Journal of Middle Eastern Studies*, 42(4): 465–480.

Osman, Tarek. (2017). *Islamism: A History of Political Islam from the Fall of Ottoman Empire to the Rise of ISIS*. New Heaven: Yale University Press.

Owen, Roger. (2012). *The Rise and Fall of Arab Presidents for Life*. Cambridge: Harvard University Press.

Paciello, Maria Cristina. (2011). Egypt: Changes and Challenges of Political Transition. Mediterranean Prospects Technical Report No. 4. European Commission's Seventh Framework Research Programme.

Pang, Khee Teik. (2015). Social Policy and Social Development. In Weiss, Meredith L. (ed.), *Routledge Handbook of Contemporary Malaysia*. Oxon: Routledge.

Parchami, Ali. (2013). The 'Arab Spring': The View from Tehran. *Contemporary Politics*, 18(1): 35–52.

Parry, Geraint. & Moran, Michael. (eds.). (1994). *Democracy and Democratization*. London: Routledge.

Pierre-Filiu, Jean. (2011). *The Arab Revolution: Ten Lessons from the Democratic Uprising*. Oxford: Oxford University Press.

Postill, John. (2014). A Critical History of Internet Activism and Social Protest in Malaysia, 1998–2011. *Asiascape: Digital Asia*, 1(2): 78–103.

Potter, David. (1993). Democratization in Asia. In Held, David (ed.), *Prospects for Democracy*. Cambridge: Polity Press, pp. 355–379.

Potter, David, et al. (1997). *Democratization*. Cambridge: Polity Press.

Powel, Brieg Tomos. (2008). From Democracy to Stability: European Union Democracy Promotion in Tunisia 1995–2007. Doctoral Thesis, University of Exeter.

Project on Middle East Political Science. (2014). Islam in a Changing Middle East: Rethinking Islamist Politics. POMEPS Studies 6.

Project on Middle East Political Science. (2017). Islam in a Changing Middle East: Adaptation Strategies of Islamist Movements. POMEPS Studies 26.

Rahman, Saodah A. & Nurullah, Abu Sadat. (2012). Islamic Awakening and Its Role in Islamic Solidarity in Malaysia. *The American Journal of Islamic Social Sciences*, 29(1): 98–125.

Ramazani, Ruhi K. (1990). Iran's Export of the Revolution: Politics, Ends and Means. In Esposito, John L. (ed.), *The Iranian Revolution: Its Global Impact*. Florida: University Presses of Florida, pp. 40–62.

Rawls, John. (1971). *A Theory of Justice*. Harvard: Harvard University Press.

Bibliography

Razak, Aidila. (2013). Malaysian Spring frozen Out of M'sia Day Art Show. Malaysiakini. Available at: www.malaysiakini.com/news/238969#EfIfVSe7V6qkFtr [17October 2017].

Rivetti, Paola. (2015). Continuity and Change before and after the Uprisings in Tunisia, Egypt and Morocco: Regime Reconfiguration and Policymaking in North Africa. *British Journal of Middle Eastern Studies*, 42(1): 1–11.

Roberts, Adam, et al. (2016). *Civil Resistance in the Arab Spring: Triumphs and Disasters*. Oxford: Oxford University Press.

Roy, Olivier. (2012). The Transformation of the Arab World. *Journal of Democracy*, 23(3): 5–18.

Sadiki, Larbi. (2002). Political Liberalization in Bin Ali's Tunisia: Façade Democracy. *Democratization*, 9(4): 122–141.

Sadiki, Larbi. (2004). *The Search for Arab Democracy: Discourse and Counter Discourse*. London: Hurst and Company.

Sadiki, Larbi (ed.). (2015a). *Routledge Handbook of the Arab Spring: Rethinking Democratisation*. Abingdon: Routledge.

Sadiki, Larbi. (2015b). Towards a 'Democratic Knowledge' Turn? Knowledge Production in the Age of the Arab Spring. *The Journal of North African Studies*, 20(5): 702–721.

Sadiki, Larbi & Bouandel, Youcef. (2016). The Post Arab Spring Reform: The Maghreb at a Cross Roads. *DOMES*, 25(1): 109–131.

Said Aly, Abdel Monem. (2011). The Paradox of the Egyptian Revolution. *Middle East Brief*, 55: 2–7.

Said Aly, Abdel Monem. (2012). *State and Revolution in Egypt: The Paradox of Change and Politics*. Waltham: Crown Center for Middle East Studies, Brandies University.

Saikal, Amin & Acharya, Amitav (eds.). (2014a). *Democracy and Reform in the Middle East and Asia: Social Protest and Authoritarian Rule after the Arab Spring*. London: I.B. Touris.

Saikal, Amin & Acharya, Amitav. (2014b). The Implications of the Arab Spring for the Middle East and Asia. In *Democracy and Reform in the Middle East and Asia: Social Protest and Authoritarian Rule after the Arab Spring*. London: I.B. Touris, pp. 1–14.

Salih, Kemal Eldin Osman. (2013). The Roots and Causes of the 2011 Arab Uprisings. *Arab Studies Quarterly*, 35(2), 184–206. doi:10.13169/arabstudquar.35.2.0184.

Saravanamuttu, Johan. (2016). *Power Sharing in a Divided Nation: Mediated Communalism and New Politics in Six Decades of Malaysia's Elections*. Petaling Jaya: SIRD.

Scarpello, Fabio. (2011). Though Not a 'Malaysian Spring,' Bersih Shakes Up Local Politics. *World Politics Review*. Available at: www.worldpoliticsreview.com/articles/9671/though-not-a-malaysian-spring-bersih-shakes-up-local-politics [17 October 2017].

Schenker, David. (2015). *Beyond Islamist & Autocrats: Prospects for Political Reform Post Arab Spring*. Washington: The Washington Institute For Near East Policy.

Schumpeter, Joseph A. (1976). *Capitalism, Socialism and Democracy*. London: Allen and Unwin.

Seib, Philip (ed.). (2007). *New Media and the New Middle East*. Hampshire: Palgrave Macmillan.

Sharp, Jeremy M. (2012) Egypt: The January 25 Revolution and Implications for US Foreign Policy. In De Leon, J.C. & Jones, C.R. (eds.), *Tunisia and Egypt: Unrest and Revolution*. New York: Nova Science, pp. 46–97.
Shehata, Samer S. (ed.). (2012). *Islamist Politics in the Middle East: Movements and Change*. Oxon: Routledge.
Sheline, Annelle. (2017). Middle East Regimes Are Using 'Moderate' Islam to Stay in Power. *The Washington Post*. Available at: www.washingtonpost.com/news/monkey-cage/wp/2017/03/01/middle-east-regimes-are-using-moderate-islam-to-stay-in-power/?utm_term=.104bf4d7c6c2 [15 May 2016].
Shiozaki, Yuki. (2007). Formation of Public Spheres and Islamist Movements in Malay Muslim Society of Malaysia. *Journal of the Interdisciplinary Study of Monotheistic Religions*, 3: 98–122.
Singerman, Diane. (2004). The Networked World of Islamist Social Movements. In Wiktorowichz, Quintan (ed.), *Islamic Activism: A Social Movement Theory Approach*. Indianapolis: Indiana University Press, pp. 143–161.
Smeltzer, Sandra & Paré, D.J. (2015). Challenging Electoral Authoritarianism in Malaysia: The Embodied Politics of the Bersih Movement. *A Journal for and About Social Movements*, 7(2): 120–144.
Sørensen, Georg. (1998). *Democracy and Democratization: Process and Prospects in a Changing World* (2nd ed.). Boulder: Westview Press.
Stein, Ewan & Volpi, Frédéric. (2014). Islamism and Regime Change in the Middle East and North Africa: Looking Beyond the Arab Uprisings. In Stein, Ewan, et al. (eds.), *A CASAW-AHRC People Power and State Power Network Report: Islamism and the Arab Uprisings*. Edinburgh: CASAW.
Stoker, Gerry. (2006). *Why Politics Matter: Making Democracy Work*. Basingstoke: Palgrave Macmillan.
Storm, Lise. (2006). Islamic Fundamentalism. In Leaman, Oliver (ed.), *Biographical Encyclopedia of Islamic Philosophy*. Bristol: Thoemmes Continuum.
Storm, Lise. (2007). *Democratization in Morocco: The Political Elite and Struggles for Power in the Post-Independence State*. Oxon: Routledge.
Storm, Lise. (2014). *Party Politics and the Prospects for Democracy in North Africa*. Colorado: Lynne Rienner.
Storm, Lise. (2017). Parties and Party System Change in the MENA after the Arab Uprisings. In Szmolka, Inmaculada (ed.), *Political Change in the Middle East and North Africa: After the Arab Spring*. Edinburgh: Edinburgh University Press.
Sulaiman, Nidzam & Khalid, K.A.T. (2017). Will There Be Malaysia Spring? A Comparative Assessment on Social Movements. *Malaysian Journal of Communication*, 33(1): 43–58.
Suzalie, Mohamad Antang. (2007). Islamist Movement in the Field of Political Participation in Malaysia. *IKIM Journal of Islam and International Affairs*, 2: 57–92.
Szmolka, Inmaculada (ed.). (2017). *Political Change in the Middle East and North Africa: After the Arab Spring*. Edinburgh: Edinburgh University Press.
Sztompka, Piotr. (1998). Trust, Distrust and Two Paradoxes of Democracy. *European Journal of Social Theory*, 1(1): 19–32.
Tallon, Lewis. (2017). Second Arab Spring. Available at: https://encyclopediageopolitica.com/2016/12/09/2017-second-arab-spring/ [15 September 2017].
Tamimi, Azzam S. (2001). *Rachid Ghannouchi: A Democrat within Islamism*. New York: Oxford University Press.

162 Bibliography

Tapsell, Ross. (2013). The Media Freedom Movement in Malaysia and the Electoral Authoritarian Regime. *Journal of Contemporary Asia*, 43(4): 613–635.

Tarrow, Sydney. (1994). *Power in Movement: Social Movements, Collective Action, and Politics*. Cambridge: Cambridge University Press.

The Borneo Post. (2013). Political Observers Reject Possibility of 'Arab Spring'. Available at: www.theborneopost.com/2013/01/13/political-observers-reject-possibility-of-arab-spring/ [4 May 2015].

The Economist. (2015). Malaysia in Graphics: Economic Malaysia. Available at: www.economist.com/blogs/graphicdetail/2015/09/malaysia [20 October 2015].

The Economist. (2016). Politics in the Middle East: The Arab Winter. *The Economist*. January 9, pp. 41–46.

The Malaysian Insider. (2013). No Basis for an 'Arab Spring' in Malaysia, Najib tells BBC. Available at: www.malaysia-today.net/2013/07/03/najib-no-basis-for-arab-spring-protest-in-malaysia/ [4 May 2015].

The Star. (2013). Najib: No Basis for Arab Spring after 55 Years of Peace, Stability. Available at: www.thestar.com.my/news/nation/2013/07/03/najib-tun-razak-arab-spring-bbc-interview [19 April 2015].

The Straits Time. (2015). What You Need to Know About Malaysia's Bersih Movement. Available at: www.straitstimes.com/asia/se-asia/what-you-need-to-know-about-malaysias-bersih-movement [20 October 2015].

Totten, M.J. (2012). Arab Spring or Islamist Winter? World Affairs. Available at: www.worldaffairsjournal.org/article/arab-spring-or-islamist-winter [7July 2015].

Ufen, Andreas. (2009). The Transformation of Political Party Opposition in Malaysia and Its Implications for the Electoral Authoritarian Regime. *Democratization*, 16(3): 604–627, doi:10.1080/13510340902884804.

UNDP. (2016). Arab Human Development Report. Youth and Prospects for Human Development in a Changing Reality, pp. 37–39. Available at: www.arabstates.undp.org/content/rbas/en/home/library/huma_development/arab-human-development-report-2016--youth-and-the-prospects-for-/.

Vandewalle, Dirk. (2014). Beyond the Civil War in Libya: Toward a New Ruling Bargain. In Kamrava, Mehran (ed.), *Beyond the Arab Spring: The Evolving Ruling Bargain in the Middle East*. London: Hurst & Company, pp. 437–459.

Vannetzel, Marie. (2017). The Party, the Gama'a and the Tanzim: The Organizational Dynamics of the Egyptian Muslim Brotherhood's post-2011 Failure. *British Journal of Middle Eastern Studies*, 44(2): 211–226.

Vinod, G. (2013). 'We Are Not Afraid of Malaysian Spring' Free Malaysia Today. Available at: www.freemalaysiatoday.com/category/nation/2013/06/26/we-are-not-afraid-of-malaysian-spring/ [17 October 2017].

Volpi, Frédéric. (2017). *Revolution and Authoritarianism in North Africa*. London: Hurst & Company.

Volpi, Frédéric & Stein, Ewan. (2014). Islamism and Regime Change in the Middle East and North Africa: Looking Beyond the Arab Uprisings. In Stein, Ewan, et al. (eds.), *Islamism and the Arab Uprisings*. A CASAW-AHRC People Power and State Power Network Report.

Von Der Mehden, Fred R. (1986). Malaysia: Islam and Multiethnic Polities. In Esposito, J.L. (eds.), *Islam in Asia: Religion, Politics & Society*. Oxford: Oxford University Press.

Von Der Mehden, Fred R. (1990). Malaysian and Indonesian: Islamic Movements and the Iranian Connection. In Esposito, J.L. (ed.), *The Iranian Revolution: Its Global Impact*. Florida: University Presses of Florida, pp. 233–254.

Wegner, Kevin M. & Gainous, Jason. (2013). Digital Uprising: The Internet Revolution in the Middle East. *Journal of Information Technology & Politics*, 10(3): 261–275.
Wan Jan, W.S. (2017). Parti Amanah Negara in Johor: Birth, Challenges and Prospects. *Trends in Southeast Asia*. Singapore: ISEAS Publishing.
Weale, Albert. (2007). *Democracy* (2nd ed.). Hampshire: Palgrave Macmillan.
Wehrey, Frederic. (2013). Bahrain's Decade of Discontent. *Journal of Democracy*, 24(3): 116–126.
Weinstein, Jay A. (2010). *Social Change* (3rd ed.). Lanham: Rowman & Littlefield.
Weiss, Meredith L. (2004). The Changing Shape of Islamic Politics in Malaysia. *Journal of East Asian Studies*, 4(1): 139–173.
Weiss, Meredith L. (2013). Parsing the Power of New Media in Malaysia. *Journal of Contemporary Asia*, 43(4): 591–612.
Welsh, Bridget. (2011). Democracy is Shining in the Dark. Available at: http://bridgetwelsh.com/2011/12/democracy-is-shining-in-the-dark/ [23 July 2015].
Welzel, Christian. (2009). Theories of Democratization. In Haerpfer, C.W., et al., *Democratization*. Oxford: Oxford University Press, pp. 74–90.
Wheatley, Stephanie. (2011). From Violence to Voting: Toward an Islamist Theory of Moderation. PhD Thesis, Baylor University.
Whitehead, Lawrence. (2002). *Democratization: Theory and Experience*. Oxford: Oxford University Press.
Whitehead, Lawrence. (2014). On the 'Arab Spring': Democratization and Related Political Seasons. In Sadiki, Larbi (ed.), *Routledge Handbook of the Arab Spring: Rethinking Democratisation*. Abingdon: Routledge.
Willis, Michael J. (2014). *Politics and Power in the Maghreb: Algeria, Tunisia and Morocco from Independence to the Arab Spring*. London: Hurst & Co.
Wilson, Trevor. (2014). Democratization in Myanmar and the Arab Uprisings. In Saikal, Amin & Achraya, Amitav (eds.), *Democracy and Reform in the Middle East and Asia: Social Protest and Authoritarian Rule after the Arab Spring*. London: I.B. Touris, pp. 187–202.
Wolf, Anne. (2017). *Political Islam in Tunisia: The History of Ennahda*. London: C. Hurst & Co.
Wong, Chin Huat. (2013). Fears Grow for a Malaysian Spring. *Asia Times*. Available at: www.atimes.com/atimes/Southeast_Asia/SEA-01-290513.html [17 September 2015].
Wong, C.H., Chin, James & Othman, Norani. (2010). Malaysia – Towards a Topology of An Electoral One-Party State. *Democratization*, 17(5): 920–949.
Yasmeen, Samina. (2014). Pakistan and the Arab Uprisings. In Saikal, Amin & Acharya, Amitav (eds.), *Democracy and Reform in the Middle East and Asia: Social Protest and Authoritarian Rule after the Arab Spring*. London: I.B. Touris, pp. 143–160.
Yee, Choong Pui. (2012). *Malaysia's Bersih 3.0: Sentiments, Perceptions and Politics*. Washington: RSIS Publication.
Yusuf, Imtiyaz. (n.d). The Middle East and Muslim Southeast Asia: Implications of the Arab Spring. Available at: www.oxfordislamicstudies.com/Public/focus/essay1009_southeast_asia.html [24 August 2017].
Zakaria, H.A. (1989). Malaysia: Quasi Democracy in a Divided Society. In Diamond, Larry, Linz, J.J. & Lipset, S.M. (eds.), *Democracy in Developing Countries: Asia*. Vol. 3, Boulder: Lynne Rienner, pp. 347–381.
Zawiyah, Mohd Zain, et al. (2017). Civil Disobedience and Cyber Democracy. *Mediterranean Journal of Social Sciences*, 8(4): 9–16.

Zemni, Sami. (2015). The Roots of the Tunisian Revolution: Elements of a Political Sociology. In Sadiki, Larbi (ed.), *Routledge Handbook of the Arab Spring: Rethinking Democratisation*. Abingdon: Routledge, pp. 77–88.

Zollner, Barbara. (2016, June). The Metamorphosis of Social Movements into Political Parties during Democratic Transition Processes. A Comparison of Egyptian and Tunisian Movements and Parties. Paper Presented at the Colloquium Entitled '5 Years After the Arab Spring: The Implosion of Social Movements?', Birkbeck, University of London.

Index

Note: **Bold** page numbers refer to tables and page numbers followed by "n" denote endnotes.

Abbott, Jason. P. 6, 84, 122
Abdessalem, Rafek 101n12, 133–4, 139n33
Abduh, Muhammad 15
Abdul Hamid, A.F. 91
Abdullah Zaik Abdul Rahman 22–3, 51, 60, 69n19, 76, 103n32, 109, 117, 125, 129
Abdul Malek, Zulkifly 3, 19, 38n9, 141
Abdul Rahman, Ahmad Azam 18, 21, 29
Abdul Rahman, Kaisan 4
activism, within Islamist movements in Malaysia 89–91
'Adjustment to Change' (ACT) theory 59, 115
al-Afghani, Jamaluddin 15
Ahmad, Dzulkefly 25
Alaoui, Hicham 80
Algeria 2, 18
Ali, Ben 50, 54–5, 60, 70n35
Al-Qaeda 29, 75, 138n3
American Revolution 51
Amnesty International 12n10
al-Anani, Khalil 96, 107
Angkatan Belia Islam Malaysia 9, 18; see also Muslim Youth Movement of Malaysia (ABIM)
anti-government protests 50–1
Anwar Ibrahim 7, 12n10, 20–1, 28, 31–2, 38n8, 39n9, 142
Arab Barometer 55
Arab-Muslim world: Malaysia and 2–8
Arab Revolutions 9, 12n11
Arab Spring 1–6, 12n11, 33, 45, 51–2, 59, 62, 69n14, 69n18, 82, 85–6, 101n2, 101n4, 102n28, 102n30, 131–2, 141; *see also* Arab Uprisings

Arab Uprisings: and ABIM 83–7; and AMANAH 83–7; anti-government protests 50–1; attitudes towards Islamist movements and 59–66; autocratic leadership 55–9; and civil disobedience 83–7; economic downturn 55–9; influence of social media factors from 87–9; Islamist movements as an agent of societal change 64–6; Islamist movements in Malaysia and 83–7; Islamists and popular civil protests in Malaysia 30–5; 'Islamist Winter' 61–2; and ISMA 83–7; knowledge of, in Middle East and North Africa 45–50; Malaysian Islamists learning from 104–25; non-violent resistance movements 52–3; and PAS 83–7; political revolution 51–2; prospect for Islamist parties 62–4; reasons for not knowing about 47–9; respondents' backgrounds 41–5; rise of Islamist parties after 89–97; role of Islamist movements 60–1; role of social media 55–9; sources of information regarding events 49–50; Tunisia and 'Success Story' of 77–9; understanding general issues about Arab Uprisings phenomenon 50–3; understanding the factors that led to 54–9; *see also* Arab Spring
Arab world stability: post-Arab Uprisings and state of 79–81
Asian Federation of Muslim Youth 4
Asmuni, Muhammad Fauzi 22
al-Assad, Bashar 50, 52, 75, 79
attitudes: towards Arab Uprisings 59–66; towards Islamist movements

Index

59–66; towards post-Arab Uprisings phenomenon 72–83
autocratic leadership: and Arab Uprisings 55–9
Awang, Abdul Hadi 3, 17–18, 51, 69n14, 69n18, 77, 80, 85, 101n8, 122, 134, 141
Awang, Ahmad 26
Awani, Astro 12n9

Badarudin, Shaharudin 7, 29
Bahrain 2
Bakar, Osman 2, 12n11, 140–1
Al-Banna, Hassan 19, 23
Barnes, Daniel 125
Al-Battat, Ahmad 12n11
'Battle of Camel' 61
Bersih 2.0 event 32; *see also* 'Walk for Democracy' protest
Bersih movement 1, 21, 32; *see also* 'Yellow Wave'
Bolshevik Revolution 51
Bouazizi, Mohamed **54**, 54–5, 67
Bradley, John 30, 68

capitalism 19, 21
Case, William 6, 7, 30, 122
Cheek, A.S. 14
Che Mohd Razali, C.H. 91
Chew, Amy 38n8
Chong, Alan 12n11
CIA World Factbook 21
'civil disobedience' 83
civil society organisations 1, 25, 30
Coalition for a Clean and Fair Election 2015 (Bersih 4.0) 34
Coalition for Clean and Fair Election 2007 (Bersih 1.0) 32
Coalition for Clean and Fair Election 2011 (Bersih 2.0) 32–3
Coalition for Clean and Fair Election 2012 (Bersih 3.0) 33–4
Coalition for Clean and Fair Election movement (Bersih) 84, 125
conservative Islamism 92, 100
Currie, Kelley 12n11

Daesh (*Ad-Dawla Al-Islamiyya fil Iraq Wa Al-Sham*) 74–5, **75**, 94, 99, 134; Al-Qaeda and 75; Northern Syria 75; post-Arab Uprisings and emergence of 74–7
Del Rosario, T.C. 86
democracy **124**; consensual 103n36; electoral 104, 125; in Malaysia 122–5; 'quasi-democracy' 6, 130; semi-democracy 7, 71, 123, 137, 144
Diamond, Larry 5–7
Dorsey, J.M. 86

economic downturn: Arab Uprisings 55–9
Edward, Salmi 12n11
Egypt 1–3, 10, 18–23, 36, 42–3, 49, 53, 59–67, 72, 74, 78–9, 96, 99–100, 106–11, 113, 118, 129–31, 142–3
Egyptian Islamists 3
Egyptian Muslim Brotherhood (MB) 16, 135–6, 141, 144
'electoral authoritarianism' 123, 137, 139n21
electoral democracy 104, 125
Eljammali, Naoufel 4, 106, 132
Ennahda movement in Tunisia 3, 4, 131–5
Ennahda Party 3, 18
Ennahda Political Bureau 4
Esposito, J.L. 72, 77

Facebook 2, 49, 55, 56, 66, 87, **88**, 97, 99
Faraghat 11n2
'*Faraghat for ijtihad*' 3
Farique, Asyraf 58, 111
Filiu, J.P. 104
Fisher, Jonah 33
Foran, John 131
14th Malaysian General Election 9
Freedom and Justice Party (FJP) 3, 18, 61–4, 70n35, 72, 89, 93, 98, 103n32, 106, 110, 143
Freedom House 6, 11n8
French Revolution 51
Funston, John 19, 20, 28

Gaddafi, Muammar 50, 109
Gainous, Jason 84, 102n29
Gandhi, Mahatma 52
Gelvin, J.L. 55, 61, 68n2
Ghabra, Syafeeq 61
Ghanem, As'ad 104
Ghanem, Hafez 72, 104
Ghannouchi, Rachid 3–4, 11n1, 11n2, 64, 70n31, 72, 94, 100, 103n36, 106, 112, 131–2, 138n4, 141
global Islamism 30, 36
global Islamist movements: Malaysian Muslim Solidarity Front (ISMA) 22–3; National Trust Party (AMANAH) 26–7; PAS and connection with 17–18
Goodwin, Jeff 130

Goodwin, Robin 59, 115
Gulf War 98

Hamas 18
Harakah Islamiyyah 17, 19
Harian, Sinar 11n6
Hashim, Mohd Safar 12n11, 140
Hassan, Musa 6
Holík, Jiří 6
Hooi, Y.K. 32
Hudson, Michael 59
Human Rights Watch 12n10

ideology: Malaysian Muslim Solidarity Front (ISMA) 22; Muslim Youth Movement of Malaysia (ABIM) 18–20; National Trust Party (AMANAH) 25–6; Pan-Malaysian Islamic Party (PAS) 16–17
IKRAM Malaysia 25
information sources, regarding Arab Uprisings events 49–50
Internal Security Act (ISA) 7, 21
Iran 2, 14, 27–8, 96, 130–1, 137
Iranian Islamic community 2
Iranian Revolution 2, 10, 27, 51; Malaysian Islamists and impacts of 27–8
Isa, Nasharudin Mat 16
Islam 3; political 143–4
'Islam and Democracy' (Esposito and Voll) 72
Islamic, defined 38n2
Islamic Action Front (IAF) 18
Islamic Congregation Front of Malaysia Party 24
'Islamic Republic' 2
Islamic Salvation Front (FIS) 18
Islamic state (IS) 75–6
Islamic State of Iraq and Levant (ISIL) 75
Islamic State of Iraq and Syria (ISIS) 75
'Islamic values' 2
Islamism 40; conservative 92, 100; global 30, 36; 'ideological rigidity' of 105; Malaysia's 24; neo-Islamism 50, 69n16, 94, 100, 143; orthodox 107; 'Pan-Islamism' 15; political 26
Islamist movements: as an agent of societal change 64–6; Arab Uprisings 60–1; in Malaysia 96–7, 144–5; and Middle East and North Africa 96–7; PAS and connection with global 17–18; role of 60–1

Islamist movements in Malaysia: activism within 89–91; Arab Uprisings 30–5; emergence of 13–16; influences of Arab Uprisings on 83–7; Islamist parties and development of 89–97; Islamists and popular civil protests in Malaysia 30–5; Malaysian Islamists and impacts of Iranian Revolution 27–8; Malaysian Muslim Solidarity Front (ISMA) 21–4; Muslim Youth Movement of Malaysia (ABIM) 18–21; National Trust Party (AMANAH) 24–7; Pan-Malaysian Islamic Party (PAS) 16–18; between regime and Islamists 29–30; semi-democratic Malaysia 29–30
Islamist parties: activism within Islamist movements in Malaysia 89–91; affecting development of Islamist movements in Malaysia 89–97; Arab Uprisings and 62–4; influential aspects 94–6; and inspiration from 'Islamist Winter' trend 89–91; Islamist movements in and Middle East and North Africa 96–7; Islamist movements in Malaysia 96–7; moderation and inclusion 94–6; post-Arab Uprisings phenomenon 91–3; prospect for 62–4; rise after Arab Uprisings 89–97; strengthening cooperation 96–7
Islamist political activism 2
Islamists: necessity of cooperation between non-Islamists and 112–15; and popular civil protests in Malaysia 30–5
'Islamist Winter' 61–2, 89–91
Ismail, Abdul Halim 29
Israel-Palestine conflict 98

Jamaat-e-Islami 18
Jasmine Revolution 4, 7, 50, 55, 65, 70n36, 131–2
Al Jazeera 18, 74
Jemaah Islah Malaysia (JIM) 2, 32
Jemaah Islamiyah 29
Jomo, K.S. 14
Jusoh, Idris 88

Kaum Muda 15
Kayat, Suhaizan 11n3, 70n39, 103n37
Khalid, K.A.T. 12n11, 140
Kherigi, Intissar 4
Khomeini, Ayatollah 28
Kingsbury, Damien 24

168 Index

Lane, David 131
Levitsky, Steven 6
Libya 1–3, 6, 50, 53, 55–6, 59–60, 67, 72, 74, 82, 109–10, 115, 136, 142
Liow, Joseph 7, 12n11, 18
Lynch, Marc 64, 74–5, 79, 82, 94

Mahathir Mohamad 12n10, 21, 32
Malay-Archipelago 2
Malay Mail 22
Malay-Muslim politics: Muslim Youth Movement of Malaysia (ABIM) 20–1
Malay-Muslims 14, 34
Malaysia: and the Arab-Muslim world 2–8; Arab Uprisings 30–5; Arab Uprisings-style revolution, requirement of 118–22; Bersih 1.0 32; Bersih 2.0 32–3; Bersih 3.0 33–4; Bersih 4.0 34; domestic politics 23–4; Ethnic Riot 7; improving quality of democracy in 122–5; Islamist movements 144–5; Islamist movements in 96–7; Islamists and popular civil protests in 30–5; magnitude of stability in current political scenario in 115–18; political strategy and preparation to govern 105–11; popular civil protests in 30–5, 35; *Reformasi* 31–2; between regime and Islamists 29–30; semi-democratic 29–30
Malaysiakini online news portal 125
Malaysian Bar 33
Malaysian Hospitality Industry 12n11
Malaysian Islamisation 14
Malaysian Islamists 1, 3; Arab Uprisings-style revolution, need of 118–22; cooperation between Islamists and non-Islamists 112–15; and impacts of Iranian Revolution 27–8; learning from Arab Uprisings 104–25; political stability or regime change 115–18; political strategy and preparation to govern 105–11; quality of democracy in Malaysia 122–5; stability in Malaysia's current political scenario 115–18
Malaysian Muslims 3
Malaysian Muslim Solidarity Front (ISMA) 10, 21–4; Arab Uprisings and 83–7; connection with global Islamist movements 22–3; ideology and organisational structure 22; involvement in Malaysia's domestic politics 23–4; political activism of 83–7
Malaysian Muslim Students Solidarity (Ikatan Siswazah Muslim Malaysia) 21
Malaysian National News Agency (BERNAMA) 4
'Malaysian Spring' 1, 4–8; making sense of 125–31; reality or fallacy 125–31
Malaysian Ulama Society 26
Malaysia Workers' Party 24
Malik, Maszlee 143
Mandaville, Peter 3
Masoud, Tarek 61
Mazuki, Mohamad 28, 39n11
Means, G.P. 6, 122
Melayu Sepakat, Islam Berdaulat slogan 21
Merone, Fabio 68
Middle East and North Africa (MENA) 1; 'Arab Uprisings' factor 97–8; awareness of political issues in 97–8; Islamist movements in 96–7; knowledge of Arab Uprisings in 45–50
Middle Eastern Revolts 62
Miller, Erica 38n5
moderation and inclusion: Islamist parties 94–6
Mohd Zain, Mohd Izani 16, 38n1
Monutty, Mohammad Nor 17, 19
Morocco 1, 18, 42–3, 63, 72, 81, 89, 96, 98, 143
Morsi, Mohamed 3, 63–4, 97, 110, 138n6
Mubarak, Hosni 3, 50, 52, 60, 70n35, 138n6
Muda, Mohamad Asri 17
Muiz, Abdul 85
Mujani, Wan Kamal 12n11
Müller, Dominik 15, 27
Muslim Brotherhood 3, 10
'Muslim Democrats' 94
Muslim Ummah 27
Muslim Youth Movement of Malaysia (ABIM) 10, 18–21; Arab Uprisings and 83–7; ideology and organisational structure 18–20; involvement in Malay-Muslim politics 20–1; political activism of 83–7; *see also Angkatan Belia Islam Malaysia*

Najib, Muhammad 3, 11n2, 25–6, 62, 93, 128
Najib Razak 5, 34–5, 71, 85, 99, 119, 123, 126, 128, 141–2

National Association of Muslim Students Malaysia 38n9
National Front Party (*Barisan Nasional* or BN) 5
National Trust Party (AMANAH) 10, 24–7; Arab Uprisings 83–7; connection with global Islamist movements 26–7; ideology and organisational structure 25–6; political activism of 83–7; *see also Parti Amanah Negara*
neo-Islamism 50, 69n16, 94, 100, 143
Nepstad, S.E. 52, 70n21
non-governmental organisations (NGOs) 4, 6–7, 13, 29, 33–4, 72, 83, 100, 107
non-Islamists: necessity of cooperation between Islamists and 112–15
non-violent resistance movements 52–3
Noor, Fadzil 21
Noor, Farish 28
Nurullah, Abu Sadat 10, 19

organisational structure: Malaysian Muslim Solidarity Front (ISMA) 22; Muslim Youth Movement of Malaysia (ABIM) 18–20; National Trust Party (AMANAH) 25–6; Pan-Malaysian Islamic Party (PAS) 16–17
Organisation of Islamic Cooperation (OIC) 118
orthodox Islamism 107
Osman, Tarek 74
Ottoman Empire 28, 51

'Pan-Islamism' 15
Pan-Malaysian Islamic Party (PAS) 1, 10, 16–18; Arab Uprisings and 83–7; Central Executive Committee (CEC) 17; and connection with global Islamist movements 17–18; ideology and organisational structure 16–17; Islamic Council of Ulama 16; non-Muslim Supporters' Wing 17; organisational hierarchy 17; political activism of 83–7; Youth Wing 4; *see also Parti Islam Se-Malaysia*
Paré, D.J. 33
Parti Amanah Negara 24; *see also* National Trust Party (AMANAH)
Parti Barisan Jemaah Islamiyyah se-Malaysia (BERJASA) 24
Parti Islam Se-Malaysia 16; *see also* Pan-Malaysian Islamic Party (PAS)

Party for Justice and Development (PJD) 18
Patail, Abdul Gani 34
Persatuan Kebangsaan Pelajar Islam Malaysia (PKPIM) 38n9
Pertubuhan Ikram Malaysia (IKRAM) 15
political activism: of ABIM 83–7; of AMANAH 83–7; of ISMA 83–7; of PAS 83–7
political Islam 143–4
political revolution 51–2
political strategy and preparation to govern 105–11
politics: Malay-Muslim 20–1; Malaysia's domestic 23–4
popular civil protests in Malaysia 30–5
post-Arab Uprisings: an 'Eye-Opener' for rulers of Arab states 81–2; attitudes towards 72–83; and emergence of Daesh 74–7; influence on political approach of Islamist movements 91–3; and issue of Syrian refugees 74–7; and political and economic implications 72–4; and state of Arab world stability 79–81
post-Arab Uprisings environment: leading to another wave of uprisings in the future 82–3; uncertainties in 82–3
Postill, John 87
Prophet Muhammad 94
The Prosperous Justice Party (PKS) 18

'quasi-democracy' 6, 130
al-Qaradawi, Sheikh Yusuf 18

radicalism 22
Rahman, S.A. 19
Rahman, Saodah Abd 10, 128
Rawa, Yusof 27
Rawls, John 83
Razak, Aidila 125
Redhuan, Mukhtar 29
'Reformation Movement' (*Reformasi*) 31–2
Rida, Muhammad Rashid 15
Roberts, Adam 104
Roy, Olivier 60, 68

Sabu, Mohamad 24, 86
Sadiki, Larbi 78, 104, 138n6
al-Saghir, Osama 133
Al-Sagoff, Syed Abdul Razak 12n11, 140

Index

Saifuddin, Mohamad 81
Saleh, Ali Abdullah 50
Sami, Mohammed Badie Abdul Majid 23
Saravanamuttu, Johan 30
Sarawak Report 34
Sayid Qutb 23
Second World War 7
Sedition Act 22
semi-democracy 7, 71, 123, 137, 144
semi-democratic Malaysia 29–30
Shah Pahlavi 2
Shamsuddin, Amran 127
Sharia law 15, 25, 36, 51, 72, 92, 100, 104–7, 110, 112, 138n10, 143
Shariff, Zakiuddin 85
Shehata, Samer 35, 143
Sheline, Annelle 94
Shiozaki, Yuki 14
Singerman, Diane 65
Skocpol, Theda 130
Smeltzer, Sandra 33
socialism 19, 21
social media: Arab Uprisings 87–9; Arab Uprisings and role of 55–9
societal change: Islamist movements as agent of 64–6
Society for Islamic Reform of Malaysia (JIM) 15
Stein, Ewan 68
The Straits Times 34
Sulaiman, Nidzam 12n11, 140
'Survival of the Ennahda Party After Revolution in Tunisia' 4
Suzalie, Mohamad Antang 15
Syafiq, Mohd 23
Sykes-Picot Agreement 51
Syria 2, 6, 50–3, 56, 58, 60, 67, 72, 74–9, 82, 94, 99, 128–9, 136, 142
Syrian refugees: post-Arab Uprisings and emergence of 74–7
Syrian Revolution 76

Tahrir Square Protest 34, 87
Taliban 138n3
Tallon, Lewis 82
terrorism 29, 99
'A Theory of Justice' (Rawls) 83
Tunisia 1; Ennahda movement in 131–5; Jasmine Revolution 4; and the 'Success Story' of Arab Uprisings 77–9
'Tunisian Jasmine Revolution' 50
Twitter 2, 55, 56, **88**

Ufen, Andreas 29, 31
UNHCR 75
United Malays National Organisation (UMNO) 20, 122
United Nations Arab Development Report 82
Uzair, Ahmad 27, 39n21

Volpi, Frédéric 68
Von Der Mehden, Fred R. 13, 14, 35

Wagner, K.M. 84, 102n29
'Walk for Democracy' protest 32; *see also* Bersih 2.0 event
Wall Street Journal 34
Wan Jan, Wan Saiful 18, 24
Way, L.A. 6
Weiss, M.L. 29
Welsh, Bridget 5, 11n7
Western Hegemony 28
Willis, M.J. 68
Wolf, Anne 94
Wong, C.H. 123

Yasier, Amar 23
'Yellow Wave' 32; *see also* Bersih movement
Yemen 2, 6, 50, 55–6, 60, 67, 72, 74, 78, 82, 99, 115, 118, 136
YouTube 2, 56, **88**
Yunos, Yasin 95

Zawiyah, Mohd Zain 83
Zollner, Barbara 73
Zubaimi, Ahmad 48